D1612581

TO BE A PILGRIM

(overleaf) The author, with Adam

ROBERT COLLIS

TO BE A PILGRIM

Foreword by
Christy Brown

SECKER & WARBURG
LONDON

First published in England 1975 by
Martin Secker & Warburg Limited
14 Carlisle Street, London W1V 6NN

Printed and bound in Great Britain by
Morrison & Gibb Limited
London and Edinburgh

CONTENTS

Foreword by Christy Brown

1	Killiney	1		13	Belsen	101
2	Growing up	13		14	Troubled Peoples	124
3	Cambridge	25		15	The Inner Circle	129
4	Yale	32		16	Nigeria	144
5	Medical Student	40		17	Ghana	159
6	Daragh	48		18	Southern Africa	163
7	Johns Hopkins	53		19	East Africa	177
8	Atlantic Voyages	57		20	Life in Lagos	197
9	Research	62		21	Interlude in Israel	211
10	Ireland	66		22	The North	216
11	Writing	89		23	Sean	222
12	World War II	96		24	The Return	228

Index 237

LIST OF ILLUSTRATIONS

frontispiece

The author, with Adam

between pages 118 and 119

Killiney Bay
The author's last game of rugger
Four of the Belsen children
Sean
The young Christy Brown
Mrs Brown with Christy, her daughter and grandchild
The author and research team in Nigeria
The author at the opening of the medical school in Lagos
Abubarkar Tafewa Balewa, first Prime Minister of Nigeria
The author at Bo-Island
The author and Han
The house at Bo-Island

FOREWORD BY
CHRISTY BROWN

I believe it is always difficult to write in any way even remotely resembling a formal manner about someone whom one has known with a degree of intimacy rarely achieved for the better part of one's life.

Anyway, neither this book nor its author is in need of pale pane-gyrics from me; even *my* egotism does not extend as far as imagining that for one moment. Robert Collis has led a many-rainbowed life in so many spheres: physician, paediatrician, child psychologist, writer, playwright—a life so varied and diffuse as to be almost impossible to pin down between the covers of any book, and, like many another rare thing, the things that go unsaid are as valid and meaningful as those that are said so beautifully.

I could blithely proceed to fill page after page about my friendship with Robert Collis and all that it has meant to me, the strange and unique alliance that has deepened over the not unremarkable years of its duration, the impact it has had upon my life, the many fine insights it has given me into other people and, not least, into myself, the doors and windows it unclasped and opened that would otherwise have remained sealed and barred to me forever.

I think most of us assiduously court the illusion that our life speaks for itself when all is assumed to be said and done; we use our best energies and talents to build and sustain that illusion lest we become at last too honest or too tired to deceive ourselves and shrink to our proper dimensions. With Robert Collis the illusion was left behind long ago, and only the reality remains.

KILLINEY

Once in the thirties, at some medical function in Dublin, an elderly, rather dried-up little doctor said to me: 'Are you Bob Collis?'

'I am,' I said.

'Well,' he said, 'This is the second time we've met. The first time was during the early weeks of this century when I galloped out on a side-car to the birth of the Collis twins at Killiney.'

'Very glad to meet you now,' I said, 'it all seems to have gone off well on that occasion.'

'Apparently,' he said, 'looking at you. But you didn't breathe at first and you were pretty blue. Your mother had a difficult labour.'

'I owe thanks to you, doctor, I should think,' I said.

'Oh, I don't know,' he said, 'you were all a tough lot.'

He wandered off and I never saw him again. But this brief conversation explained to me a good deal of what had baffled me about our family life.

Clearly, the birth of the twins had been a mistake. My elder brother, Maurice, had been born some eleven and a half years before, in 1889, followed by Mary a year later and Joyce some six years after that. My mother believed in sexual intercourse only for procreation; my father, being a Victorian, thought he should have 'husband's rights' when he needed them. Having had three children and several miscarriages, neither of my parents wanted any more. In consequence when my mother found herself pregnant again when she was no longer young, and this time with a very uncomfortable pair of twins, she was anything but pleased. Then when, as might have been expected, she had a difficult confinement, ending with the second twin, me, being born somewhat narcotised due to the sedative she had been given to allay the severity of the labour pains, it is not surprising that she received the newcomers with mixed feelings. When after a struggle I breathed and went on

I

breathing and was handed to her, now a pink new-born baby, her maternal love poured out to me. The other twin, Jack, was forgotten and hardly seen for several days. From that moment she accepted me and rejected my brother. This grew into an over-love and an under-love, almost a dislike in Jack's case, which clouded all our lives thereafter. On me she bestowed her complete devotion in every conceivable way from tiny gifts of love to hours of reading as I grew older. She read me most of Scott, much of Dickens and a selection of other great English writers. I was completely enthralled and used to regard these times as the most precious moments of the day. If I showed my love for her by little acts, like arranging a bunch of flowers or coming back to give her a second kiss after leaving the room, she would sparkle with pleasure, her love flowing about me like an aura. This happy love between two people is the greatest gift of joy that can be found in the world. That she hated my twin, often fought with my father about apparently trivial matters, behaved in many ways without mental discipline, was true, but she loved me, and in return I loved her. At that early age she filled my life, and perhaps I gave her life a meaning. The only cloud was her obvious dislike of my twin brother whom she excluded from her life. She would not even kiss him good night unless I particularly asked her to and when she did it was so unlovingly that it was painful to see.

As a child she had never been disciplined. My maternal grandfather was a surgeon of some distinction being, I believe, for several years president of the Dublin College of Surgeons. Apparently he had listened to his daughter's heart when she was quite young and heard a murmur of some sort. It must have been a congenital valvular abnormality of a mild variety if he heard one at all. Combined with this my mother had a tendency to violent temper tantrums as a child. Her doctor father, in consequence, had pronounced her as 'delicate' and on account of her weak heart said she must never be crossed lest a tantrum prove fatal. After marriage she continued to indulge in tremendous tantrums as a personal right. Even my father, who was pretty tough, was made to feel guilty if he resisted in a male manner which he was apt to do. When these rows occurred at the dinner table we children would be reduced to miserable silence while our parents said things most likely to hurt each other but which hurt us more. If a maid entered the room on one of these occasions my mother would say in a strangled voice, 'No, Willie, not in front of the servants,' and a deathly silence would fall on the room. Terrible battles sometimes raged, their egos clashing and battling for supremacy. I remember awaking one evening when my mother

entered my room and flung herself down, burying her face on my
bed, shaken with violent sobs. She said nothing, not knowing I was
awake, and crept away quietly after a time. But I have never
forgotten the anguish of her face.

My father belonged altogether to the Victorian age although he
survived the death of Queen Victoria and into the middle of the
twentieth century. Recently that remarkable television series, *The
Forsyte Saga*, has made me understand my father's outlook. He
belonged to that world of property, class, family and code. He had
been born, however, with no property, no silver spoon in his mouth.
His father was also a surgeon of some renown. He inherited the
position of Surgeon to the Meath Hospital and County Dublin
Infirmary from his uncle, another well-known Dublin doctor whose
time dated back to the days in the nineteenth century before the
introduction of anaesthetics and aseptic surgery. In the Meath
Hospital there is an old illustration of a surgeon operating for a
malignant tumour, the victim being held down forcibly by medical
students while he was cut up.

It is said that my grandfather's coffin was followed to Glasnevin,
the great Dublin burial-ground, by four miles of cabs which suggests
that he was loved by the people of Dublin.

This grandfather belonged to the famous Dublin Medical School
of the late-nineteenth-century period along with Abraham Colles,
Corrigan, Graves and Stokes, the latter two being also his colleagues
at the Meath Hospital. He had been trained partly in Paris whose
medical school led the world of medicine at the time before the rise
of the great German, British and American schools. He had the
distinction of being made a Surgeon to Queen Victoria at the age of
forty but shortly afterwards cut his finger while operating on a
facial tumour. He died a week later of septicaemia, leaving his widow
and young family almost penniless. My father was educated by one
of his uncles but was so hard up as a boy and a young man that he
never got over it and for the rest of his life had the feeling that
unless he economised he would end in the workhouse. This resulted
in literally taking the cream out of life for himself and us. When we
were boys, for instance, and we had lunch with him at his club the
whole excellent meal, rich surroundings and general comfort of the
place would be spoiled by his refusal to allow us to have cream with
the apple tart as he felt this to be an extravagance which he had
learned to renounce and must teach us to do also if we were to
survive the rigours of life. Cream on the tart became 'a thing' which
now I can see came up from his subconscious. At the time, however,
it just seemed a meanness which would sour the moment and take the

joy out of the day for us. I did not realise then the incredible struggle my father had been through or his courage and splendid physique, mental and physical. For not only did he get the Gold Medal in the Law School in Dublin University but he largely supported himself by working in a lawyer's office and even at the same time played for Ireland at Rugby football. He had an iron constitution. He was never ill from the time he had mumps at the age of fifteen until he was seventy-three when he fractured his skull in a motor accident, though even that did him little harm except to stop him hunting with the Ward Union Stag Hounds, one of the most dangerous packs in the world. Indeed he lived on until he was eighty-seven when he arranged his own funeral. He said to his man, 'John, I shall walk up and down the drive for five days. I shall stay in bed on Friday. Arrange for my funeral on Saturday, you have all the other directions.' John told me this. 'Well,' I said, 'he always does what he says, but we needn't order his coffin yet!' He did exactly as he said. He walked up and down the drive for five days, stayed in bed on the sixth, went unconscious at 10 a.m. on the Saturday and died at 1 p.m. At that moment I was at the christening of one of his great-grand-children. I rushed back to Killiney and ran up to his room. The rather shrivelled corpse in the bed wasn't him. When Maurice arrived from London and went up to pay his last respects he only stayed a minute, and when he came down he said, 'But he wasn't there—he's gone, he's taken his leave!'

As I grew older, particularly when I came to live in Ireland, I discovered him on a number of occasions helping impecunious persons, and after he died I found several unfortunates who had depended on him. When I found out I thought his secrecy was because he was afraid his acts might encourage us to be extravagant ourselves but now I think it was, in part anyway, a shyness of exposing his real feelings. He once said to me, 'It's all right for you, Bob, you have all sorts of friends, but I've never really been able to have a close friend in all my life.' The fact was he just could not reach out to people. I'm sure he wanted to but there was a psychological block or something missing in his make-up which shut him off from those about him and made it impossible for him to experience the great joy of joining another in friendship which means giving and taking without thought or reason.

Maurice we as children hardly knew for he had been sent to Rugby School by the time Jack and I were old enough to appreciate an elder brother. Like Jack and me later, he had an undistinguished academic career there. None of us got into the sixth form. Most of our time was spent desperately acquiring the necessary routine memory stuff. Recently I found a letter in an old family bureau by Maurice's Rugby Housemaster to my father in which he deplored Maurice's capacity only to be interested in Rugby football since he got his cap. Remembering what happened to us later at Rugby I am not surprised at his inability to appreciate the academic side of that great school. The fact that he left home at nine and went to school in England made him appear to me a superior person of exceptional ability and grandeur. His subsequent First at Oxford in History and later career in the East followed by his success as a writer and an art critic gave him a god-like position in my sub-conscious so that I have always accorded him the top literary laurels in our family until recently when Jack's book *Bound upon a Course* following Maurice's *Way Up* has put Jack out in the lead.

My elder sister Mary was born a year after Maurice. She shared with my father his passion for horses and my recollection of her as a child is almost always associated with a horse. I can still see the picture of her being brought home by all the cabmen who used to stand at Killiney Station; she fell off her pony riding side-saddle, her foot catching in the stirrup, and was dragged for a hundred yards along the stony station road. Mary always was a glamorous being to me. She married into the famous Hone family, all of whom are artists to a greater or smaller degree including two Masters, Nathaniel Hone and Evie Hone, one of the greatest stained-glass artists of this century. Mary painted quite well herself. I always loved her, though until her last illness I never knew her as a close friend. My other sister Joyce was only four years older than us and we were much closer to her. Both the good looks and the great physical stamina of the family passed her by. To us she was just Joyce who, though not in our age group, was always there as our sister. She was simply accepted as part of the surroundings. She had little sex-appeal and never got married and so remained in the home as a mother's companion-help, a fate not uncommon for daughters of all classes. My mother naturally accepted this as a God-given part of her life and being a person of tremendous egocentric ability she dominated Joyce completely for a time. But Joyce was not a Collis for nothing. If she could not resist the onslaught of my mother's personality by direct means she achieved it subconsciously in the most satisfying and complete manner imaginable. She outdid my mother's 'weakness' by acquiring what the Irish used to call 'the delicacy'—tuberculosis of the lungs with a secondary in the bone. It was in the days before the modern drug therapy of tuberculosis, when the disease was treated by sending patients to the top of Swiss mountains, giving them quantities of milk and eggs and if possible putting part of one of their lungs out of action by a method of pumping a jacket of air into the chest around it. Joyce had a good resistance to the infection and managed to have quite a reasonable life for twenty-five years after diagnosis. It killed her in the end when her lungs literally ceased to function as organs to take in oxygen from the air. Without being conscious of her victory by this means, she had placed her health as number one delicacy in the whole family, putting my mother into second place without anything being said.

Her other reaction to my mother's dominance was equally complete. She joined the Roman Catholic Church. This at one blow side-tracked my father's Victorian protestantism and my mother's religiosity. My father, once he had got over the shock of having a Catholic daughter, in no way interfered with her observances, and she found herself free to meet that other Ireland that had been living around her without her being aware of it in the past. Politically and personally it opened a new world to her. But most of all it was a complete shield for her personality against my mother. Once the shock of her conversion had worn off at home it led to considerable easing of her relations with both her parents and gave her a life she could never have found otherwise. Like us all she had an artistic touch and a capacity for expressing herself. She even wrote a little book describing her new life, *A sparrow findeth her nest*. She never left Killiney. My father built her a little house of her own on his land and she died there at about fifty years of age.

*   *   *

My father bought Kilmore in 1898. It was an early-nineteenth-century house built some quarter of a mile from the beach on the side of the hill. He added a new wing and put in numerous bow-windows which were the fashion of the time. Though they added to the amenities of the inside they destroyed the severe Georgian lines of the exterior. The inside of the house contained a number of splendid rooms, including a great dining-room in which hung the portraits of our Collis doctor-ancestors. For years it was spoiled by the back portion being filled with a billiard table which my father installed. Billiard tables were a status symbol at that time and my father whose struggles as a young man had now led him into a lawyer's well-to-do practice was very aware of the importance of class. Later the billiard table was transferred into the new wing where the big downstairs room had been a children's play-room. Billiards is one of the few games I have never learned to play. For some reason it annoyed me, perhaps because my father and later Jack became implacable experts and I was always a poor outsider while they continued to cannon or pocket the red while I watched, my near-misses endangering the cloth, and evoking growls of wrath from my father.

The basement of the house containing the kitchen, with its coal range on which all cooking had to be performed and which heated the bath water, was of a type which is never used any more now that the upper classes have to cook themselves. Numerous maids lived in the basement and struggled to keep us supplied with quantities of food and hot water. Our only bathroom-lavatory being at the other end of the house from my mother's room, and a most depressing place, she had hot water carried up daily to a hip-bath in front of a fire in her own room. I remember being put in this bath myself backwards when my mother had read that hot hay soaks prevented colds.

The drawing-room was the real joy of the house. It had a number of good pictures but its great feature was a mirror which covered a complete wall. In front, it was my father's greatest joy to arrange a mass of giant chrysanthemums which he had grown in the back-garden green-house. From the centre of the ceiling hung an ancient oil-lamp with a brass support from which was suspended a round handle to touch which with your head was to graduate as a man in the Collis clan. The room had two bow-windows, one giving onto the garden with its flower-bed immediately below from which grew a profusion of climbing geraniums around the window itself. The other looked out across the garden, over the tennis ground. Beyond the court a row of copper beech-trees stood through which vistas of blue sea or purple headlands could be seen.

There at Kilmore for all the years of our childhood and young manhood we learned the pleasure of physical endeavour amid almost perfect surroundings. In my memory the sun was always shining and the sea was always deep blue. Through a gap in a grove of very tall eucalyptus trees one could see to the north-east Dalkey Island with its Martello tower. To the south-east was Bray Head which is really a spur of the Wicklow mountains which juts out into the sea and rounds off Killiney Bay. A number of peaks of entrancing rounded beauty join Bray Head to form the background of the bay, their lower slopes uniting together to form the Vale of Shanganagh. The whole effect is one of almost perfect symmetry, a natural setting unsurpassed anywhere in the world. It is an area with the smallest rainfall anywhere in Ireland, but its Gulf Stream climate brings a moist warm air in which a profusion of rhododendrons, fuchsias, palms and blue gum trees and all manner of semi-tropical flowers flourish along with daffodils and the more hardy flowers and trees of the northern climes.

The garden of Kilmore was some three acres in extent and in those days surrounded by fields stretching down towards the sea. It was noted for its famous giant Himalayan rhododendrons which, set on a grass slope from which in spring grew hundreds of clumps of daffodils, were a sight so arresting that people passing up the private avenue to the big house above ours often used to stop and stand gazing starry-eyed at our garden as if it were a miracle.

In a long low house further up the hill from us lived in those days a couple of old brothers called Harris. They and my father carried on an internecine war. If we children trespassed on their fields or watched their cows being milked they would shout at us and utter dark threats. They were splendid bogey-men to us and in the nursery we used to tell each other awful stories of their foul deeds. On one occasion their rubbish dump fell down the slope into our hen-house. My father sent them a solicitor's letter. They settled out of court. The refuse was removed by a gentleman whom my mother said also removed the vegetables out of our back garden.

My father's triumph, however, occurred when Professor Lyons, who had built a house below ours, allowed his septic tank to overflow into the Harris field. Harris's horse drank the professor's drains and died. The Harris brothers were so enraged that they opened their own cess-pool and allowed it to run down the steep hill of the private road which led to all our houses hoping that it would run in at the professor's front-door. Unfortunately it took a wrong turning and came down our drive instead, thus providing my father with a perfect case to take to the sanitary authorities. I never heard what damages he got. We were never told that sort of detail as it might have led us into extravagances.

Later the Harrises both died and the house was taken by the charming O'Sullivan family. In my early twenties I knew Maureen O'Sullivan, their daughter, and used to take her out to dances sometimes. She was very pretty in a classical Irish way and I was attracted to her. But along came John McCormack and swept her off to Hollywood to partner him in his Irish film *Song of my Heart* which with its glorious sentimentality, added to a puckish Irish humour, won all our hearts. Maureen naturally never looked or came back. She went on later to partner Tarzan and was continually dragged by her hair through pools infested with crocodiles, and became an international film star.

*   *   *

Into this disunited family life set in a world of Irish beauty Jack and I awoke gradually to consciousness. No doubt our family make-up with all the tensions it engendered affected our psychology and to this day is responsible for repressions and complexes in our characters. But so complete was the beauty of Killiney that its meaning has never left us. Indeed, all the Collises possess so strong a nostalgia for Killiney and the Wicklow mountains that wherever they go they carry it with them, and whatever they produce Killiney gets in somewhere. If it is an oriental picture painted by Maurice with strange Burmese figures in the foreground there will be the Powerscourt waterfall in the background, while in all our writings we come back again and again to the picture of Killiney deep in our minds. The impact of that beauty on me as a child has never left me.

I remember the first time I found myself alone in the world. We had gone on a picnic to a wooded valley. I don't know how old I was, but I remember we went in some sort of horse vehicle, and that it was late summer.

After the picnic meal I escaped from my elders and scrambled up a beautiful, small wooded hill. It was mysterious and I was afraid. I came to a gap in the hedge at the opposite side of the wood and looked out upon a field. Suddenly for the first time in my life I became aware of beauty.

I can still see the scene quite clearly. Standing looking out of the wood which at that point consisted of a circle of ancient oaks, I saw a steeply rising field through which a brook gurgled. About twenty yards away a rabbit was sitting with cocked ears. The evening sun was slanting down but it seemed as if the earth itself was emanating if not exactly a light, a sort of luminosity. I have read in a book by Robert Benson, called *The Light Invisible*, of a vision he had in which the earth suddenly looked like a cloak worn by a living spirit. That perhaps is as near a description of what I saw as I can find, though I did not at that time think of it in those terms. Rather amazement, joy, awe, almost fear was my childish reaction. I gazed for a while, transported as it were into a wonderland, and then turned and ran back through the wood to my family. I never tried to tell anybody what I seemed to have seen. I can only remember one other occasion as a child when I had the same kind of vision. Again I have always remembered the place. This time it was in another little valley away up in the hills. Here the scene centred on a spring from which a brown stream ran away gently. On each side of the valley were wind-blown beech-trees under which and enclosing the spring was a great profusion of wild fern. The colours were greens of different shades, from very light green, almost blue, to dark green, almost black, with here and there a flash of golden gorse or purple heather. Again the scene seemed to shine with a light of its own so vividly that I never forgot the actual spot. Many years later I came riding into the same little valley early one morning before people were about. By the spring I saw a hind standing motionless, head high, sniffing the air. I checked the horse and for a moment we all remained still. Then with a bound she was gone, disappearing into the bracken. It seemed to me that she was the spirit of the place. I rode home remembering my childhood visions and feeling again that I had glimpsed another world.

These visions made me vividly aware of the creatures both animate and inanimate in that world of beauty in which I came to consciousness at Killiney. Whether it was this or some inherited doctor gene I don't know but I found myself passionately on the side of the wounded, the sick, and the suffering. At first it chiefly took the form of a deep attachment to animals whose mere closeness brought a thrill of delight to my mind, as when I saw a hare with pointed ears sitting in a field, or I was put on my father's great hunter and walked up and down the drive when only three years old. I can still almost feel, almost smell that horse whose great muscles under me gave me a satisfaction, a comfort and a feeling of security.

But the suffering or the killing of a creature tore my heart. My father once shot a rook in the garden. It is the only time I remember him shooting though he regarded the possession of a double-barrelled shotgun as another necessary status symbol. I found the rook lying dead on a gravel path, its black-blue feathers sticky with blood. I felt an utter desolation which even now, over sixty years later, has not completely vanished. It was not the shock of death or the blood which covered my hands as I carried it away and buried it in my own small garden that upset me. Even then I was not worried by gruesome bloody messes, nor have these sights, ordinary in a doctor's existence, ever affected me. But for the first time I had met with the cruel destruction of one living creature by another.

Naturally with this feeling for creatures I had the closest relationship with the family pets. The most vivid memory is of Towser, our Aberdeen terrrier, who must have come into the family about the same time as the twins. He was very much a Scottish character and didn't put up with any nonsense. If he was not taken everywhere with us he would sulk on our return and pretend to be more interested in a bone than in any of us. On these occasions I was usually given the job of placating him. This had to be done very gradually with saucers of milk and many words of endearment. After a time if I was successful he would wag the tip of his tail whereupon I would fall down before him and he would lick my ears.

Many other animals influenced my childish mind at Kilmore

such as the wild out-door cats who roamed the garden, an occasional hedgehog who, coming out at night, sometimes got entangled in the tennis net. But of all the creatures, the birds came closest to my heart. The garden at Kilmore was a tremendous refuge for all kinds. In spring the air was full of the song of blackbirds and thrushes. Gulls circled and called when storms drove them in from the sea, rooks cawed and there was never complete silence in the garden. A family of perky robins always was around when the gardening was in progress. They would perch on a bough above the broken ground with heads on one side and small beady eyes. Sometimes they would fly up on to a branch above and sing. On several occasions they flew into my room in the house, and one evening one sat on the top of the chest of drawers and sang to me. It was on an occasion when I was worried about a decision I had to make. While the bird sang my mind lost its turmoil. I fell asleep. When I awakened my problem had vanished and the bird had flown away.

When my mother was sinking in her last illness she said to me one day, 'Oh, I remember the nicest thing you ever did.'

'What was that?'

'One day some boys came up the road to Kilmore with a cage with two singing birds, a thrush and a robin, which they had caught. Their idea was to sell them. They met you near the gate and showed you the birds in the cage. Suddenly you jumped forward and opened it. The birds flew away up into the trees. The boys jumped on you and were pounding you when I came round the corner and they ran away. I don't remember how old you were, but you were pretty small at the time.' The incident flickered back into my memory. I could remember the spot where it happened, being frightened of the boys and being rescued by my mother but I had no memory myself of the birds.

When I was adolescent and, like so many others at that age, occasionally overcome by fits of deep depression for which the reason is usually more glandular than psychological, I had so vivid an experience that I can still, even now, remember the small details of the scene.

On this particular occasion I can only remember that I was deeply unhappy. At last, finding no relief at Kilmore I took the dogs, two Cairn terriers called Rags and Tatters, for a walk. Like all Kilmore dogs they were part of the family, Tatters being a particular friend of my twin brother in whose room he spent much of his time. The dog comforted him through his childish troubles which were much more severe than mine.

I went down to the shore of Killiney Bay and walked along to its

great white granite rock. On this afternoon the sky was grey, the
sea was grey and my mind was grey. I sat on the rock for a time. A
bigger wave than the rest came in and hit the rock below covering
me with cold wet sea spray. I shook myself and got up feeling still
more depressed and began to run back along the shore preceded by
the two small dogs. Suddenly Tatters stopped before something
white that moved close to the edge of the sea. I called to him and
the object, which was a small sea bird, opened its wings and circled
out just over the waves, coming back to the shore a little distance
away. I called the dogs to heel and approached the bird slowly. It
lay on the wet sand quite still, one wing extended. Obviously it was
sick or injured. I picked up the little creature whose body seemed
tiny under its feathers. It did not move so I held it under my coat for
warmth. What to do? I might bring it up to the house and try and
nurse it, but how? What would such an animal eat? No, that would
only frighten the creature which was obviously very weak. I looked up
and saw behind me the clay cliff which comes down at a certain
point to the back of the beach. I turned and carried the bird there
and clambered up for a short distance and placed it on a little ledge
looking out over the sea with the wind blowing about it. It had
folded its wings. I looked down at it. Its beady eyes were open. It
moved its head but did not try to rise or fly away. I put out a hand
to flatten its roughened feathers then withdrew it lest my touch
should scare it. I stood there silently. At that moment a ray of
sunshine came from between the clouds and was reflected as a
brilliant path across the sea and the whole beauty of Killiney Bay
shone round about us. As I stepped down from the cliff I found the
depression had left me.

It was about this time that these experiences made me realise
that I must be a doctor when I grew up, that I must try and battle
against the pain and the cruelty of the world. At this age the death
and pain inflicted on the animal world by man wrung my heart.
Birds driven over butts to be shot down by gentlemen with double-
barrelled guns seemed horrible to me. Even the sight of a salmon
panting out its life on the bank of a river after having been landed
by a fisherman hurt me.

I remember the exact day, when I was nine years old, when these
feelings crystallised in my mind. I can remember the exact spot, the
rusty iron supports of the railway bridge over the road along which
I was walking at that moment with a friend.

'What are you going to be when you're grown up?' he said.

Suddenly I knew. 'A doctor,' I said, and never afterwards has it
ever occurred to me to be anything else.

CHAPTER 2

GROWING UP

As Jack and I grew older we acquired bicycles on which we learned that a fabulous world lay outside Killiney. We discovered we could ride off into the Wicklow mountains to lovely lakes such as Lough Bray. Lough Dan was some twenty miles away. To reach it we had to walk up desperately long hills pushing our bicycles. Now the young stand at the side of the road-junctions thumbing lifts; bicycles are considered too hard work; walking is absolutely out of the question.

Today when Jack comes to stay with me at Bo-Island in Wicklow he is inclined to disappear. I can always find him, however, knowing that he will have gone up into the high field, where he can sit down against a hay-stack and see the road to Lough Dan.

At nine years old we went as day-boarders to a school at Bray, a few miles from Killiney. This meant catching an early train which resulted as a rule in having to run down the Kilmore hillside and along the station road, often crossing the line after the incoming train had passed. On reaching the platform we would fall gasping into the last carriage before the train started again. The guard and the local porter used frightful threats but they never stopped us.

Of what I learned at that school I can remember absolutely nothing which has later had any bearing on my thought processes. Whether the Latin and French grammar and arithmetic I learned there have really made any difference to my subsequent life I now doubt. The Headmaster was almost completely deaf. He was English and believed in what he called 'British Honour'. In some ways I managed to establish the myth that I never told a lie. It was not easy to keep this up and at times I got very near the line. Sometimes he would indulge in a quiz. If you failed to answer you were beaten on the hands. Sometimes half the form would be sitting literally wringing their aching hands, a sort of 'battered hand syndrome'. On these occasions it was not uncommon for the victim to call out to other members of the form who might know the answer. If the Headmaster saw your lips move he would shout 'You're talking'. If you denied it he'd call you a liar and make you hold out your hand. On one such occasion he saw my lips move.

'Collis major' (I was 'major', Jack 'minor' because, though the second twin born, I was the bigger), 'you're talking,' he shouted.

'Yes, sir,' I replied with a broad honest smile. 'I asked my brother the time.'

'All right,' he growled. And I had got away with it again.

What I did learn at the school and what became one of the greatest experiences of my life afterwards, was Rugby football. There, on a little ground under Bray Head, I got that oval ball into my hands for the first time at the age of nine. After that game the old master, who was refereeing, said to me:

'Collis, you will play for Ireland.' And when I did, fifteen years later, I sent him a wire.

From that first game I never looked back and found myself playing for the school by the time I was eleven although at that time it kept some boys up to seventeen. The Aravon School fifteen was the first I captained, though during my football career of twenty-two years I captained or led every side I played for except Ireland. This included Rugby School, the Cadet Battalion of the Brigade of Guards, Cambridge University, the Dublin Wanderers, the Harlequins, King's College Hospital, the United Hospitals, the London Irish, Surrey, London and Leinster. I managed to survive in spite of a severe attack of primary tuberculosis, a dislocated knee and a broken arm. At times I felt unequal to the strain of very big matches but managed not to show it during the actual games. I learned more self-discipline through Rugby football than in any other way. I grew to appreciate what it means to be really fit and feel clear-headed and untired, a state which once experienced is never forgotten. It means no drink or drugs or odd women as an escape from the tensions of manhood. Above all it means not eating too much. Food kills many more people than drink. When I see baggy-eyed, aged, unexercised gentlemen sitting down to a four-course meal at the age of forty I know that in ten years they will be panting at a round of golf and really incapable of life till after lunch.

Rugby football teaches you to think quickly, to make up your mind in a flash, and, if you are a leader, to convey your decisions in a way that others can and will follow. Every first-class player

must have a good athletic build of course. The more of such attributes
he has the better. If he weighs two hundred pounds and can run the
hundred yards in ten seconds he has a great advantage over the
ordinary player and it may be worth putting him in the side even if
he lacks the mental attributes that in some way mark him out as a
real champion. When the selectors have enlisted almost a complete
team of such brutish giants, as is not uncommon these days, the
game sometimes deteriorates into a dirty brawl. This is not to say
that it should be a kid-glove affair, or a stylised, stately performance
like cricket. It requires a degree of fearlessness, of readiness to suffer
pain, and great physical discipline when the body is crying out for a
let-up but at that moment the game needs your last breathless
effort.

One of the bravest physical things I ever did was to dive down and
seize the ball away from the feet of three rubber-like New Zealand
giants as they were approaching the Irish line in a wild forward rush.
In some way I managed to snatch the ball away from their feet and
pass it to our full-back, Ernie Crawford from Belfast, before those
awful knees crashed into my ribs and knocked all the wind out of me.
The most splendid moment was at Twickenham when I held
Cove-Smith, the English captain, by the knees, while Jammie
Clinch, the giant Irish wing-forward, had him by the neck and was
banging his head against our goal-post. He dropped the ball. In
the subsequent scrum which was under our posts the ball came loose
and I kicked it into touch. It was time. 6–6 and fifty thousand
spectators rushed cheering on to the ground to carry Jammie off
shoulder high. But perhaps the best moment of all that Rugby
football brought was when I was Captain of Rugby School. On a
certain February day I had received my running colours. I felt very
happy, so to celebrate the event I went down to Jack's study and
gave him the most sought after distinction of all at Rugby, his
Rugger cap. Then fellow house-companions celebrated this double
Collis success by according the two of us what was called 'hall-
cheering'. When my brother and I came into the house hall at tea-
time they beat on the tin baths they had brought in from the 'tosh'
room and broke all the crockery. It was the last time that the ancient
ceremony of 'hall-cheering' was allowed in the house. The authorities
felt that our double event had an Irish touch about it not altogether
in accordance with the Arnold tradition.

*　　*　　*

When we reached fourteen years our father felt that Jack and I
should follow Maurice and go to Rugby School. Except for one

15

summer when we had spent a few days in London we had never been in England before though our schooling and general family up-bringing had been along English lines. We knew very much more about English than Irish history and what we did know of the latter was chiefly to the discredit of the Irish. We had never heard of the Irish famine during the nineteenth century, or the associated million deaths from starvation which were largely due to the English administration of the country at the time.

My clearest memory of Rugby School is of the friends I made there. The best that England bred were there then. I described them in *The Silver Fleece* as 'the chivalry of England, the envy of the world'.

*   *   *

In the middle of my indoctrination into English thought and ways of life I was suddenly brought into contact with the other Ireland which I had only glimpsed as a child and knew nothing of. It occurred when I was home for the Easter holidays in 1916. The Irish rebellion headed by Padraig Pearse and James Connolly broke out suddenly in Dublin. Of all Irish risings this was probably the most gallant. Certainly the leaders who were chiefly visionaries, poets or, like Connolly, representative of the Dublin poor, were quite exceptional. That they did not have a chance, particularly at a time when the British war machine was fully geared for action, left them quite undaunted in what they had set out to do. I do not suppose any of them really thought they could win. They probably hoped for much greater support in Ireland and from abroad but fundamentally their thought was that if Ireland was to be saved from being completely Anglicised before another generation had passed it was necessary for them to sacrifice themselves as a demonstration that the spirit of ancient Ireland was not dead.

The whole rising lasted only a week, but during that time the centre of Dublin was burned and a lot of severe street fighting took place. My father was back from the Italian front where he had gone with a group of University men as an ambulance driver. He was in his fifties at the time.

He did his old car up with red crosses painted on table-napkins and took me to the Meath Hospital where he was chairman. After that I went there on my bicycle from Killiney every day during the fighting. I had acquired Red Cross armlets which got me through both sides. I saw death and destruction of the human body for the first time. The pictures of the city with its pall of smoke hanging over it, the awful noise of small-arms firing, the whine of bullets and the fear I felt are not far from my conscious memory, but it is the last day of the fighting that I remember most clearly. I had been helping at the Hospital. Quite stiff fighting had been going on round Jacobs' biscuit factory which was held by MacDonagh, one of the poets. I went down there from the Hospital and helped to bring in a girl who was hurt. I had got through the English lines by wearing a Rugby O.T.C. badge in my button-hole and forgot to take it off when I got into the Irish lines. The Irish were evacuating the factory and slipping off into the old Coombe slum area. One of them came up to me, looked at the badge and said 'You're the kind of lad who gets shot.' He said it with a smile on his face. I took off the badge quickly and picked up the wounded girl and helped to carry her into the Hospital. Then realising that it was late and my mother would be wondering what had happened if I didn't turn up at home I left the Hospital and set out for Killiney. It was a very bad moment to be out in the Dublin streets. The English party who had stormed Jacobs' now pulled down the Tricolour—green, white and orange—which had been floating in the breeze from the factory tower. I saw it flutter down as I stood at the Hospital gate. I had never seen the flag before and it had no overtones for me. Somebody cheered. I turned angrily round as if I had been hit. Then I set out along Camden Street to try and get home. The road was completely empty. The storming party were returning down another parallel street, firing volleys whether at people or not I couldn't see. Bullets were passing overhead with a whine. I was too afraid to ride my bicycle so I walked pushing it. When I got to the canal at Charlemont Street Bridge some soldiers in a house at the opposite side of the canal shouted at me to get back. I shouted that I had a pass. Somebody fired; a bullet sang by my head. I don't suppose the sniper meant to hit me as he could hardly have missed but I got off that bridge as quickly as possible and ran into Kelly's at the corner where the military had a post. There they asked me to dress a wounded British sailor. It was the first wound I had ever seen close up. I looked pretty useless. One soldier said I was a very poor Red Cross person and should be investigated. Another pointed out I was only a kid. In the end I helped the sailor into a nursing home close by and stayed there for the night.

The soldiers in Kelly's were the same party as had captured MacDonagh's flag over the factory. They gave me a little bit of it. I kept this in my wallet for the next ten years, until the wallet was stolen by a pick-pocket in France.

During the fighting I had gradually changed sides, finding myself an Irishman rather to my own surprise. But the actual moment

17

when this was borne on my conscious mind was some days later when I was in the centre of Dublin. There was a boy calling 'Stop Press'. I bought a paper and read that Padraig Pearse and a number of the others had been court martialled and condemned to death and that the sentence had been carried out that morning.

I stood quite still. Nobody in the street was smiling. Everybody stood silent. The tension closed me in. Here I was in the centre of Dublin with the Irish people all around me. An Irishman had been executed again. I remembered that close to that spot Robert Emmett at the end of the eighteenth century had stood on a lonely scaffold ladder hoping for rescue at the last moment. The executioner had at last lost patience and kicked the ladder away and Emmett had been left jerking out his life at the end of a rope. His rebellion had been a very poor thing but he had immortalised himself by his speech from the dock—perhaps one of the best speeches from the dock ever made.

As I walked up Grafton Street I suddenly realised that I was an Irishman. I knew that I was on the side of the people of Ireland. I did not realise much more then. I did not feel any violent national-istic surge of feelings. It was a deep compassion for the people, particularly the poor of Ireland. Class and religion had no part in it.

*   *   *

At the end of these holidays I went back to Rugby. After a few days I shut up about events in Ireland as I realised that the English naturally regarded the Irish rebellion occurring in the middle of their desperate struggle with the Germans as a stab in the back. The boys were completely ignorant of Anglo-Irish history—had not even the little knowledge I had and naturally no sympathy for Ireland. Nor did my Dublin experiences make me for a moment feel that I should not join the British Army as soon as I was old enough. My elder English friends were just beginning to be killed and wounded then. Nearly all the generation of boys a year older than I were killed or wounded during the next two years, as were most of the form masters in the school who had joined the army.

At the school life went on as always. There was so much to do. Every day was filled from morning till night with class work, games and military training in the school O.T.C. Time passed and I reached my last term.

During this term I led a sort of double life. As an Irishman, I was working for the University Entrance Exam to Trinity College, Dublin, but at the same time I was fully accepted as the captain of the Rugby School rugger fifteen. Rugby at that time was the most English of English institutions. Provided you conformed to the set rules, written and unwritten, you were accepted whether you came of the same stock or not. But if you deviated from their code of behaviour in any way you would be regarded with suspicion and excluded. In my case my athletic prowess made it possible to be completely part of the inner life and thought in spite of my experiences during the Dublin Rising in 1916. On one occasion at that time, I found two small boys fighting. I separated them. They were fighting for the honour of carrying my boots down to the ground.

I had two other great friends then. One, E. A. Montague, was the cleverest boy and head of the school; the other, Boughton Leigh, an Englishman of the country gentleman type. He was captain of running. Boughton Leigh also played for the school at Rugby football with me. None of us three went into school on Saturday mornings. Rather we met and arranged the next week's athletic events. That term there were five Rugby football matches, four inter-house runs of eight miles, two inter-school cross-country races, the Crick race and the sports. For the latter I was the official starter, and I only had live ammunition for the pistol. But nobody questioned me.

The Headmaster of Rugby at the time, Dr David, was an idealist but not a very astute headmaster. He treated Montague, Boughton Leigh and me with extraordinary trust which we didn't abuse though we were never able to cross some barrier which separated us from him. In my case this may have been due to the fact that he had the lowest opinion of my academic ability. He told me that I just might be able to realise my ambition of becoming a doctor as that did not require any great intelligence. He had an even lower opinion of Jack's academic attainments. Remembering Maurice's similar position in the school and the subsequent careers of the three brothers Collis, it is difficult to understand what happened to us at Rugby. To say we were 'late developers' doesn't really help. Our brains just didn't react to the method of instruction we were subjected to at that time. Our subsequent academic attainments do at least demonstrate that we were not stupid. Except for a very few, most masters simply tried to get facts fixed in our memories without reference to their meaning. One famous old cleric glorified in grammar (English, French or Latin) and dates (chiefly of English kings). All the Collis brothers in turn reached the bottom of his form. To this general criticism of the masters one exception must be made. I was taught history by 'Tiger' Hastings, an enthusiast with a bristling moustache and a capacity for arousing interest in his pupils I have never seen excelled.

*　　*　　*

Four years before when Jack and I were tough new boys we had befriended a very clever sensitive boy called Levens who eventually became a don at Oxford. Now he was Head of the House and a member of the Upper Bench Sixth Form which had been made into a sort of schoolboy senate by Dr David. This body had passed a law forbidding any School boy to buy food in the town. There was a national food shortage in 1918 due to the German submarine campaign.

As Captain of the School XV I had to entertain to tea visiting teams. This I did by procuring extra food with money obtained by fines such as those for boys walking over the cricket pitch. The new rule seemed to preclude this and we were very short of food anyway as our House butler was selling some of it in a shop in the town unknown to our housemaster at the time: the situation became desperate so I said to Levens, our House representative on the school senate, 'You'd better go and get us some stuff yourself as you made this horrible rule.' Off Levens went but he was reported to Dr David by a snooping master. David was enraged and said a lot of unpleasant things about untrustworthiness and told Levens he would remove his sixth-form power and make me Head of the House in his place. Levens was almost in tears. There was only one thing to be done so I went straight round to the Headmaster and bearded him myself in his tower room looking out on the Close, the playing field where William Webb Ellis had inaugurated Rugby football a hundred years before.

I told David that it was my fault and he mustn't blame Levens. I also mentioned that the food was abominable in our house and I had to do something about it when outsiders were being entertained. When I finished a kind smile came over Dr David's face. 'Collis,' he said 'thank you, I wish you were staying on and I'd confirm you as Head of the House.'

'But, Sir . . .'

'No,' he said, 'not another word. It was fine of you to tell me.' I staggered down the turret stairs to the waiting Levens and friends. 'O.K.,' I said, 'it's all right, he nearly kissed me!'

A few days later, however, Levens got ill and I took over the Headship of the House anyway for the rest of the term. During this time I saw still another side of Dr David before he became Bishop of Liverpool.

At that time we had a number of unusual personages as boys in our House. The most remarkable of these was Ionides, an English-born Greek. His father, thinking unwisely that the Arnold tradition might turn his son into a proper member of the English middle class, had sent him to Rugby. His hopes and plans were dashed, however, for young Ionides remained Greek in spite of anything the Arnold tradition could do, and not just ordinary Greek at that. His Rugby career came to a climax one night when I was Acting Head of the House. While the boys were out playing games our pockets in the changing-room were rifled and all our small change removed. This we reported indignantly to our housemaster who told Dr David. The latter came round late in the evening and I was called into the housemaster's study. 'Collis,' said David, 'I have decided to search the studies of the only two boys who were off games in your House today.'

'Yes, Sir,' I said.

'But,' he said, 'remember the Arnold tradition: a Rugby boy's study is his fortress and anything we see there which does not pertain to the stolen money must not be noticed.'

'Yes, Sir,' I said.

The first boy's study only produced several packs of playing-cards which the Headmaster made sniffing noises over but no comment. On arriving at Ionides' study he said, pointing at the top drawer of the desk:

'Open that.' I did. A pungent smell struck our nostrils. There lay a partly degutted bird of sorts.

'Open the next.' I did. There was a loaded Colt revolver.

'Open the next.' I did. And the head and neck of a snake slowly rose from the drawer.

'Close that drawer at once, Collis,' said David, backing away. I did so, with some difficulty avoiding being bitten while getting the snake's head back in. I followed David and the housemaster to the latter's study where we stood in sticky silence for some time, till David said, 'Thank you, that will do, Collis.' (Later it was discovered that the money had been stolen by the house butler's help.)

Next day, in spite of the Arnold tradition Ionides was put through the third degree by the Head. Later his father was requested to remove him from the school. He refused and Ionides remained for another term when he joined the Indian Army where he became a celebrated disposer of man-eating tigers, but not a very typical regimental officer. When after World War I he said he wanted to become a game warden in darkest Africa his Colonel made no objection. He found his real home in Africa and became perhaps the

most famous game warden of all time having several books written
about him.

✻   ✻   ✻

In the spring of 1918 nobody was expected to survive for very
long. The period of expectancy of life at the front for a subaltern in
a crack regiment in the British Army was about fourteen days then.
Most of the boys immediately ahead of us were already dead or
mangled with wounds.

The Easter Term of 1918 came to a sudden end. My childhood
and adolescent life during which I had been protected completely
from the rigours of real life came to an abrupt stop one afternoon.
For a couple of weeks I went home to Killiney. Then, like all the boys
of my generation and upbringing, I joined the British Army to help
fight the Germans for the mastery of the world. I found myself
sharing a tent with Boughton Leigh in a cadet battalion outside
London in training for the Irish Guards.

The next six months were the most unreal of my life. I was
supposed to become conditioned so that I could act as second
lieutenant in one of the European armies who were slaughtering
the young men of our generation by the million at that moment.
That meant I must be trained so as to acquire the conditioned
reflexes which would result in my obeying orders automatically and
without question. When the order came I would climb out of my
trench in France or Flanders in front of a group of private soldiers
and advance across a stretch of country called 'no man's land'
against a hosing-like machine-gun fire. More than likely I would be
hit by one of the flying bits of metal and lie dying between the opposing lines of young men. To accomplish this feat I had to be trained
to obey, and how to kill others. The method used to create the
necessary reflex in us young men was continuous drill where orders
were shouted at us. We were taught to obey meticulously and with
precision. This went on day after day. You became proficient if you
could abolish every other thought from your mind and just shout
or be shouted at and react accordingly, but if you allowed yourself
to think of anything but forming fours or whatever you had been
ordered to do you were lost and would be roared at by the drill
sergeant as if you had committed a deadly crime. Neither Jack nor
I ever acquired the right mental attitude to platoon drill.

I was even worse psychologically at killer training. At this you
were taught to bayonet other young men by bayoneting sacks. To
make this life-like, or death-like, you were encouraged to shout
indecent profanities at the sack while plunging your bayonet into it—

'Goddamm you, you fucking bugger'—you were expected to stick your bayonet into the sack furiously and kick it in its imaginary balls while cursing. I could not work myself up into the necessary frenzy. The sack just remained a sack to me. I just couldn't make it in this violent world at all. I tried; I boxed for my platoon. In the finals, during the first round, my opponent hit me with a swing, lifting the skin off my cheek bone and almost closing one eye. He tried to do it in the third round but this time I was ready for him and ducking at the right moment I came up inside his guard and hit him with a right–left on the chin. This knocked him silly but did not knock him out. He just staggered about for the rest of the bout which I won on points. The Colonel, who was a dessicated specimen from the Grenadier Guards, sent for me afterwards and said in the clipped voice of the Guards, 'Carlis, I am surprised at you. Why didn't you knock out that feller when you had him at your mercy? How the hell do you expect to bayonet half a dozen Huns if you can't finish off a chap in the ring?' I wondered too!

The war ended so suddenly in 1918 that we were left out of breath. It took some time before anybody anywhere was able to realise that dynastiscism was dead. The Kaiser had fled. The Czar of all the Russias had been murdered. Franz-Joseph and the Austro-Hungarian empire had gone. In the mêlée even the Ottoman empire had disintegrated. As yet it wasn't at all clear what had happened. Actually the birth pangs of a new world were only half over. The cessation of slaughter was only a pause in the struggle which after an uneasy period was to start again.

In England in 1919 that tricky Welshman, Lloyd George, was proclaiming that England must be made a land fit for heroes to live in while preparing to meet the aspirations of the poor people of Ireland with the Black and Tans.

Trinity College, Dublin, had not commenced to function again as yet. Jack and I found ourselves demobilised and for a moment unemployed. All our friends who had survived the war were in England. Jack's were planning to go to Oxford. Elmhurst, later of Darlington Hall fame, persuaded me that Trinity College, Cambridge, was the place for me. Our father, who found himself in the unusual position of having three sons of killable age still alive at the end of the war and also being somewhat suspicious of our Irish Nationalist sentiments, decided that it would be best if Jack and I went to Oxford and Cambridge respectively. This was the real parting of the ways for the twins. From now on Jack's course was literature and mine medicine from which we have never deviated for the rest of our lives. But the vision of ultimate beauty that we both received in our childhood at Killiney and the knowledge of that creation other than man which exists round about us always has remained with us. Both of us still share the same joy and wonder in our hearts when we stand together on a sunny evening and look out upon Lough Dan from her silver strand or walk up through the old oak-wood past the lower lake towards the upper lake at Glendalough in the Wicklow mountains.

CHAPTER 3

CAMBRIDGE

Early in May 1919 I went up to Trinity, Cambridge. It was an extraordinary moment to be young and to be alive. A million of our generation from Great Britain and Ireland lay dead in Europe where millions of other young men's bodies lay rotting in the ground —French, Russians, Italians, Germans, Austrians and even a few Portuguese, and some of America's best.

It was a moment of tremendous joy. Up to Cambridge came the survivors of the conflict, casting aside Army discipline, the Army way of life, Army thought, waking, as it were, from a nightmare. To us, the reprieved, Cambridge that spring was a miracle. It sparkled in the dawn of every new day. Never in their history have the Backs looked so beautiful. We floated in punts under Queens' College Bridge, through the King's Meadows under Clare Bridge to the Trinity Backs, and beyond to John's with its Bridge of Sighs and finally to Magdalene. Above this the river stretched away to Grantchester through lush fields in which old Cambridgeshire horses with long lips and very hairy legs cropped the fresh grass in the sunshine. There was no hurry any more. No orders to go and kill anybody, no danger of being horribly murdered oneself, stuck in the stomach with a bayonet after being kicked in the balls by a German. Among us were some who would never completely recover mentally. There was the young man who not uncommonly awoke screaming from a bloody dream. He took hours to recover each day. There was the young captain whose hair had gone quite white. During that summer term he became bald. But for the rest of us, the reaction after the war had not yet set in in England, and in Ireland 'the troubles' had not as yet boiled up. For a moment we all lived for the day, trying to forget the past without daring to think of the future. Jack in Oxford experienced the same joy. The vision of nature which we shared in Ireland he took with him and was able to find again

25

where the Cherwell flows through its 'green and pleasant land'. He wrote this little poem at that time. It expresses the mood of that moment so perfectly that I quote it here:

> They slope, they curve, they swell
> They rise in waves, they flow
> They wash against the roads.
>
> They swirl around the single trees
> They compass cottages and farms
> They island out the copses
> They beat against the woods
> The green fields of England.
>
> The green fields of England
> Her secret and her sign
> Her word to all the world
> Her heart, her song, her flag
> Her deepest truth divine.
>
> J. S. C.

Because of my athletic prowess I found myself with Geoff Conway, later the English Captain, the first to be given Rugby football Blues at Cambridge after World War I. Greenwood, the only surviving Blue from before the war, suddenly said to us one day when we were leaving the field after a game: 'Go and order your things.' We didn't know what he meant for a moment but on our way home it dawned on us what had happened. We went wild with joy. Conway was no awful brute of a man but the sensitive son of a University professor of Greek. He himself later was to get a First in Classics. Our other companions at that time were gorgeous young men like Noel Hudson who had been acting brigadier at twenty-one and been wounded over and over again. He lacked one knee-cap and always looked as if he would break in two when tackled by Rugby forwards. He didn't quite get a Blue. He was studying for the Church and I expect is now a bishop if still alive. There was also a New Zealander with one arm who couldn't quite get into the side either and all sorts of others including boys just up from school who had missed the Army altogether. It was an odd mixture. We enjoyed ourselves travelling all over England and playing against all the clubs with famous names which were reviving again.

As a leading Blue I found myself caught up in all sorts of unusual activities. Somebody came into my rooms one day and asked me to help restart the Cambridge University Officers' Training Corps. I pointed out that I was an Irishman and anyway that it was ridiculous as we were all already officers. 'Never mind,' he said, 'the War Office want it started and if we do George and Henry are promised free University education. Look Collis, with your influence you could rally the rugger crowd.'

'Well,' I said, 'for George's sake I'll do what I can but no infantry, absolutely no drill parades or foot-slogging route marches.'

'All right,' he said, 'we'll just have cavalry and horse artillery.'

And so it was. We found forty-seven old horses which served for cavalry charges before breakfast, and were used in pulling field-guns in teams, though not very successfully, at the gallop. The trouble was that some of my rugger friends couldn't ride and had to be put through an Army riding-school which meant riding round and round the enclosure without stirrups or reins till they fell off. We never had a proper parade and towards the end of the term George said we must do something to show we really existed.

'Right,' I said. 'What do you suggest?'

'Night operations are the thing,' he said.

'Yes,' I said, 'nobody will be able to see us.'

So night operations it was. We took the field-guns out of Cambridge and unlimbered them in a fen. Our instructions were to put down a barrage with dummy ammunition.

All went well for a time and the drill was carried out successfully even in the dark. We were getting bored when suddenly there was a terrific explosion. Our gun fired, a blaze of flame leaping from its muzzle; the gun itself running backwards with the backfire. George fell off his horse. He was wearing the kilt. Everyone crowded round me. I was the No. 3 who had actually pulled the trigger.

'It seems to have gone off,' I said, opening the breech and striking a match. 'No. 2 must have put in a live round.'

'How was I to know the difference in the dark,' he said.

'Well,' said George, 'this is very serious. It may cost me my Army Fellowship. We'd better get out of this quick.' And we did. We got our old horses into a gallop on our way back to Cambridge where we put the guns away as quickly as possible and went and got rather drunk together. We discussed very seriously what we should do next.

'We must do something quickly,' George said.

'Why not give a dinner to all the Commanders of all the armies in the last war,' someone suggested.

We sat down then and there and wrote out the invitations and went to bed. To our consternation about a week later we got replies from the generals all of whom accepted except Haig who declined regretfully. Now we realised we had six or seven generals coming to dinner but we had no money. However, we remembered that there was always the Old Man, a famous heavyweight don. He weighed twenty stone, and was the patron of the Rugby Football Club. We went to him and told him what had happened. He was delighted. It was his moment.

'We'll give the dinner in Pembroke,' he said. 'We'll open the cellars—get out some pre-war wine. This will be a great day for the Cambridge University Rugger Club. We'll entertain our gallant generals who won the war!'

The dinner was tremendous! The Pembroke head chef provided a meal fit for heroes and the wine was very good. The generals lapped it up.

Sir Henry Wilson, the one really brilliant soldier among them, a Northern Irishman who was to be assassinated by a Southern Irishman shortly afterwards, made a rousing speech. He said he was glad to see we were preparing for the next war as it was sure to come. He knew the Germans and he was sure that the present moment was only a pause in the struggle for the mastery of the world and the Germans would attack again as soon as they got their second wind. He spoke extremely well but we didn't like it and felt uncomfortable, not guessing how right he was.

As the Hon. Secretary of the Cambridge University Rugby Football Club, I was considered an important person, more important than Noel Hudson who had merely been a Brigadier in the last war. I was therefore seated between two of the Army Commanders.

Lord Horne turned to me when the port was going round.

'And where do you come from, my boy?' he asked with a smile.

'Dublin,' I replied.

'Oh,' he said, 'the only thing to do with your bloody country is to put it under the sea for a week.' That was a usual remark at that time when the Irish Republicans were battling with the Black and Tans for the soul of Ireland. I had heard it before. Not feeling very competent to dilate on the Irish situation, I decided on the spur of the moment to carry the attack into the enemy's quarters. I had heard that there was considerable ill feeling between the Army Commanders of the Western front about certain episodes concerning liaison between their respective wings in certain battles. I happened to know the details of one of these unfortunate affairs. So I turned an open enquiring face to the general and asked him why he had left the right wing of the Army next to his in the air on a certain occasion.

He flared up at once and said, 'I'd have you know, young fellow, my army was the only one which didn't retreat.'

'What's that?' said old General Lord Plumer who was sitting opposite. He was reputed to be the darling of his troops. And his army was said to have had three hundred thousand casualties. 'Retreat—I suppose you mean run away?'

'Well,' said Horne, 'I didn't say that the Second Army *ran*. I only said . . .'

The other generals now joined in and fought the campaigns of 1916–1918 all over again. They weren't nice to each other. We sat silent. For the first time I realised what had really happened. A whole generation of young men had been ordered to their death by incompetent men of the generation before, not one of whom could give a convincing answer if you asked them why. Why did they give those orders? What was the war being fought for anyway?

It was a sobering experience. Afterwards we walked silently back to our respective colleges through the moist Cambridge air.

Trinity was different from all the other colleges. It had eight hundred students and one didn't know half of them by name. There were at least a hundred Fellows, some of whom had sat drowsing in their rooms so long that the College seemed to have forgotten them. It had no esprit-de-corps as a College. Nobody got at you about anything. You had a director of studies. Mine was Dr Adrian, a most distinguished scientist, later to become Master of the College and a peer. He remained my friend ever afterwards though I can't remember that he taught me anything definite. At that time he was working on 'sleep' as a physiological problem. He once said to me, 'Anyway, Collis, I can assure you that sleep is an instantaneous phenomenon. I have often observed a student fall asleep in one of my lectures actually in the middle of writing down a word.'

J. J. Thompson, the then Master, is supposed to have been the first person to split the atom or at least to do the work which made that possible. He knew everything about everything but was vague in a Trinity way. He always thought I was a rowing Blue and used to ask after the boats when I dined at the High Table with the dons. It would obviously have been bad manners to have corrected him so on those occasions I was always reassuring about the boats although I only once rowed in an eight and then caught a crab.

My work in the medical school in those days was very pre-liminary. From the scientific point of view I was only learning the language, and medicine as the art of doctoring was not taught at Cambridge. Hopkins and Barcroft led the world in physiology at that time and I looked on from the fringe. I only glimpsed the fascination that research might bring later to my life while I stayed at night helping Barcroft in his experiments.

Suddenly something happened which was to influence the rest of my life. I awoke one morning after a night full of queer dreams feeling very odd. My head was burning. I had a headache and I couldn't eat my breakfast. I felt so dizzy that I didn't go down to the medical school. A doctor came. He found I had a temperature of 104°F. He examined me and could find nothing. He enquired where I had been travelling with the football club. He spoke darkly about fever—perhaps typhoid fever. The temperature persisted for some days. Then red, raised eruptions like blotches appeared on the front of my shins.

'Ah,' said the doctor, relieved at being able to make some sort of diagnosis, 'you have erythema nodosum, a symptom of rheumatic fever.' He examined my heart and my joints and shook his head. He went away, looked up the subject and now gave me a bottle of most unpleasant medicine, actually a strong solution of salycilate, the treatment for the painful joints in rheumatic fever. Soon my ears were ringing and I was nearly deaf. Gradually my fever came down but I felt very weak. I could scarcely walk across the room. My two friends Bill Daggett and Charlie Green nursed me. Eventually my mother came over from Ireland and took me off to the South of France where I lay in the early spring sun in a garden at Cap Martin between Monte Carlo and Menton and gradually recovered. A friend of mine called Omio Iyangur, an Indian, had come into my room while I was lying sick with the fever. He sat down by the fire looking very ill and shaky. He told me his awful cough which I had often noticed had been diagnosed as tuberculosis and that he was going home to India with his mother. He then got up and said goodbye. I heard later he had died on the way. His mother sent me a little ivory case in memory of him. At the time I was far too sick myself to realise his dangerous condition, far less connect his cough in any way with my own state. But in years to come the whole sequence became plain to me during my research into the cause of rheumatic fever which led me to unravel one fact of scientific medicine: the mechanism of erythema nodosum.

Now I joined Bill Daggett in Paris where we dissected the head and neck of a Frenchman whose body had been recovered from the Seine. It had been so imperfectly pickled that we disarticulated the neck and took the head into the garden to avoid the smell. It was my first experience of French medicine.

When I got back to Cambridge for the summer term I found my illness had caused me to be passed over for the captaincy of the

Cambridge side for the next season. This was a very natural reaction as it was doubtful if I was well enough to play again but it seemed a crushing disappointment to me. Hence when Harry Davison, an American officer war-veteran and son of one of the partners of the New York millionaire J. P. Morgan, asked me to come to Yale University in the U.S.A. for the next year, to help to set up a group of scholarships for Oxford and Cambridge men to go to Yale, Harvard and Princeton, I accepted immediately.

CHAPTER 4

YALE

One morning towards the end of September 1921 I found myself aboard a Dutch liner, the *Noordaam*, creeping up into New York Harbour. The first sight of New York from the Narrows shimmering in the vivid sparkling American sunshine is so overpowering that one is reduced to silence as thousands of immigrants have found.

On this particular morning the whole scene was accentuated by the Davisons meeting me, as we came alongside in Hoboken, in a fast, long, electric yacht that carried us rapidly up the East River, under the vast bridges to Long Island Sound and their palace there.

Coming from a professional Irish home, the immense wealth that the city presented and the personal riches of the Davisons were frightening but I had no time then to think out my position. After a night's stay at Peacock Point I was taken across the Sound to New Haven and presented to the Yale football squad which was already in training. Harry Davison felt this would be my best introduction as a Cambridge Blue to Yale University. One is not eligible to play for Yale in one's first year, a rule invented to eliminate would-be athletes from getting into the College on their muscular prowess alone. I found myself in a squad of 'ill-eligibles' who were organised to form an opposition to the official University Squad. We had a coach of our own, a Dr Bull, and in consequence were known as 'Bull's bastards'. In those days to an outsider such as myself the whole concept of American football was a complete mystery. It presented a mystique of its own representing many of the forces behind American life. First of all comes violence—in this case straight, physical violence. The players are heavily armoured though in those days we did not sport crash helmets with barred face protectors which give the present players their appearance of knights of old in modern dress. Secondly, complicated tactics are the order of the day. The code to be remembered, denoting each play, the drill necessary for each member of the side to remember his particular part in the complicated manoeuvre to be carried out, are such as to make the game into a veritable 'business'. The propaganda build-up of the teams, the vast arenas of the stands around the grounds, the tremendous spectacle finally evolved are all on such a grandiose scale as to leave the poor European intensely bewildered.

Harry Davison's introduction by means of the football squad certainly threw me into the centre of Yale life with a bang. I met a splendid group of young athletes some of whom have remained my friends for life. They were fearless, great players in every sense of the word and friendly and warm-hearted beyond the ordinary. It was almost like belonging to a group of young men in some army ready to sacrifice themselves for a cause. My own part with Bull's squad, however, did not last long, for the first time I was sent out into the field to stand up against the Yale team my left arm was torn backwards out of the elbow joint with such violence that all I could do was to carry it off holding it up by its little finger. To begin with there was no feeling in it at all. But soon an excruciating pain began to wrack me. The ulnar nerve had been pinched between the bones and a blood vessel in the tissues torn so that they went black right down to the wrist. The pain was so bad that I have ever afterwards known what torture means—an agony like a bright burning flame with a dark wall behind it which can only be borne as long as the mind is steady.

Out of the game, I was rapidly driven to a hospital and given morphia. It was the first time I had experienced the extraordinary effect of the drug. Torn by agony I was clinging to my mangled arm to prevent its slightest movement. The jolting journey in the ambulance had been so bad that I had only just refrained from yelling by remembering what I was supposed to be representing: a Cambridge athlete in America. But now the morphia began to act— the pain gradually subsided. Whole minutes passed when it went altogether and I lay back relaxed. They came and cut my playing clothes off me, removing my steel knee-guard, thigh-, shoulder- and kidney-protectors, and laid me on soft pillows with the broken arm extended on an electrically warmed bandage. In a few days I was about again with my left arm in a sling. Harry Davison had been right, I was now a Yale man. I was elected to two clubs—secret societies—allowed to dine at Moray's with the élite and treated as one of themselves. But I do not recommend this form of entering into American life to any Cambridge or other Blue if they find themselves at Yale.

When the academic term proper started I found my position at

Yale somewhat equivalent to a second-year medical student nearing the end of his physiology and anatomy studies. But the idea of the Davison Scholarship was to get British undergraduates to go to an American university for one year and then return to their own university for a final year bringing, it was hoped, an understanding of American life and thought back with them. Clearly this was almost impossible as far as a medical student was concerned. But as the first scholar from Cambridge I felt I must do my best and at least try and see what it was like to be an ordinary undergraduate in an American university. I therefore not only entered the medical school and went on with my anatomy and physiology studies but I also chose two courses on the academic side: Lewis' course in English poetry and Phelps' famous course in Modern Drama.

Lewis was a real master and his course a complete joy to me: Byron, Coleridge, Shelley, above all Wordsworth whose clarity of line in telling of his vision of infinite beauty in the natural world about us put into words the meaning of the visions I had seen in Ireland as a child.

Billy Phelps was a complete contrast to the academic, charming, erudite Lewis. He was a showman. On Tuesday afternoons he came bounding in to give a lecture to the adoring ladies of New Haven in a large auditorium. His conduct of classes was in the same vein, but he made us read the whole of Ibsen and Shaw, many of the other great playwrights of our time, and write him essays every week on what we had read and thought. The best of these he read out at his lectures with his own pungent comments. On several occasions he read out an essay of mine which made me feel that I was grasping the meaning of the subject of drama with some understanding though I did not realise then what the effect this brief introduction to this form of expression was to have subsequently on my life.

In the medical school I found the teaching a great contrast to Cambridge. Here the art of teaching had itself obviously been studied and the means whereby a subject could be conveyed intelligibly to the students' mind and memory worked out. This resulted of course in the classes resembling in no small degree school teaching: the student was taught by the teacher rather than by himself. At Cambridge the teaching was very poor. The teachers were primarily interested in advancing their own subjects. Teaching undergraduates the elements of physiology was just a bore to people like Hopkins and Barcroft. They inspired you and left you to learn if you could. In the end you taught yourself how to master a subject so that in future nothing, save perhaps higher mathematics, was insurmountable. The American high school method, however, when added to the personal Cambridge approach, was very effective and the few months I spent in the Yale medical school brought the subject far more into my open consciousness which after all is what is needed if you are to pass the necessary gruelling examinations. I learned enough in anatomy to satisfy the examiners later even in the pure memory test at Cambridge, and Mendel, who made bio-chemistry mean something to me, helped me to get over seventy per cent and to be among the first few in the physiology examination at Cambridge.

During the last two years the Irish Troubles had been raging. After World War I the Irish-elected members of parliament met in Dublin and declared a Republican parliament of their own. Lloyd George proclaimed this illegal and arrested the leaders. An underground rebellion followed. Lloyd George recruited a vicious ex-World War I group of soldiers into an auxiliary force which became known as the 'Black and Tans'. Violence and subsequent death became the order of the day on both sides. After a period during which American opinion made itself felt the British decided to make terms with Michael Collins, the brave leader of the Irish, and a truce was brought about followed by a treaty.

During these years I had been away at Cambridge starting my medical course and coming back to Ireland only rarely. Previously my education had been largely in England, I had obtained a commission in the British Army (Irish Guards) and although I still remembered the feelings I had had during the 1916 rebellion, I was not caught up in the struggle. I remember now, however, opening the *New York Times* one day in my rooms at Yale and seeing that the Irish Free State had been created and that peace between the two countries had at last come about. The whole room seemed to sway about me and memories of Ireland crowded my mind. I remembered the famine, the penal laws, the executions which the Irish had suffered—I wept for joy. I think I realised at that moment more than at any other that deep in my subconscious was a passion for my country that all the English education I had had, all the English friendships I had made, could not overlay, and that somehow, some time, I must get back and work for my own people.

But at that moment Yale activities filled every moment of my days. I had not yet completely recovered from my illness of the last year at Cambridge and I sometimes found myself so weary that I would lie down in my room in the new Harkness building and fall asleep during the day. Then suddenly, some time in the early spring, I got a few days off and went with a friend, Arthur Bingham, to New Hampshire. It was very cold there and we got frozen coming down from a snow-covered mountain one evening. We both collapsed and ran high temperatures. We took the train back to New York and arrived next morning feeling very ill and retired to bed in Dr Bingham's house in New York. Arthur rapidly recovered but I did not. My chest began to hurt when I breathed and I developed a severe pleurisy, my left chest rapidly filling up with fluid which had to be aspirated. I was put in the old Presbyterian Hospital and full examined. I told them about my previous illness at Cambridge, the erythema nodosum which I had been told was a symptom of rheumatic fever. 'Well,' said the chief physician, 'pleurisy like this is almost always a symptom of tuberculosis.' The bottom seemed to drop out of my life. No more Rugby football! I had a vision of life in some sanitorium on top of a Swiss mountain. The memory of my sister's fate must have shown in my face for the professor of medicine added kindly, 'Of course, in your case it might only be a reaction to influenza in a rheumatic subject.' 'Yes,' I said to myself and grasping this straw like a life-line I assumed this unlikely diagnosis to be correct and so put tuberculosis completely out of my mind, thus enabling me to get on with my life as if I had merely had a minor illness. It was years later after I had miraculously recovered that my own research into rheumatic fever, tuberculosis and erythema nodosum proved that both the erythema and the pleurisy were, in fact, caused by tuberculosis. If I had realised this at the time it would have wrecked my life as it was then developing. However, assuming that all that was wrong with me was a rheumatic tendency, whatever that meant, I accepted the Davisons' invitation to go down to Georgia, near the Florida border, to convalesce at their place deep in the forests. Though I took the New York doctor's advice when he said 'Go home as soon as you can' and I booked a passage home in a month's time.

My stay near Thomasville in Georgia is vivid in my memory still— the wonderful warm balmy pine-scented air after the cold, biting winds in New York; the birds—humming-birds, cardinals, blue birds. Then the horses—'Ginger-snap' whom I rode daily through the Everglades; the perfect food, served by the Davisons' immaculate staff, including a valet, once a corporal in the Coldstream Guards; and finally, the amazing Davison family themselves.

H. P. Davison, the father, was dying at the time, of a tumour of the brain, but was still perfectly in command of all his thinking faculties. He had been operated upon and decompressed and his condition diagnosed as hopeless, though I don't think he knew this. He often sat and talked passionately of his work. He was one of the great American money kings being a Morgan Bank partner, all of whom were said at the time to be making a million dollars a year. How anybody could or can make a million dollars a year by honest work still baffles me. If it is done on what is called 'the stock market' it must mean, I suppose, that other people have lost a million dollars. How can a bank lend money it hasn't got? What exactly is credit? Until Stalin murdered all his friends I used to think that state ownership was better than capitalism. But now Russian communism doesn't seem the answer either. Somebody recently described capitalism as a 'jungle' full of surprises and containing wild beasts, a land of adventure, and communism as a 'prison' for the individual. At that time in my life, I said very little, just sat and listened in awe to this leader of American money. Trubee Davison, his eldest son, was there also and several of the charming daughters came and went. Trubee had broken his back in an air crash into Long Island Sound in World War I and had been rescued by Dot, the daughter of the Headmaster of Groton School, whom he later married. The accident left him with great weakness in the legs, but, like Roosevelt, he overcame this disability and became a Senator. The most remarkable member of the family, however, was Kate Davison, H. P. Davison's wife. If ever a woman knew that she should be the centre of a family, she did—the centre to whom all members could return for comfort and support from whatever battering the world might have in store for them.

At that time she was taken up with nursing H. P. Davison through his last illness with all its hopes and fears, and with death always looming before her. Later I was to see her freed from this awful tension in the centre of the Davison home on Long Island surrounded by the families of her children. She had a simplicity and a goodness which completely transcended her wealth, making her a woman of great heart loved by us all. She was adored by all the subsequent Davison Scholars and all the different people whom I have sent to her down the years. She is dead now but her memory does not fade and I often recall her warmth and real greatness, particularly whenever I run into brash American tourists abroad, destroying the peaceful beauty of some sacred spot such as the Sea of Galilee with their harsh loud-voiced acclamations of approbation or dislike out of tune with the place they are in at that moment. Then instead of feeling anti-American, as is all too easy on these occasions, I remember Kate and let my battered senses relax.

The Davisons belonged to the Republican hierarchy of the United States and knowing them made it more possible to understand the astonishing position which these families of great wealth can reach, the latest example being the Kennedys.

In those days I was only a young undergraduate recovering from a severe set-back and I did not realise how privileged I was to have got a glimpse of America behind the scenes. Later, however, I have realised how much these few weeks in Georgia taught me, particularly when I returned to America in subsequent years or became involved in American affairs in other parts of the world.

I don't know whether the other Davison Scholars learned as much as I did, or got to know the best side of American life which is all too easy to miss amongst the vast numbers of semi-educated and over-moneyed people there. But the Davison Scholarships, which now have been amalgamated with those presented by the Harkness family, were a very fitting memorial to H. P. Davison who believed in the friendship of the peoples of the English-speaking world as being the best hope for the future.

After four weeks in Georgia, a week at sea and two or three weeks at home in Killiney I had recovered enough to go back to Cambridge for the May term. I did not tell my family that the American doctors thought my pleurisy was connected with tuberculosis. In fact, I made very little of either of the illnesses I had had. My father, having the Collis constitution and never being ill himself, asked no questions. My mother accepted my assurances, and so I found myself once more at Trinity, Cambridge, in May 1922.

My medical friends welcomed me back. We were all due to take the gruelling second M.B. medical examination in anatomy and physiology sometime in June and nobody had time to think of anything else as our medical futures depended utterly on the result.

Trinity being Trinity, my re-entry was accepted without comment. I might not have been away. The young man to whom I had left my room got up and very affably found himself digs somewhere in the town. My tutor, a classic, who was supposed to be responsible for me as a pupil, but who obviously regarded medical students as a lower form of life, indicated by certain growls that he regarded anybody leaving Cambridge and going to an American university as a person with a damaged brain. Adrian told me some more about sleep and J. J. Thompson, the Master, said kindly that the boats must have missed me. In Hall at dinner I was now at the B.A.s' table having acquired a B.A. in physiology. Here I sat with a brilliant group of young men, like the Lister brothers and Roseveare whose conversation was so quick and stimulating that those evenings when we discussed the meaning of the world seem to be with me still.

It was heaven to stroll out after Hall on the Backs behind Hewell's Court and wander up and down on the green lawn by the water's edge with some companion or amble across to a close friend in

John's next door and sit talking over cups of coffee late into the night. I had to husband every ounce of strength because my side ached where I had had the pleurisy and I still used to become so tired that I couldn't take in what I was reading after ten o'clock at night. I needed twelve hours' sleep at this period. But my Yale teaching on top of my Cambridge knowledge of how to make myself tackle a subject stood me in good stead and I passed the second M.B. examination without difficulty, came up for a special medical course in bacteriology and pharmacology during the long vacation, and then packed up my books and set off on the real medical course in King's College Hospital in London at the end of the summer.

CHAPTER 5

MEDICAL STUDENT

King's College Hospital is situated at Camberwell, the heart of the Cockney world. Here were crowded into dingy dirty streets in little houses the poor English Londoners. In Whitechapel and the East End were to be found the Jews and immigrants of all kinds, but from Camberwell to the Elephant and Castle is the home of the real English. I was told that in one area off the Walworth Road they were crowded sixteen thousand to the acre in those days. I had already got to know the Cockneys through the Rugby Clubs which were situated in Notting Hill which in those days was still English. There shortly after the war I had met C. S. Donald, a Scotsman who ran the clubs. He taught me to love the Cockneys. One picture of the Rugby Clubs remains in my mind. It was during the famous General Strike of 1926. Many of the men and boys in the club worked at the rail termini around, looking after the then horse-drawn transport. In an immense establishment near Paddington were stabled some hundreds of magnificient dray horses, huge creatures with a vast expanse of back and very hairy legs. The General Strike was the most English of English affairs from beginning to end. Everybody 'played the game'—the strikers, the volunteers and the lookers-on. My friends and I volunteered to look after the horses in this particular stable. Far from being stopped by the pickets and turned back we were greeted with pleasantries of an earthy variety, and asked to look after certain horses particularly, to whom we were not uncommonly asked to bring sugar and turnips by the pickets themselves. Admittedly some young gentlemen who went up to the East End and did more or less the same thing there at another stable had their trousers removed by the strikers and had to make their way back on buses to the West End in their shirt-tails. But everyone laughed, including the young men.

On arrival in London I found that Rugby House was too far

away from King's College Hospital for convenience. So I started by living at Toc H House in the Lambeth Road. Then I went to Cambridge House in the Walworth Road, nearer still to King's and Cockneydom.

The Cockneys are the kindest people in the world. They are really the most quietly civilised people you can meet whether as soldiers in Ireland, or helping to rebuild the towns of Germany after World War II. In the shattered Europe of those days the English private soldier seemed the only civilised human creature left in all the world. About the time I went to Camberwell they fined a man in the Walworth Road half a crown for ill-treating a goldfish by leaving the bowl in the sun. People said that this showed they were sentimental. Maybe it did. But I was less sure, after the London Blitz in World War II.

Living at Cambridge House and working down the road at King's College Hospital I became part of this Cockney world. As a medical student you served in the wards, clerking, which meant writing up the notes on the cases and acting as dressers on the surgical patients— anything from helping to dress wounds in the casualty department to assisting at operations. You were thrown into the closest contact with patients of all kinds from those with urinary stoppages to others with acute pain or loss of muscular control. You saw men reduced to such weakness that they would cry; you encountered bravery where you might have expected despair and fortitude instead of panic. We learned that each man suffers and dies alone.

The teaching staff at that time were all honorary physicians and surgeons. That is to say they gave their services free to the hospital including the teaching. They made their living by seeing private patients in their Harley Street consulting rooms. It meant that they taught the practical practice of medicine. This was the method in all the medical schools in Great Britain and Ireland in those days. Nowadays there are a great many full-time physicians and surgeons who spend their time advancing the subject of their choice and teaching, but the main motif has remained the same. The result of this approach has been that the doctors turned out in these islands are better attuned to practise medicine in the field than doctors qualified by many of the European and American schools where the training, if more scientific, is more theoretical than practical. It has been my experience in latter years, when helping to organise medicine in developing countries, that doctors whose training has been along such lines in Great Britain or Ireland find it easier to cope with health problems generally in these states than doctors trained elsewhere.

King's, at that time, had a number of men who have left their mark on modern English medicine as leaders in this field of the practice of medicine. Among these the most notable were Sir Cecil Wakely and Sir Frederick Still.

Wakely, when I was at King's in the twenties, was an assistant surgeon of enormous vitality. He had been a medical student who served more or less as a qualified doctor in the British Navy during World War I. He acted as an assistant to the then senior King's College Hospital surgeon, Sir George Lentel Cheatle, who had been Surgeon-Admiral in the war. Wakely told outrageous stories about Cheatle which delighted us students, as when the great man cut off a sailor's wrong leg. He was so grand that when he operated on a battleship everything had to be ready for him when he came aboard, the patient laid out, anaesthetised and on the operating table. On one of these occasions the job was the amputation of the left leg at the hip. Sir George did it rapidly with some fine sweeps of the knife. Then the rumour began to spread. Finally Wakely was told to tell him. 'Sir,' he said, 'I'm sorry. You've cut off the wrong leg.' But Sir George was grand that day. 'No matter, my boy,' he said, 'we all make mistakes. I'll cut off the other one tomorrow.'

Fortunately when the seaman came round from the anaesthetic he refused to have anything of the sort done.

In World War II, of course, Wakely also became an Admiral himself.

Still was a great contrast to Wakely. He was a shy Cornishman who had never married and had no children of his own. He was the first real paediatrician in Great Britain. To adults he was pernickety and shy and many of his house-physicians and students found him unsympathetic. But early in my internship I saw him take on to his knee a child who was screaming with pain when Wakely was trying to examine her. In Still's hands the child ceased to cry and lay quietly so that the diagnosis could be made. A kind of aura seemed to hang round Still transforming the tidy, clean impersonal ward into a place of beauty so that everybody smiled suddenly. I never forgot this vision of the man and later when I became his house-physician at King's and he invited me to become his last house-physician before he retired at the Hospital for Sick Children, Great Ormond Street, I immediately accepted and, instead of becoming a psychiatrist which was my intention at that moment, I became a children's physician for life.

* * *

During my first winter in London I learned the language of clinical medicine and found my way around the wards of King's College Hospital and did little else. I had been told not to attempt to play football and although my health seemed to have recovered I only played a couple of games towards the end of the season. However, when the following season began to loom up I decided to play again properly, putting out of my conscious mind the warnings I had received and being careful not to get examined by any of the Hospital doctors. I was immediately asked to lead the Harlequins who were at that time the gayest and most lively London club. They had the tradition of particularly attractive open play. I also agreed to captain the Hospital at mid-week and in the Hospital Cup matches. But far more important to my life was the fact that Rugby football now brought me back to Ireland. Solomons, the famous Master of the Rotunda Hospital in Dublin and an old international himself, got me a trial for the Irish team. One of the great moments in my life happened when, after the last trial match in Dublin, I rang up the Wanderers' Club in Dublin from the Goat Club in London where I was lunching with Halloran, the heavy-weight champion (boxing) of the British Navy. We heard that both of us had been picked for the Irish team to play against France. The Dublin voice read out the names slowly. Mine was the last.

The Irish team which in the old days had been composed entirely of Anglo-Irishmen now consisted of a cross-section of Irish life from Dublin, Belfast and Cork. And in spite of the differences in background of the players—Catholics, Protestants, Republicans, Orange-men—all were Irish on these occasions, proud of their green jerseys with their embroidered shamrocks, and thrilled to the core when the tens of thousands of voices shouted 'Ireland' as they ran on to the ground. Now, though part of the London world, particularly the London medical world, I knew where I belonged and that sooner or later I must return to Ireland. My first step in that direction was to take another piece of advice from Dr Solomons and to do my practical midwifery course at the Rotunda Hospital in Dublin.

Now suddenly at the age of twenty-two I found myself in the city of my forbears where my family had been doctors for over a hundred years, whose old Georgian houses formed subconscious images in my brain as I walked through its streets in the hospital district.

It was a moment of disillusionment and despair in Ireland. The struggle with England had ended in a Treaty which had not satisfied the Republicans who had continued to fight on against their recent comrades. Collins had fallen by an Irish bullet and in revenge the Free Staters had executed many of the Republican leaders such as Rory O'Connor and Erskine Childers. The country was wellnigh bankrupt, but still had to pay England the land annuities under Gladstone's old Land Act whereby the Irish farmers were able to purchase back the lands of Ireland. In Dublin the poverty, the slums, the dirt and the smells were appalling. As students on the Rotunda district we found ourselves face to face with conditions of squalor and grinding poverty which plucked at the mind and tore at the heart.

One desperate scene stands out in my memory. It was on one of my last cases. My companion was a Scot. It was his first case. The woman, whose husband was a young Free State soldier, lived in a single room in a house which had been battered by shell-fire in the recent fighting. The room was lit only by a poor oil-lamp, there was no heating and the windows were shut. In consequence the smell in the room of stale sweat, general dirt and unemptied slops was very nauseating. On arrival I made an examination of the patient. I knew just enough to know that something was very wrong. So I ran all the way back in the rain to the Rotunda Hospital through dark, wet streets. I got the doctor on duty to come back with me. When we arrived a second lamp had been brought in and there was more light. It was easy to see that the woman was now in extremis. The doctor gave her an injection. She did not rally but cried out and then sank down on her pillows and died before our eyes. There we stood in the flickering light. Gradually the room filled up. The young husband burst into loud wailing. For a moment pandemonium reigned. Somebody said we'd killed her. Then an old gnarled woman entered. She raised her hands and keened. Silence fell. She came to the dead girl, covered her face and then knelt down and began to recite the rosary. The others knelt also in the room and on the landing outside. We stood silently with bowed heads; the Scot by the fireplace with a look of horror on his face, alone, an outsider. I stood by the door among the people feeling a oneness with them, a Dubliner among Dubliners.

The old woman got up from her knees, said a few words and began to clean up the mess and lay out the dead girl.

I took the Scotsman by the arm. We went silently out and walked back to the Rotunda.

The English companions who had accompanied me to the Rotunda from London for the midwifery course were disgusted with the conditions in Dublin. Their comments hurt me. I couldn't explain or defend my own city, but the experience of those days sank into my subconscious with such hard lines as to make my decision in years to come automatic when the opportunity to return to Dublin presented itself.

*　　　*　　　*

Back at King's I became immersed in medicine, in learning how to become a doctor, though this took me nearly ten years during which I became qualified, did my residences in England and in America, and learned the meaning of research along scientific lines upon which the basis of modern medicine is founded.

At King's as a house-physician I was left very much on my own to work out my doctor–patient relationships. My chiefs came round the wards twice a week diagnosing, explaining and teaching. The patients regarded them as gods and seldom ventured to speak to them. The consultants left the personal side of doctoring largely to their residents. Dr Kinnear Wilson, the world-famous neurologist who has a disease called by his name, said to me one day after examining a man who was dying slowly of disseminated sclerosis (a fatal degeneration of the nervous system which takes a long time to kill): 'Collis, will you look after this man, talk to him and give him a course of injections if you feel that will help his morale. I have so many of these patients I'd go mad if I got too close to them.'

So for months I lived beside the sick and the dying, saw pain and got used to the valley of the shadow of death with all its agony and grandeur. I also experienced the happiness of people who recovered from a disastrous illness.

It was in the children's wards that I learned the joy of being a doctor. There was a little girl of twelve who was called Ivy, a case of rheumatic fever associated with heart failure. She had been admitted into the adult women's ward and was surrounded by older women mostly in pain or weakness. She was very unhappy and used to cry most of the day, her heart beating very fast so that the veins in her neck pulsated, giving her a frightened appearance. At that time I met Coué, the famous French auto-suggestion man: 'Every day and in every way I am getting better and better.' He taught me how to give suggestion under light hypnosis by a simple method which ever since I have found useful in removing pain or putting people to sleep. In Ivy's case I came up five nights in succession and put her into a light sleep and then suggested to her that she was 'getting better', that soon she would be well, that next day she'd feel happy. From that moment she ceased to cry and became the radiant, smiling, adapted child of the women's ward. She even began to recover. She loved me quite simply as a child and I loved her back.

At the end of my residency at King's, Dr Still, the first famous British paediatrician, brought me, as I have already written, to the Hospital for Sick Children in Great Ormond Street as his last house-physician. Here I found myself amongst a group of outstanding young men who were to create modern paediatrics in Great Britain.

Among them were Alan Moncrieff, later to succeed Still as Professor of Paediatrics in London University, and Wilfred Sheldon who became Sir Wilfred when he found himself children's physician to Prince Charles and Princess Anne. At this time they were both registrars, that is to say, senior housemen, though not resident. None of us were really paid anything in those days. As house-physician one got £50 a year which was taken away for laundry; as a registrar, perhaps £350. One was expected to work day and night with no official time off at all.

On my arrival at Great Ormond Street, Sheldon, who was also a King's man, said to me, 'Collis, I think you are intelligent, though with all this football other people doubt it! What about doing some real work while you are here? Why not publish a paper and take the Membership examination for the College of Physicians?' This was a completely new thought as far as I was concerned. I had never considered myself very bright, particularly after what Dr David had said to me at Rugby, but I had a great respect for Sheldon whose knowledge of paediatrics impressed me enormously.

"All right,' I said, 'I'll try.'

I got together a clinical paper on a group of interesting cases and as Sheldon was away showed it to the third registrar, Reggie Lightwood, who made me completely rewrite it in proper form a second time. I was surprised actually how easily writing came to me. Then I set out to work for the examination for the Membership of the London Royal College of Physicians which is one of the most gruelling tests of its kind in the world.

You had to get the whole of child, adult and old age medicine with their physiology and pathology into the forefront of your consciousness so that you could reach down into the folds of your memory quickly enough to be able to produce the right answers at a moment's notice.

For three months I worked for four hours every night after I finished my rounds in the hospital wards. I never left the hospital precincts even to go out to a movie or have a drink, though I kept fit by playing tennis on the hospital court under the splendid old plane trees.

The eve of the examination arrived quite suddenly. I met Sheldon on the stairs of the hospital.

'Oh, you're taking the Membership tomorrow. Good luck, Bob. By the way, do you know old Jones is examiner again? He's a bit cracked. He always gets in a question on the ovaries though it's a medical and not a gynae exam.'

'Thanks,' I said, and having nothing else to do I went up to my room and took down a Scottish gynaecological work I had. I realised that I knew nothing about the ovaries, one way or the other.

To my amazement I discovered that there were seventeen ovarian conditions of importance. I read on, becoming entranced with this completely new subject to me. I forgot all about the exam and looked up nothing else.

Lo and behold, next morning on opening the paper in the Royal College of Physicians I found to my delight that the first question in the paper was 'Classify ovarian tumours'. I started my answers by boldly proclaiming: 'I shall approach this question under seventeen headings.' The second question in the paper was one concerning children to which I knew the answer completely but the last question was about tuberculosis of the skin and the only thing I knew about it was its Latin name, 'Lupus Vulgaris'. I left that question out and concentrated simply upon the others.

I heard much later that the examiners were delighted with my paper. 'Here is a well-known athlete, actually an old Blue and an international footballer, who could approach the ovary under seventeen headings. The man must be a genius!' For the rest of the examination they pulled my leg benevolently to such an extent that after the final viva I thought I must have failed. But the Secretary of the College assured me that I had passed. I was so overcome by this that I missed the first step of the stairs on leaving his room and slithered down on my bottom into the College Hall. Here I was picked up by the Cockney porter who said, 'Pubs don't open till six o'clock, guv'nor!' I staggered out into Pall Mall and walked into Trafalgar Square. There I slapped one of the immense stone lions on his large front paw. He almost smiled.

The winter now was approaching and I flung myself for one last time into the athletic world and played again for Ireland at Rugby football. At the same time I applied for a Rockefeller Research Fellowship of which a few were available at that moment and was elected to one. I made arrangements to go to the Johns Hopkins Hospital's Children's Department at Baltimore the following autumn. There I was to be introduced to the world of research, where one pursues an idea towards its source through days and nights of work, often in dark frustration and only sometimes towards the dazzling light of discovering a new fact, a new conception, another facet in the strange mathematical imagination of the Creator. Before setting out upon this voyage of discovery I had a moment in Ireland when the mystery of nature came back to me with all the vividness of the creature world.

CHAPTER 6

DARAGH

People who have never owned a dog themselves are apt to regard such relationships as sentimental or phoney. But the creature–human relationship can be a transcendental experience of life and death like no other.

My first acquaintance with a dog of my own was in my twenties when I was a post-graduate young doctor. I acquired an Irish wolfhound called Daragh. He belonged to Caragh's family. Caragh was the Bruce Lockharts' mother wolfhound and of extraordinary beauty. Rufus Bruce Lockhart had taken over the House I had been in at Rugby School after World War I and when I came down to stay at the school again after the war I met him and his family for the first time. He was a most distinguished Scottish character later to become headmaster of the famous Sedbergh School in the north of England. Mona Lockhart, his wife, was half-Irish and they had four magnificent sons. Lockhart himself was not only a linguist, an international rugger player before and after World War I, but was also a painter of some distinction. Mona was a painter as well but excelled really at being the mother of these four sons all of whom did everything better than anybody else. As far as I remember they all played for Scotland except one who had a tuberculous knee, and excelled in their careers whether schoolmastering like their father, in medicine or the Secret Service. When their recounting of legendary achievements became a little too much their mother used to look up and say, 'Let us have a little less B.L.G. (Bruce Lockhart Genius) please!'

I naturally stayed there as often as I could get invited by them or could find an excuse. They always said I came to see Caragh and not them. Certainly she was one of the attractions of their family. She had a number of famous puppies who won every sort of prize so that the car they could at last afford was said to belong to her. How

I heard that one of her descendants could be purchased at a price I could pay, I don't know. I think the owner had died. Anyway, I got Daragh. He was tall, fair and very lanky when I saw him first, and suffering badly from rickets, his legs bowed and his ankle joints very loose due to lack of proper food and vitamin D. He was growing at a rate of a pound and an inch a day and had to be given a pound of raw meat and four tablespoonfuls of cod liver oil every day.

He looked at me with his soft wolfhound eyes when I came in, so I gave them all the money I had and brought him back to Ireland. Soon he knew my voice and could pick up my scent and track me down for miles. His strength and beauty grew very rapidly and he gained an almost regal appearance so that people would stop us in the street and ask if he was really a Royal Irish Wolfhound that they had read of in books about the days of Erin.

I took him on holiday to the West of Ireland to join my family. We arrived one evening in Galway, an ancient city full of history and wonders such as the water under the bridge where you can see many salmon stationary in the current, washing off the sea lice in the fresh water before proceeding upstream to their appointed breeding-grounds. I thought Galway romantic and beautiful but we were rudely repulsed by the hotel manageress of the Railway Hotel who looked at Daragh very doubtfully and absolutely refused him permission to sleep in my room. I didn't know what to do so I just got into the family car and drove out of the town. I had never been there before and I had no idea where to go. We drove westwards. As it was getting dark we reached a part of the road that ran close to the shore of Galway Bay. It was summer and very warm. I had a sweater and two rugs, so I put on the sweater and made an impromptu bed in the sand of the shore. Daragh and I lay back to back for warmth; I rolled myself up in one rug and tied the other by its fringed edges round his neck.

The night was clear and bright with stars reflected in the still water of the Bay. We fell asleep. Shortly after midnight some fisher people passed along the shore towards a hamlet some hundreds of yards away. I was awoken by a 'woof' from Daragh and saw their dim figures. Daragh roused himself and stood up, the rug clinging round him like a cloak and gave tongue to the ancient bay of the wolfhound which echoed and re-echoed around the shore. The people seeing a queer draped creature silhouetted against the night cried out, afraid they had seen the banshee, and fled into the darkness beyond the rocks.

We lay down again and fell asleep once more. I awoke early as the sun was rising red through a mist over the sea. A feeling came over me that I had done all this before, that it was natural to be lying by Galway Bay with a wolfhound by my side.

I caught up with my family on Achill Island where they were staying in the old Sheridan's Hotel where the tariff at that time was 10s. 6d. for Bed and Breakfast.

It was here that our man–dog relationship was created. I had to feed him myself which meant cutting up sheep's heads and the like, not all that easy to obtain on the island. If I left him for any time he would get restless and come into the hotel and walk along the wooden corridor swinging his great tail, knocking on the doors on each side so that the occupants would shout 'Come in!' On reaching my room he would snuffle around and lie down until I came in when he would jump up and welcome me with endearing little noises and great wags of his feathery tail. At Doogort there is a semi-circular silver strand below the mountain where I used to take him daily. There he gambolled or lay in the soft sand then fell instantly asleep. I still have an entrancing picture of him there looking at me with a half-expectant puppy face.

Not long after this I had to leave Ireland. Leaving Daragh was one of the hardest partings of my life. I arranged for him to go and be mated to Bran, a slim grey wolfhound bitch which Lady Talbot de Malahide had given to my sister Mary who lived in an old Georgian House at Leixlip on the Liffey, about twelve miles from Dublin.

The last night before I set out for America I spent in my old room at Kilmore with Daragh sleeping on the rug by my bed. Each time I awoke that night, and it was many times, he awoke also to push his soft muzzle into my hand or lick my face.

I left him next morning on the railway platform beside my mother. The train started; I crossed the carriage and looked out on the beauty of Killiney Bay with the Wicklow mountains rising beyond, but I could see nothing.

When I came back from America it was not possible for some years more for me to pay more than occasional visits to Ireland as I was very intensely concerned with an important project of research (see p. 62) which did in fact determine much of my future medical career. So Daragh stayed at Leixlip and sired numerous famous and beautiful wolfhounds which brought joy to many people. He was complete and happy in my sister's family but whenever I came he would greet me in a particular way, placing his great paw in my hand and intimating that he and I shared a secret.

It was fitting, therefore, that when he reached the end of the wolfhound span of life and had passed into his last fatal period of illness I should be on hand. I had just come to Kilmore for a few days when my sister rang me up and told me that he was very ill and that the vet felt he must be put down that night—would I come?

When I arrived it was evening. The tall beech-trees stood whispering about the old grey stone house at Leixlip. All was silent as I passed under the gloom of the trees and entered the stable behind the house. A candle was burning with a yellow light in one of the stalls; the ground was spread with fresh hay. There lay Daragh, his body much wasted but his great head and shoulders still magnificent.

He looked up when I came in and greeted me with his hazel eyes and a feeble wag of his tail as he lay crouched in the hay.

I knelt down and took a little bit of chocolate out of my pocket: this was my way of greeting him. He licked it and swallowed a tiny portion, as it were to please me because he hadn't been able to keep down anything, even water, all day. He put his paw in my hand and looked into my eyes. We sat thus together for a little time. Then they came and told me the vet had arrived with prussic acid to inject into his lung as the quickest and most painless end. I explained to him that I was going to give Daragh an anaesthetic and that he was to stand by with the injection until I gave him the signal.

He protested that it would be hard to administer an anaesthetic to such an animal, that he would struggle and that prussic acid injected into the lungs was more or less instantaneous.

However, I believed that if I treated my hound like a child he would not suffer or struggle. Again I knelt down and talked to him. My sister held his great paw in her lap. He looked at us trustingly. I took up an open anaesthetic mask, sprayed on it ethyl chloride scented with lavender which I used at that time to induce light anaesthesia in children, and held it lightly over his nose. He snuffed it and breathed deeply. I sprayed a little more; he breathed it in. I moved the mask closer; he was asleep without a struggle even in the second stage of anaesthesia. Now I commenced chloroform and soon he was well under. The vet said he would have a horrible convulsion when given the prussic acid so my sister, feeling she could not bear that, crept out of the stable. Now his head lay in my arms. His eyes were shut; his breath became feeble; it stopped. 'Now, if you think it necessary,' I said over my shoulder to the veterinary surgeon. The needle went in between the ribs. Daragh never moved. The vet got up and went out without a word. I was alone. Daragh's body lay stiffening in the fragrant hay. I put out the candle and walked out under the stars. The trees were silent; no breath of air disturbed the leaves. It was a silence when the breathing of the spirit of the earth might be heard. I stood up and stretched out my arms towards the stars.

CHAPTER 7

JOHNS HOPKINS

The Johns Hopkins Hospital at Baltimore was a great contrast to King's College Hospital. The latter belonged to the great English, middle-class, professional world. There the old Harley Street establishment ruled with all its taboos and unrestricted power based upon its intimate knowledge of the most important facts of life and death which transcend class. Kings and peasants are born similarly and finally die crossing the same river alone. The very fact that the Harley Street specialist gave his time free to the great hospitals while gaining a living in private practice made him understand the patient's point of view much better than the whole-time physician or surgeon at the Johns Hopkins. The latter, however, were trained in brutal honesty and were therefore more able to advance medical science than the Londoners.

The Johns Hopkins was one of the first great medical centres in the United States to go over to the conception of the whole-time medical teacher and researcher. When I went there in the late twenties it was still amongst the best medical centres in the U.S.A., or indeed in the world. Certainly the Paediatric Department, known as the Harriet Lane Home, was the leading paediatric centre in the country. Ned Park had just been called to the Chair and was gathering about him a team of young men and women who were to help to create modern American paediatrics. Such names as Rustin McIntosh, Emmett Holt and Helen Taussig are now world-famous. Park has been called the father of modern American paediatrics. He was a Lincoln-like figure of great height, rather ungainly, slow-spoken, New England in thought, utterly honest. He was by far the best leader of a group of intelligent men I have ever known. He knew instinctively our good points, our weaknesses, our hopes, and by little understanding acts, an occasional word of praise or a gentle rebuke made us completely loyal to him, and even to each other, so that we have remained comrades in arms for the rest of our lives wherever life in the twentieth century has taken us, from Belsen Camp in Germany to the Near East or Lagos in Nigeria.

My project was to write a thesis for my Cambridge doctorate. The subject I had chosen and which had been accepted was 'Allergy', which was just then coming into prominence in medical thought. Allergy, the reaction against external foreign matter including germs, was only beginning to be understood and the concept that it was an over-action in the body's protective reactions of a harmful nature was not fully grasped though the work of the young men of the Hopkins, such as Rich, was moving in that direction.

For my part I took over the children's allergy clinic which consisted of many cases of asthma, hay fever and skin conditions such as eczema. As I was writing my thesis on allergy I naturally read the literature on the subject. This opened up the wide field of scientific investigation to me. I was enthralled, surrounded as I was by others bent upon the same quest, exploring the complicated mathematical systems upon which our third-dimensional world has been created. We were concerned with the 'how' rather than the 'why'. Our job was to find out how the world works, how its parts fit together, not to speculate why the Creator imagined it like that. I learned that the pursuit of ideas towards their source can be absolutely absorbing and completely fill the mind, waking or sleeping. As yet I only stood on the edge of this scientific world of discovery and my time at the Hopkins only opened my eyes upon this new vista which was later so largely to fill my life.

The clinical side of the allergy clinic was interesting in a different way. It opened a window into the American immigrant world which at that time in Baltimore was composed of tens of thousands of poor Slavs and Latins who had escaped from the wretched slums of Europe where the poor were still crowded in conditions of horrible squalor. They had come to America in high hopes of escaping from bondage. America in those days was a land where men could rise by their own efforts. Admittedly the weak were often pushed to the wall in the rush to gain a place in the sun, but it still was a land which could be called free. I greatly enjoyed looking after the children of those immigrants. They were rapidly becoming American, often to the shame of their parents who found their children's new manners almost too much to bear. It was a great experience for me to see the collision of the old and the new cultures. My training under Still as a children's doctor stood me in very good stead. Asthma is a very difficult thing to cure but can be greatly ameliorated so I was constantly called in to help children whose breathing had suddenly become very laboured. Nothing makes a patient more grateful to the doctor than being helped in one of these attacks. I made many friends among this section of Baltimore society and was received into their homes with great kindness.

I saw America from the inside during these years for, apart from the clinical and research side of our work, the department under Park was organised socially as well.

The Parks lived outside Baltimore in a not at all grand house near Towson Town. It stood in grounds of its own. The fact that American gardens are not divided by railings from each other gives them the appearance of parkland. The Parks' house was called La Paix. There at weekends all we assistants forgathered. I organised the riders and we would set off on horseback to a rendezvous by Loch Raven, a lake some six miles off. The others would go there on foot or by car. There we would all meet, light a fire and cook sausages, potatoes and heat coffee. In the evening we would again foregather at La Paix where a great wood-fire would have been lighted. Rusty McIntosh, who was an eminent musician as well as a great doctor, would play to us divinely Schumann's *Carnival*, sitting in the dark, his hands finding the keys. Park would read of the American Civil War—*John Brown's Body*—or I would read them Irish poetry. Sometimes we would indulge in 'shop', and an evening was given over to discussing what we were trying to do in the hospital. We had no rules. The Parks, including Mrs Park and their three children, Rollo, David and Sally, became part of our lives.

I played an insignificant role in a great event which occurred at that time at the Johns Hopkins. Park said to me one day: 'We should have a children's heart clinic. I know you are interested in rheumatic heart disease. There is also the wide field of children born with abnormalities of the heart. I wonder if you would go round the other cardiac clinics and come back and get one started here?'

I went to New York and saw May Wilson whose children's heart clinic was one of the most interesting at that time, and others elsewhere, and came back with the necessary detailed knowledge and helped to set up one in the Children's Department of the Johns Hopkins.

This clinic started quite simply but rapidly gathered a wide circle of children with different forms of cardiac disease. In years to come it was to develop into the most celebrated heart clinic, for it was here that Helen Taussig and Blakelock were to introduce modern cardiac surgery for congenital heart conditions which was to be taken up everywhere in the world. It has now saved the lives of thousands of babies with deformed hearts and given many others a full life who would have been condemned to a half-existence by the handicap with which they were born.

Then one day when I was working in the Johns Hopkins I got a letter which suggested that the Rockefeller Foundation might be interested in giving a grant to Irish medicine in the new Irish Free State. I went to New York and discussed the possibilities. It was thought that the project might be sponsored by some well-known, non-political Irish personage. And as at that moment George Russell (AE) was then on a lecture tour in the States it was thought he might be the best man.

CHAPTER 8

ATLANTIC VOYAGES

I had been introduced to AE the last time I had been in Ireland and when he agreed to the plan it was suggested that I should act as medical liaison for the project and should travel back with him to Ireland and put the idea to the authorities in Dublin.

Park made it easy for me and I took temporary leave from the Johns Hopkins and sailed back to Ireland with Russell. The project never materialised. It was a very bad moment in Irish medical history. During the nineteenth century Irish medicine had played a leading role in the early days of modern medicine and surgery with the coming of anaesthetics. Names like Stokes, Colles, Corrigan and Graves were known all over the medical world. But since then Trinity College School had remained conservative medically and politically and the new National University Medical School in University College, Dublin, was divided inside itself after the Irish civil war. Henry Moore was the young Professor of Medicine at University College. He had himself been trained largely in the Rockefeller Institute. He belonged to the Free State side and was anti-Republican and also anti-Trinity College. The then Irish Minister of Health was thought of as an ex-guerrilla leader by the Trinity men, and, though highly intelligent, knew nothing about modern medicine. He belonged to the same political group as Henry Moore. Between them they managed to pour cold water onto the Rockefeller proposal of forming a medical research centre in Dublin run by both Trinity and University Colleges. Like many other proposals in Ireland it foundered on the incapacity of us Irish to work together. At that moment we couldn't even speak to one another whether we were of Republican or Free State or old Anglo-Irish stock.

As far as I was concerned I found myself out of my depth in Dublin. I knew nothing of local conditions or politics. AE knew everybody and was respected by all sides but he knew nothing of

57

health problems, less still of medical research. A more inept pair than the two of us it is difficult to imagine when it came to putting the Rockefeller point of view to a group of Irish medical leaders who were antagonistic to each other medically and politically.

It was not surprising that our mission ended in failure. But to me it had one great compensation. On the journey to Ireland I had the inestimable privilege of having AE as my companion. It was during the off-season and the boat was half empty and I had him very much to myself for the whole week of the journey. AE held a special position in the Ireland of that time. He belonged to a group of Irish writers and poets who with Yeats had gone back into the mythical past of Irish history and by their writings made the Irish conscious of themselves as a nation again. Along with Synge, O'Casey and others he had created a stirring renaissance of Irish literature. AE was himself a poet and a painter but, par excellence, he was a seer in the Tagore mould. He had a vision of the Infinite, a kind of paranormal sight, the images of which he described in strange poems of great beauty and on canvas. He was greatly loved by everybody. Indeed he was about the only person about whom that could be said in Dublin, a city which has killed or mocked most of her great men. That brilliant men, who were also technically proficient, such as Yeats, both loved and respected him is proof of his real quality of greatness. He belonged to the days when the spoken word was considered an art, before radio and television had taken its place. Intellectual evenings were still popular when expert talkers such as Gogarty or Yeats himself would hold court in their homes and where a group of friends and acquaintances would gather to hear the Master talk. Sometimes admittedly the Master's discourse became a monologue, and unless he had considerable powers of self-criticism it was all too easy for him to become a bore. In AE's case, however, his peculiar vision combined with a knowledge and great love of the country of Ireland made his evenings memorable for all who came to him.

In my case, his fourth-dimensional vision of what he called 'the elemental world' around us fitted in exactly with the memory of the visions I had seen as a child and caught glimpses of since. His paintings of shining figures, rising out of the sea or the woods of Ireland never conveyed to me what he had seen but his poetry put into words my own visions of the Infinite which I had seen myself. It seemed to express what I had always been groping towards. In consequence, when he strode along the deck of the Cunarder while his long hair and beard blew in the wind, intoning one of his poems, or sat and told me of his visions in Donegal, I became his disciple and experienced the joy which young men knew when they sat at the

feet of Socrates. I asked him about the actual visions of spirits which
he had painted into his pictures. Were they exact? Were they really
as he had portrayed them or were they imaginary?

'These visions come to me near Marble Hill in Donegal,' he said,
'and in a few other places in the West of Ireland. That is what makes
the West different from anywhere else. If you have been there you
may have seen a kind of emanation from the earth round about you.
I know a few other people who can *see* with whom I can discuss what
I have seen.'

'What do you really see?' I asked.

'You don't see, in that sense,' he said, 'not with your eyes. Yet
you see forms as I have drawn rising from a wave or sometimes a
spring in a wood. I once came upon a lonely pool in a wood surrounded by flowering shrubs and it seemed to me I saw a form
rise out of it and finally sink back into the pool while the scene was
lit by a kind of light.' This so corresponded to one of my childish
memories that I knew what he was trying to explain.

One poem of his more than any other expresses to me the beauty of
the elemental world about us which we have all but lost in our cities
and built-up areas. One day he walked up and down the ship's
deck, his head thrown back, his hair wild while he intoned, 'The
Wings of Angus' (Angus is the Gaelic God of Love):

The grey road whereupon we trod became as holy ground:
The eve was all one voice that breathed its message with no sound;
And burning multitudes pour through my heart, too bright, too blind
Too swift and hurried in their flight to leave their tale behind.
Twin gates unto that living world, dark honey-coloured eyes,
The lifting of whose lashes flushed the face with Paradise
Beloved, there I saw within their ardent rays unfold
The likeness of enraptured birds that flew from deeps of gold
To deeps of gold within my breast to rest, or there to be
Transfigured in the light, or find a death to life in me.

So love, a burning multitude, a seraph wind that blows
From out the deep of being to the deep of being goes.
And sun and moon and starry fires and earth and air and sea
Are creatures from the deep let loose, who pause in ecstasy
Or wing their wild and heavenly way until again they find
The ancient deep, and face therein, enraptured, bright and blind.

I was to meet AE many times afterwards in Dublin and go to the
evenings at his home in Rathgar, and like all Irishmen who knew
him I loved him.

On the way back to Baltimore to finish my Rockefeller Fellowship I had another experience as profound as my meeting with AE. Being short of funds I obtained through my Clyde-Cambridge friend, Joey Maclay, a passage on a tramp steamer carrying china clay from Cornwall to Philadelphia. I was the only passenger and occupied the cabin of the absent third officer.

Off the North American coast we encountered a hurricane of stupendous violence, the wind reaching eighty miles an hour and the waves piling up into mountains over fifty feet from trough to summit. It became impossible to proceed through such a tempest and we had to heave to, that is to say to face into the hurricane about two points off the direct line of the wind with our engines running at about half speed, which left the ship stationary, or at least not lunging forward. So tremendous were the seas that the boat wallowed and shook like a creature struggling to survive. It was impossible to lie down as one was thrown out of one's bunk and I spent much of the next day and night on the bridge. Here I stood with the wind howling about me, the seawater spray and the rain pouring off my oilskins, but I was not cold because we were in the Gulf Stream. At times I felt half in, half out of my body, somewhere between sleep and waking consciousness, like being hypnotised. Gradually I became part of the great sea world which we landsmen never encounter ordinarily in our lives. Here we were surrounded by hundreds of miles of sea, cut off from mankind while wild elements, unconcerned with man, roared and danced about us.

After hours of battling in the wild shouting wind there was a sudden silence. The wind dropped completely, though the mountainous seas still broke over us. Then suddenly the storm burst in on us again from another quarter. 'Turn her fifteen points a' starboard,' the captain said to the steersman standing behind him. He was a silent Yorkshireman, not given to light conversation, master of his ship. As I stood watching him I realised that he belonged to the breed of captains who had sailed the ships of Drake and Raleigh in the great days of seamanship when, inspired by that motive to conquer that lies deep in the heart of man, these seamen along with Columbus and Magellan, had driven on their sailing ships through hurricanes like this—on and on into the unknown. As I stood behind our captain I glimpsed something of the indomitable courage that such sea-triumphs create.

The storm ended as suddenly as it had begun and we started to move ahead once more. Suddenly out of the now near silent night a great seventh wave appeared like a mountain. Now we were before it, deep in its first trough; we started to rise to climb up its mountainous unbroken side; we rose and rose; then as we reached towards its breaking crest our nose went in under the mass of water. The sea came crashing across the forward holds like an avalanche. One moment I was forty feet above the torrent, the next its crest reached us even on the bridge; it passed; we heard the hiss as the water splashed against our hot funnel. Then the ship seemed to rise out of the deep, shaking herself. The phosphorescence of the Gulf Stream cascaded off us in streams of diamond light.

CHAPTER 9

RESEARCH

When finally my American scholarship came to an end I returned to Europe with my thesis complete but no definite job to come to. I had applied for a post as Child Welfare Director of a new clinic in Dublin but had been turned down as having insufficient knowledge of local conditions. However, at that moment the post of Research Fellow into the problems of rheumatic fever in children at the Hospital for Sick Children in Great Ormond Street, London, was advertised. I applied and was appointed.

The salary was minimal. The previous Research Fellow's health had broken down and he had decided to be psychoanalysed. The laboratory was only partly organised and consisted of an old ward previously used for communicable diseases. The research funds available were very meagre.

My appointment was baffling. Great Ormond Street Hospital was still run by an honorary staff who gave their services free, both as doctors looking after the sick poor and as teachers. They made their living through fees charged in their Harley Street rooms. They belonged to a class apart in the British establishment akin to the great lawyers. Many of them received titles in recognition of their position in society.

The senior physician, now that Sir Frederick Still had retired, was Dr John Poynton, who was noted for having played cricket for a West County side in his youth and for having written a book on rheumatic fever before World War I. He was now elderly, crotchety and not at all easy to approach, particularly on rheumatic fever as his previous work on the subject had not been received very well. He gave me a copy of his discredited book on rheumatic conditions in childhood. In this he claimed that he had recovered the causative germ from the blood of a child with rheumatic fever.

I felt that I must start by repeating his work and see what we could find in prolonged blood cultures from children with the acute disease, of whom there were usually at least ten in the hospital.

I went to Sir Walter Fletcher, Secretary of the Medical Research Council, and an old Trinity College, Cambridge, man, and put my case to him. He was sympathetic and helpful. He augmented my miserable salary and gave me a grant-in-aid which enabled me to employ a laboratory technician.

Now began for me one of the most exciting periods of my life. So far I had learned to be a doctor at King's, and at the Johns Hopkins I had caught a glimpse of fundamental scientific research where the seeker after new thought pursues an idea towards its source. This is exploration in modern dress.

I realised that before I could set out upon my own journey of exploration into the meaning of the rheumatic fever disease syndrome I must learn the bacteriological techniques necessary, and also must read all the previous literature on the subject. For a year and a half I read while at the same time carrying out some seventy blood cultures on rheumatic fever patients. I kept the cultures for six weeks each and plated them out weekly to see if they had grown anything. I recovered a number of harmless germs and only one belonged to a dangerous variety, a so-called haemolytic streptococcus.

About the same time, Dr Schlesinger, another Great Ormond Street doctor who looked after a convalescent home for rheumatic fever children, observed that in children who had had one attack and were recovering, relapses occurred in a certain very definite sequence. A child who had apparently recovered from an attack would show a sudden rise of temperature lasting two or three days. Then after a period of ten to twenty days he would suffer a full-blown rheumatic fever recrudescence associated with fresh inflammation of the heart.

I studied these charts and came to the conclusion that we ought to be able to find out the germ causing the first rise in temperature.

At this time Sheldon was looking after another convalescent home for rheumatic fever children at Cheyne Walk on the Embankment and found the same reaction taking place in his cases. I linked up with him. Our first plan was to find out what germs would grow from the throats of all the twenty children in the home while convalescent, so as to be able to discover the germ involved when the rise in temperature occurred. We took weekly cultures from all the children and thus knew the normal flora of germs in all their throats. We continued this method for some months. Then suddenly a child showed the characteristic rise of temperature that we were expecting. We grew a pure growth of the haemolytic streptococcus from his throat. At the same time, we found that a nurse had an attack of tonsillitis with the same germ as the child and must have infected him. Gradually the germ passed round the ward. Ten children in all were affected, one after another. They all behaved in a similar manner: rise of temperature at the time of the infected throat, followed by a silent period of ten to twenty days and then a rheumatic relapse would occur. We recovered the nurse's germ from all ten cases. The heart symptoms were severe and four children died. What was happening? The picture was quite unlike the ordinary symptoms found in infections caused by the haemolytic streptococcus. We were completely mystified. We performed post-mortems on the bodies in the Hospital for Sick Children. I used to bring them across from Chelsea in my battered Austin Seven. I often wondered what a London policeman would say if he stopped me and found a dead child in my car.

Sometimes these examinations took all night. My results were very surprising. I found the germs which had caused the acute sore throat at the time of the temperature, in the tonsils always, in the glands of the neck, sometimes in other glands, the spleen and occasionally in or around the heart. These results were so unusual that for years I was very careful about proclaiming them until a worker from Edinburgh carried out similar post-mortem investigations on rheumatic fever patients and found exactly the same thing.

There was no doubt in our minds now what the infecting germ was.

Quite suddenly a new light on this conception was given me from a completely different angle.

Dr Donald Paterson, one of the most successful of the younger staff of the hospital at that time, had said to me when I took up the position of whole-time research worker, 'Don't give up clinical medicine for anything. Come and work in my clinic once a week.' I had followed his advice and suddenly two sisters we saw in the clinic appeared with erythema nodosum. I remembered my personal experience of that illness years before at Cambridge and got the girls admitted into Sir Robert Hutchison's ward. He didn't believe that erythema nodosum was caused by the tubercle bacillus, as propounded by Wallgren of Sweden and the other Europeans, or in the British-held theory that it was of rheumatic origin, but rather that it was caused by some specific infectious condition of unknown origin. However, he let me take over the sisters. I found both of them were very sensitive to tuberculine, they had tubercle germs in their stomach washings and their X-rays showed primary tuberculosis. We found that their mother had active infective lung tuberculosis.

This seemed confirmation for Wallgren's hypothesis. 'But,' said Sheldon, 'I have a little girl who has had erythema nodosum already four times and is not sensitive to tuberculin before, during or after an attack and has no clinical signs of any tuberculosis.'

I immediately obtained her address and asked her mother to bring her up to the hospital. The mother came and said, 'She will have an attack of erythema nodosum next Monday because she has the sort of sore throat which always comes first.'

I took the child into hospital. She did exactly what her mother said she would and got an attack of erythema nodosum two days later.

We tested her and found she was quite insensitive to tuberculin germs but highly sensitive to an extract of streptococcus which Sheldon and I had prepared. Indeed, a small injection of this extract into her skin not only produced an erythema nodosum-like swelling around the injection site but vividly brought out the other eruptions again which were fading at the time. We weren't at all sure of the significance of what we had observed or what this sensitivity meant. Could it be that we were witnessing a new type of body reaction to disease, an over-reaction, if you like, to certain substances foreign to the body tissues. Could these germs we had found be the cause of such bodily reactions? Could different germs produce similar body reactions?

Without further speculation Sheldon and I published our results which were confirmed simultaneously in America and later again on this side of the Atlantic. We had, in fact, added one fact to the modern understanding of disease, though at the time we had no idea that we had actually entered the ranks of the discoverers.

CHAPTER 10

IRELAND

Suddenly towards the end of my research period at Great Ormond Street Hospital, I received a letter from the then only children's physician in Dublin, stating that he was retiring and suggesting that I take over his house and his practice.

When my father heard this he offered to buy the house for me if I would return to work in Ireland which, he pointed out, would be following in my grandfather's footsteps and the Collis doctors before him. I did not hesitate but resigned as soon as I could and set out for Ireland with joy in my heart.

The moment I returned home was at one of the turning points in the history of Ireland. De Valera's Republican Party had come into office for the first time. Great anxiety was felt in many circles. Many English-minded people both inside and outside the professions got up and departed for England. For instance, my father's senior legal partner, who came from a middle-class Protestant family, retreated to Tunbridge Wells in the south of England leaving the firm in my father's hands. Even more apprehensive than the Anglo-Irish were the Free Staters. They had come out on top in the civil war with the Republicans in the twenties after the latter rejected the Treaty with England. The civil war had left great bitterness, as such conflicts always do. Michael Collins, the gallant leader of the Irish guerrilla forces who had fought the English regular army and the Black and Tans, had been killed in a skirmish between the two Irish sides. This led to a toughening of the Free State attitude and some seventy Republican leaders had been executed. Now, in 1932, it was felt that once the Republicans came into power they would revenge themselves on the Free Staters. But when de Valera took up the position of Prime Minister nothing happened. Life went on as before outwardly. New policies were introduced; a struggle with England about the Land Annuities ensued but no Free Staters or, for that matter,

66

Anglo-Irish were molested. Many years later when on returning from Nigeria I brought a message from General Gowon, the Chief of the Nigerian State, to de Valera, then President of Ireland, he said to me: 'I'd like to tell you something, Dr Collis. When I came to power in the thirties by replacing Mr Cosgrave, a very critical moment arose which isn't in the history books. The Chief of the Free State forces approached Cosgrave and said, "We'd better not let the Republicans in. They are bound to revenge themselves. Let's have a coup d'état." But Cosgrave answered "I am a democrat. I have been defeated at the polls and I am going to go out." ' And, de Valera said, 'I sent for Frank Aiken, the chief of our forces and said, "Now Frank, we've got in—NO revenge." Cosgrave and I were then not on speaking terms but we both believed in the same thing. A new Ireland was born that day though neither of us knew it.'

The English always complain that the Irish have too long memories and always bring up the past when discussing the present. But the fact is that the ordinary Englishman knows nothing about Ireland or why it has apparently always been such a vexed question. The reason may be that it has always been the fashion everywhere to present history to the next generation in such a way as to make the boys proud of their own country above all else. And as Anglo-Irish history, if told at all truthfully, is discreditable to the English to such a degree that the myth of the superiority of the British to all lesser breeds might be seen through, silence is best.

It is quite unnecessary for the Irish historian to go back to Elizabeth I or even Cromwell who tried to impose by force a form of Protestantism on the Catholic Irish people, or those who came after with their Penal Laws against the Catholics whose property and very lives were at stake if they did not turn over to Protestantism. One has only to study the history of the nineteenth century when the Penal Laws had been repealed and the people of Ireland were supposed to have the same privileges as their English counterparts and were governed by the English Parliament from London under a British Civil Service: then, when England was the most prosperous and powerful state in the world and her population quadrupled, she governed Ireland in such a scandalously inefficient and degrading manner that the Irish population was halved and a million people died of starvation while cereal crops were actually removed under police escort from the country. Probably no great power in the modern world has ever treated a cousin people as badly as the English have treated the Irish. But it is only since Liam O'Flaherty's *Famine* and *The Great Hunger* by Cecil Woodham-Smith have been widely read that the English conscience has been stirred and some feeling of guilt has been felt in regard to the 'Irish Question'.

That the Irish people should have been driven from time to time to resort to force rather than to persuasion is not to be wondered at. That force by the few rather than the decision of the majority has become recognised as almost hallowed in Ireland is not surprising either. In this century the Irish question has been enormously complicated by this mystique which first resulted in the Northerners resisting the perfectly reasonable Home Rule Bill of 1912 which would have allowed the Irish to manage their own affairs. These Ulstermen are closely related to the Lowland Scots but unlike their Gaelic cousins their forefathers embraced a very Protestant faith at the time of the Reformation. They still believe in the old Jewish scriptures as being the actual Word of God, and consider the Roman Catholic belief in the Virgin Mary and the saints to be idolatrous. Perhaps their fear of the Catholic claim that the Pope is the final arbiter of what is right and what is wrong is not unreasonable.

In the early thirties, however, the Ulster question was not in the forefront of Irish affairs as it had been before and was to become again later. At this moment, once de Valera was firmly in the saddle, the problem was economic.

In the 1880s Gladstone had passed his Irish Land Bill whereby the Irish farmers could buy back the land from the landlords, most of whom had received it as gifts from the British Crown down the years. A long-term loan of some two hundred million was raised in the City of London to cover the compensation necessary. This then enormous sum had kept Ireland poor for some fifty years; any profits made by the small farmer tended to go to pay the annuities on his land. De Valera now stated that he was going to stop this tribute to England for land they had stolen from Ireland in the first place. In retaliation the British Government slapped a penal tariff on Irish goods, such as beef and butter, which, as Ireland had no other market, more than compensated for the annuities. Finally, in 1938 the Irish Government came to an agreement with Mr Chamberlain for a down payment of ten million pounds and the rest of the debt was cancelled.

The immediate result in the early thirties of this economic war was to leave Ireland very poor which meant no money for social services, and the most extreme suffering among the poor whose plight was very grave, particularly in Dublin where because of political troubles little had been done socially for fifty years.

I returned into this Ireland completely ignorant of the society I was to find myself in. Coming back, now in my thirties, I came with wide open eyes unbound to any side: Anglo-Irish, Free State or

Republican. But the scene I found myself in was very baffling, both medically and socially.

*   *   *

In Dublin in 1930 there were three medical schools, Trinity College founded by Elizabeth I, the College of Surgeons, and the University College of the National University.

Trinity was an old Protestant stronghold, University College a comparatively recent Catholic foundation, and the College of Surgeons one of the oldest medical schools in Europe. Dublin contained more hospitals for its size than any other capital city. There were ten general hospitals, three maternity hospitals, two children's hospitals, a fever hospital, an ear, nose, throat and eye hospital, a huge municipal hospital, an enormous old-fashioned lunatic asylum, and a number of what were called convalescent homes. The doctors who ran this vast medical service were not paid by the hospitals and had to make their living outside in private practice, either general or specialised. In most hospitals there was no pension scheme or retiring age and the staff, if they were unable to retire for financial reasons, often had to cling on to their appointments into their second childhood.

One of the old general hospitals founded in the middle of the eighteenth century was known as the Meath Hospital and County of Dublin Infirmary. It had been largely built up during the nineteenth century by a series of Maurice Collises, and my father, though a lawyer, was still Chairman of its Board.

It had the most unusual staff. Sir John Moore was the oldest member, somewhere in his eighties. Next came Dr Lennon. Nobody knew his age and it was said that he and Sir John could only remember things clearly which had happened forty or fifty years before. Then there was Dr Boxwell who was physician and pathologist, and was great friends with the matron who was up-stage-and-county English. On the general surgical side was the last of the Stokes, one of the most famous medical families with a disease called by their name. Henry Stokes, the present family representative, was a gentleman of the old school. He was too kind to charge the poor any fees and too grand to charge his friends. In consequence he was exceedingly poor. I once heard an old woman from the Dublin slums describing him to a friend. 'Ah, Mr Henry Stokes,' she said, 'there's no rhyme nor reason in him, he's like the love of God.'

Gogarty, poet, literateur and talker known all over the world, was ear, nose and throat surgeon, with a great reputation in every direction. He was said to be a surgeon of ability though his method of chopping off tonsils rapidly without an anaesthetic frightened me. Lane, though a physician, was a urogenital surgeon of considerable renown. There were also a number of younger men.

The entrance hall of the hospital was very impressive, particularly to me as the old bearded busts of two Maurice Collises stood by the inner pillars flanked by other busts of such famous people as Stokes and Graves (of Graves' Disease). It was presided over by a famous porter who served the hospital eventually for fifty years. He did everything from explaining tactfully why a certain member of the staff might be away that day and couldn't see some important patient to keeping the Chairman, my father, exercised by playing tennis with him on Sundays.

A few hundred yards away was the National Children's Hospital, also an ancient foundation, occupying a number of converted houses in an old Georgian street. Behind it there was a large, cold damp hall used as an out-patient department. Since the departure of Dr Crighton, whose place I eventually filled, it seemed to possess no paediatric staff at all.

The Rotunda Hospital, founded by Bartholomew Mosse in 1741, on the other side of the river, was at that time still the most famous maternity hospital, if not in the world, at least in these islands. Mosse had had very original ideas apart from a great heart moved by the distress of the Dublin mothers. Although he had no fortune he always did everything in the grand manner. The hospital was planned and built regardless of expense. He is said to have gone bankrupt several times in the process. But so well did his architects plan for him that the main hospital building and the Assembly Rooms next door, which he built to support the hospital on the snobbery of the age, are among the architectural gems of eighteenth-century Dublin.

The hospital up till the twenties had been run by a Master who was the leading Protestant obstetrician of his day. He served for seven years during which time he received all the fees of the students coming to the hospital which, as its fame grew, amounted to quite a lot in any one year. At the same time he was allowed private practice. But his term of office only lasted for a limited period, after which he had to retire on whatever practice he had left. In consequence it was generally agreed as reasonable that he should make as much as he could during his term.

At the time I arrived Dr Bethel Solomons had become Master and broken the Protestant succession. He was immensely good-looking and had the most wonderful hands for surgical procedures.

*　　　*　　　*

On my arrival in Dublin my father said I must come on the staff of the Meath Hospital. I pointed out that I was a paediatrician. My father didn't know the term but said that if it meant I was interested in children, although there was only one ward of ten cots for children in the Meath, there were plenty of sick children attending the hospital, and anyway as a Collis I must now take my place in the family hierarchy. It was no use arguing so I became assistant physician to Sir John Moore.

At the same time I applied for a post in the National Children's Hospital where there were two other applicants, one a young Trinity College man with higher qualifications similar to mine, the other a lady of some forty-five years who had recently taken up medicine and qualified when over forty. Her husband had been shot down on Michael Collins' orders I was to discover later when Frank O'Connor was writing Collins' life (*The Big Fellow*). He showed me a despatch which read 'Get Lee Wilson'—the lady's husband, a police superintendent. He was shot down in front of her, getting into his car. She received twenty-five thousand pounds compensation from the Irish Government and took up medicine. She was the strongest character I have ever met, a lady of indomitable force who literally could not be stopped if she decided on a course of action. She had worked herself into an invaluable position in the hospital by years as a house-officer and was, in fact, the only real doctor in the place though up till this moment not officially appointed to the staff. She was a Catholic. Most of the governors were Protestants. She had no special degrees, and was not a real paediatrician at all. But she personally interviewed every member of the Board with such vigour that when it came to the actual election the Board was unable to choose between us. I had the best outside qualifications, Dr Steen the best Dublin qualifications and Dr Lee Wilson the greatest general pull otherwise. The Board was composed chiefly of ancient Anglo-Irish aristocrats, chaired by Lord Powerscourt who was chiefly known for the waterfall in his deer forest which is one of the beauty spots of the world. He knew absolutely nothing about child health, but he was a gentleman of the old school and very courteous to us all.

After considerable argument the Board appointed all three of us.

* * *

These appointments took some time to materialise and it was over a year before I could be said to have really settled down in Dublin medicine though I started work immediately at the Meath Hospital.

I can still remember my introduction there. At eleven o'clock each day the staff forgathered in the ancient Board Room with its portraits of famous old doctors and illustrations of early operations. There the matron dispensed coffee like a grande dame before the French Revolution. As I entered the first time the matron was handing Mr Henry Stokes a cup: 'Can I press two lumps on you today, Mr Stokes?', while holding up one in a pair of silver sugar-tongs. Sir John Moore seemed to be explaining to Dr Murphy, one of the younger doctors, something important in the construction of Greek irregular verbs. In another corner of the room Dr Lennon, surrounded by a group, was in the middle of an anecdote. I listened. 'I took my four-in-hand and galloped down to Howth,' he said, 'there I found the Boss, Old Boss Croker, in bed, would you believe it, with three girls. "Boss," I said, "what are you doing?" "Trying to keep warm," he said.' I never heard any more because at that moment Gogarty entered and everybody turned towards him. He made some Wildean kind of brilliant quip and everybody laughed. Behind him Lane stood rather stiffly. He whispered to Henry Stokes and drew him away to some surgical emergency. As they went out together I realised that I was in a hospital in the twentieth century, not in a coffee house in the eighteenth as it had seemed a minute before.

My duties were equally baffling. I was supposed to be assistant to Sir John Moore who held the first Diploma in Public Health to be bestowed in Ireland and was in consequence in charge of the infectious diseases wing. Things had changed since his young days, however, and it was no longer considered good medicine to admit all kinds of infectious patients into beds beside each other and the ordinary patients. When a child with kidney disease whom I was looking after developed diphtheria from a case admitted into the next bed and I protested and made a scene, the matron intervened, saying, 'Sir John calls it "Hospital throat".' Nor did my modern biochemical approach in certain conditions go down well with the old physicians who regarded such new tendencies in medicine as very unsound and preferred the old pharmacopaeia which consisted chiefly of concoctions of inorganic salts whose action in the body has now been altogether questioned. At that time we were ignorant of antibiotics and the modern concepts of medicine had not yet appeared.

In other ways, however, the Meath was a great education to me. In the Out-patients I was expected to refill with air the chests of the tuberculous patients who were undergoing the artificial pneumo-thorax treatment. This was rather outside my experience of the last few years as a children's physician. But the patients belonged to the poor strata of Dublin society and their care brought me in touch with a whole side of life I had never known existed which opened my eyes to the suffering which poverty brings. Each week on entering the Out-patients I would find a group of silent men waiting their turn. They would come into the clinical room, climb on to the couch, wince, perhaps, when the needle went in and maybe become a little breathless. But they seldom complained or caused any difficulty and went away quietly to their poor, often cold homes. There were no anti-tuberculous drugs then and the pneumothorax treatment was only an adjunct to aid their general resistance which was often very poor due to their living conditions. Some got better. Others continued to go downhill and died. Few complained. I learned to respect courage in that clinic.

The sisters in the wards were women of great skill and greater heart. They took care of the poor sick of Dublin with a kindness and a gentleness I have never seen exceeded. They must have found me sympathetic for they often called me to difficult cases at night when the nursing staff needed a doctor's support, perhaps at a death bed. The following description which I have recently come across in an old diary illustrates the participation in the life of the people which these old Dublin hospitals possessed. This was rare enough then anywhere but now with the coming of modern scientific medicine it has become almost extinct. The scene took place in one of the old wards of the hospital. There a girl was dying of a painful abdominal complaint. She had come to rely upon me to help her when the pain got too severe and I was accustomed to drop in to see how she was as often as possible. 'On the evening of the 8th I entered the ward and found her very weak. She was surrounded by her mother, younger sisters and brother. Immediately I appeared she asked for a sedative. I called the nurse and she was given one. She felt cold and almost pulseless to my hand, but now she began to feel more at ease. She thanked me for helping her, said she would pray for me. Then closed her eyes and lay back exhausted. Suddenly she was racked by an acute pain. She cried out: "It is like a fire in my back." Then she said "Are the lights on?" I knew then she could no longer see. Her lips moved. I heard her whisper "Jesus help me". Her breathing became long, then irregular. She became unconscious at last.

'Seeing the change the elder sister, a little person with a pretty, small, strong face with clear-cut features, knelt down at the end of the bed. All the others knelt including the ward nurse and all began to recite "Hail Mary". A moment before the ward had been an ordinary surgical ward—in one end a woman was vomiting continuously, in the next they had just passed a catheter on another patient . . . Now all was changed with the clear voices intoning. All was hushed. The responses were taken up by the mother, brother and sisters and joined in by the nurse and the other patients. The soft cadence filled the old room and quiet peace descended. The candles flickered. Shadows like ghosts hovered in the summer air. Fear fled, terror retreated as the ancient ritual went on. I sat on as her unconsciousness deepened and her soul slowly freed itself from her body. Gradually, it seemed, she left us as she lay breathing less and less till she needed us no more.

'I got up stiffly and walked down the stairs and past the two old Maurice Collis busts, crossed the eighteenth-century hall and came out into the Dublin night. I walked down the street where the bullets had whined around me in the fighting in 1916. It was empty.'

*   *   *

My father said, 'Bob—look, you must understand if you want to get on here you must show that you are a Dublin man. It's no good coming home with all these grand foreign degrees. Membership of the London College is all very well but if you want to succeed here you must become a Member of our own College.'

'You mean I must take the Irish M.R.C.P. exam?' I said.

'Yes,' he said.

'All right,' I said. I asked Dr Boxwell at the Meath about the Irish examination. 'Oh you shouldn't have any difficulty, having your London Membership,' he said. 'But when you come up for the exam don't be too modest. Show the examiners that you know what you are talking about. The first part of the exam is quite simple, straightforward clinical medicine, the second part more specialised.'

I took what he said literally and went up for the examination without much reading, thinking I probably knew enough. I found the papers none too easy as I had done very little adult medicine for five years, but it was in the clinical viva that I met my Waterloo.

This part of the examination was conducted in a particularly old-fashioned Dublin hospital. The first case I got was an ancient gentleman who intimated that for a small donation he would tell me what was wrong with him. I gave him half a crown. He said, 'Alkaptonuria'. I knew at once who he was, the only case of this rare condition in Dublin. He was one of the professional examination patients.

'All right,' one of the old examiners said to me when I had started off on alkaptonuria in great style. 'How much did he charge today?

What else is wrong with him?' Quickly I examined my man again—
every system, heart, lungs, abdomen—I was struggling with his
nervous system when the old doctor came up again.

'All right, all right,' he said. 'What's wrong with him?'

Desperately I said he had an irregular pulse, one pupil was larger
than the other.

'Yes, yes! But what else? What's obvious?'

I hadn't been examining adults for years and I couldn't see the
obvious.

'Emphysema,' he said. 'Can't you see his whole chest is like a
barrel? He can hardly breathe.'

'Yes, sir,' I said.

'All right,' he said. 'Come over here—examine that child and tell
me what you think.' The case I was given now I found was one of
rheumatic heart involvement in a little girl of ten.

Well, I thought, the old boy is being decent to me and has given
me a case of rheumatic fever, my own subject!

So when he and the other examiner came back to me, remembering
Boxwell's advice, I gave them a regular exposition on rheumatic
fever, clinically, in regard to the actual case before us and generally,
mentioning the haemolytic streptococcus as the causative factor.
As I talked I noticed that their faces became blanker and blanker.
They said absolutely nothing but when I finished they just walked
away muttering to each other.

Subsequently, as was customary in Dublin at that time, I attended
the College of Physicians where the president and the examiners
were gathered. There each candidate was called in and informed
personally how he had done in the examination. I was called in last.
The president was a very old physician, very polite and urbane.
'Dr Collis,' he said, 'I'm afraid we can't pass you. Your papers were
not very good but with your children's experience perhaps that
could be overlooked, but in the clinical you were given a straightforward case of rheumatic fever in a child and you did not know the
first thing about it. You talked arrant nonsense. In Dublin we pride
ourselves on our clinical acumen. Perhaps we are a little old-fashioned
but honestly all this semi-scientific stuff that seems to be the thing
now is not what we feel will make a good doctor of you. I'm sorry
as you have your London Membership but . . .'

I lost my temper. 'It's not me that knows nothing about rheumatic
fever,' I said. 'It's you people, who haven't even read the *Lancet*.
But I'll be proved right.' And I got up and went out banging the
door.

I came back to my father at Killiney in a defeated rage and poured out my feelings. All he said when he could get a word in was, 'Well you failed, didn't you, Bob? Take it again.'

I looked at him. I felt like being sick. He made no further comment. This time I went out of the room without banging the door.

Next day I wrote to the president apologising for my rudeness and saying 'the candidate is always wrong'. He wrote me back a charming letter in which he advised me to try again.

This failure made my position in the Meath very unpleasant. It had got around that I was a bumptious young fellow with a lot of high-falutin' foreign ideas who talked too much but didn't know his stuff. The Anglo-Irish consultants cut me or spoke sadly to me. Only Lane and Gogarty were kind. Lane advised me to go back to London as all my Protestant Anglo-Irish compatriots disliked me. Gogarty was kindness itself. 'Never mind the bastards,' he said. 'We all suffer from those old cods.' He insisted on me keeping the whole five guineas which a family had paid for a child with an earache whom he had seen with me. 'You look hungry,' he said.

I ignored Lane's advice, for I had got the feel of Dublin by now. Perhaps something in my disposition drove me on. I took a correspondence course with a London group for the M.R.C.P. exams and settled down to read up medicine again.

I resigned as assistant physician from the Meath Hospital. This enabled me to concentrate on two hospitals instead of three, and allowed me to be only a children's doctor and cut out adult medicine altogether.

The position of paediatrics at that moment in Dublin was very much at its beginnings and the prospects of being able to support oneself rather slim.

Both in the National Children's Hospital and in the Rotunda real paediatrics had to be organised from scratch. It was in the new infant department of the Rotunda Hospital that I really came to grips with the problem of paediatrics in Dublin. There the attitude had been extraordinary in the past. The emphasis of the old foundation had been only on the successful extraction of the baby from the mother's womb. The fact that the infant might suffer from complaints while in the womb, that the actual method of birth was all important to his healthy afterlife, and that the neonatal period was one of the most important periods in his existence, were completely ignored. The Master of the Rotunda was a personage in Dublin society due to his known wealth together with his academic prominence. Solomons sent for me.

'Collis,' he said, 'in spite of the fact that I have been warned by a member of the Board that it is a bad precedent and might lead to

a lowering of the status of the Master I have come to the conclusion that I must recognise your position as a teacher of paediatrics to the students here and I would like to give you an honorarium for your lectures of forty pounds a year and I will send you any difficult infant problems that occur in my private practice.'

'Make it guineas,' I said. He did, generously.

At that time the forty-two pounds was very welcome as my father's allowance of a hundred pounds a year did not go very far, my British Medical Research Grant which had continued for a year after my return to Ireland while I wound up my rheumatic fever work had now come to an end, and I was making only about five hundred pounds a year in consultant paediatric practice. I was in fact at a very low ebb in my fortunes but at that moment I had one piece of good luck which outweighed everything else. The staff nurse who was appointed to work with me in creating a proper neonatal department in the Rotunda Hospital was a Tipperary farmer's daughter who came from the slopes of the Galtee Mountains. She had all the drive and intelligence of those splendid people. During the forty years which have passed since our first meeting she has created one of the best neonatal departments anywhere, certainly the most human, and generations of students both nurses and under-graduates are eternally in her debt. At first neither of us really knew anything about the subject of neonatal paediatrics and in those days the literature was scant and at variance. We had to learn as we went along.

The necessity of keeping premature babies warm was immediately borne in upon us when we found babies with temperatures below 90°F. We invented a cheap (five pound) wooden cot, electrically heated, in which the baby lay in a temperature of 80°F, while being easy to nurse. These cots have now gone all over the world. I came upon one in the middle of Africa recently, but it cost a lot more than five pounds. The nurse, now Sister Moran, found that it was much easier and safer to feed these premature babies by stomach tube than by any other way before they had learned to suck. She introduced a simple method which could be taught in a few minutes to young nurses. It saved time, the whole procedure taking less than three minutes. It was much safer than the risk of drowning the baby when fed by spoon, and was altogether satisfactory.

A vast number of other procedures of a sometimes very complicated nature such as blood transfusions on the newborn were worked out.

At first the neonatal nursery consisted of only some twenty-five cots for abnormal babies born only in the hospital. Later a little neonatal hospital was built in the grounds where it was possible to take in newborn babies born outside who were suffering from one of the many critical abnormalities of that period, needing extremely complicated operations, as when the breathing and swallowing tubes from the mouth into the chest were joined. In these cases the baby was likely to die from the lungs being filled with secretions from the stomach unless a very difficult operation was performed, in which the chest wall itself had to be opened.

All this took years but gradually the unit took shape.

The Masters of the hospital came and went down the years. Solomons was very magnificent; his successor suffered from low blood pressure and we had to keep him alive by building a squash court off the great hall to keep him exercised; another's blood pressure got too high and he died; most over-taxed themselves with over-work, teaching, operating and making money.

Yet it was a great institution to belong to, a society in itself with its Christmas shows and dances, its beautiful eighteenth-century chapel services, its ever crowded student quarters, and the hospital, situated as it was in its own square right in the heart of Dublin, held a special place also in the hearts of the people. Once, during World War II when I was reduced to a bicycle, I was looking for the mother of a baby down Moore Street where a market was taking place along each side of the road. As I reached a certain point I called out to a young man selling meat, 'Where does Mrs Murphy live?'

'How the hell would I know?' he said. An old Dublin woman sitting at a stall in front selling fish got up holding a mackerel by the tail and slapped him across the face with it. 'That's no way to be answering a Rotunda doctor,' she said.

About that time John Betjeman, the poet, was cultural attaché at the British Embassy. He was greatly interested in the remarkable architecture of the Rotunda. On one occasion when I was taking him up to the chapel we were met at the top of the stairs by a strong smell of ether. 'Where are we?' he gasped. 'Just outside the labour ward!' I replied. He fainted. It took all the ward brandy to bring him round.

✳   ✳   ✳

The early 1930s were a very difficult period for Ireland in every way. After years of conflict the economic war with England over the annuities still further reduced our resources. Free Staters and Republicans of the New Ireland were hating each other and what was left of the old ascendancy Anglo-Irish did not know where they stood. By being out of the country virtually for the last twenty years while I grew up into manhood I found I did not belong to any group. Not having been brainwashed into any particular way of looking at things, I was able to see the good in every party's aspirations and to some extent their weaknesses at the same time. I had not been sickened by personal loss in the bitter feud that rent the country. I was free to make my own assessment of the situation. This did not make me popular with anybody as everybody I met seemed to belong to one or other hating group. Everybody regarded me with suspicion. If I opened my mouth to a Republican he felt I must be a Free Stater, and vice-versa, and to the so-called loyalist Anglo-Irish who were loyal to England I could not say a thing without calling down upon my head the foulest imprecations. I felt very lost at that moment but the beauty of Ireland and the great qualities of humour and imagination of its ordinary people touched something in me that carried me beyond these irritations and brought happiness and a certain kind of peace to my mind.

More particularly I found this in the Western Seaboard districts where as yet the people had not been involved in the modern scientific age of pollution. My father used to take a house, belonging I suspect to some impecunious legal client of his, each summer at a place called Glenlossera on the north coast of Mayo, near the little village of Belderig. I got to know the country round there very well, and the fishermen of Belderig particularly. Whenever I could I used to slip away and spend a night or two with Padraig Caulfield, the schoolmaster. Here I would go out with the fishermen along that incomparable sea-coast of iron cliffs in which are hundreds of deep caverns where the seals bred in the spring. It was Anthony McHale who usually took me out in his four-oared curragh which I would steer with another long oar.

On a summer day with the sea calm and the sun shining it was possible to go out round the headland where the cliffs rose above the water for hundreds of feet. The sea itself in the evenings would be full of seals, some asleep with only their noses above the water. Now and again you would see a sinister dorsal fin denoting the presence of a long grey shark body moving below.

At one point there was a place called Lady Cove where on entering a narrow channel in the rock below a high cliff one found oneself in an entrance to several caves. In one of these a stalagmite had formed in the shape of a woman's dress which shone white from a shaft of light coming down from a slit in the rock face above.

The rise and fall of the water from the Atlantic rollers in the entrance was sometimes as much as four feet. A queer sighing filled the air, mysterious and frightening as if the cave was haunted by spirits. As a rule the fishermen avoided the place but one very still evening Anthony guided the curragh right into the cave through the narrow channel. We landed and almost immediately came upon a newly born seal which could hardly move or see. It had a white fur covering, like cottonwool. I picked it up. As I did so the father rose out of the water behind, followed by his mate, and barked wildly. The seals' angry fearful sounds echoed through the caves. The baby seal struggled. 'Let me knock it on the head,' Anthony said. 'It would make a nice bit of fur for a lady.'

'Oh no,' I cried, feeling that that would have been murder. So I placed the small creature carefully between two rocks. As we retreated through the entrance in our curragh I looked back. The parent seals were flippering over the rocks to their baby.

Most vivid of all the sea pictures of Belderig was one night I spent in midsummer with the fishermen when they were catching salmon.

Led by some instinct, these fish come swimming along the coast for a number of weeks each summer, looking for the particular river up which they will swim and there spawn. How or why a salmon from the sea who has been born in a certain little stream in the West of Ireland will return years later to spawn in the same place is one of the mysteries of the creature world. Following similar instincts the eels which you find in your pond have got there by swimming up the nearest river and even crossing land to reach their destination. Later they will leave the pond again, reach the river, swim down to the sea and swim westwards across the ocean to their spawning grounds in the Caribbean and there sink down to the correct depth where they spawn and die.

The Mayo fishermen have learned that during these summer weeks the salmon looking for their river mouths will be swimming along parallel to the shore. So if you lay a four-feet-deep net (the fish swim near the surface) for some hundreds of yards out at right angles to the shore, the salmon coming along will swim into it. The darker the night and the rougher the sea, the more fish will be caught as they will be unable to see the net. You may pull in as many as eighty salmon into one curragh, weighting it right down to the gunwale or you may catch none at all. It is a difficult and risky business. If a storm gets up you may lose your nets. If you hang on too long you may be swept out to sea and drowned if the wind is off shore. At about the time I am remembering there had been such a storm and all the men from one village had been drowned and from another a curragh had been carried out and cast up on a distant shore in Donegal, the crew surviving. It was said the fishermen from our village had not gone out that night. Some said it was because Seamus had seen 'the black pig', others that 'the bottom had fallen out of the priest's barometer' and he had persuaded them not to go out.

On the evening I went with them there was no gale and only a slight wind ruffled the water. I steered the curragh as directed by Anthony to a place below a dark cliff where the water rose and fell against the rocks. The net was then let down for what seemed an immense distance along the top of the sea at right angles to the dark land behind. We hung on to the end of the net and remained thus for some hours. The curragh rose and fell with the Atlantic swell till I became nauseated. At last a greyness appeared between sea and sky away to the East. Summer dawn was approaching so they began to haul in the net. Every now and then a salmon would be disentangled from it and thrown into the bottom of the curragh. Suddenly there was a commotion and a struggling creature was lifted in. It was a small shark or a very big dog-fish. It was difficult for me to see what was happening as it was still dark. The four rowers unclasped their knives and with queer oaths plunged them into their enemy, the shark, and tore its tough skin, killing it gradually. Suddenly they looked up and saw me watching their primitive vengeance on the creature and somewhat disconcerted they desisted. The fish lay twitching for a time at the bottom of the boat and then was still along with the dying salmon.

As we approached the little harbour jetty and came through the breaking rollers it was just getting light.

In spite of the motion of the boat filling me with such abdominal discomfort as to dull most other feelings, I experienced that night an understanding of the sea itself and the live creatures in it. It was as if I had travelled into another dimension. I had glimpsed a vastness almost beyond the imagining of man's mind which made the little matters that must be attended to on landing seem petty. But the moment after coming ashore a woman hurried up and said I must come quickly for her child was very sick. And I was a doctor again. The night had gone and the sea receded from my mind. As the fishermen gathered their fish together into baskets they waved to me as I went up the hill with the mother. The sea world and its spell had already fled.

An even more terrifying vision of the sea and the western cliffs of Ireland came to me one day when I lay down on top of the cliffs of Moher in County Clare, on a flat rock, and looked down at the Atlantic breaking against the rocks seven hundred feet below. The height mesmerised me so that I had to shut my eyes lest I throw myself over. I opened them again and saw the waves like shadows on a screen come in and break against the foot of the cliff which seemed far away. The agony of fear gripped me again so that I was paralysed and unable to move. Inch by inch I wriggled myself backwards until I could see over the edge no more. I lay still until I could move myself into an upright position and then gradually retreated from the edge of the cliff. I realised in that moment what panic, what fear means. I had often seen it affect other people but never before understood it sufficiently to sympathise with the man or creature overcome to the stage of paralysis by fear.

The West of Ireland is the most westerly point of Europe where the great seas meet the land, where the water meets rocks, where man's life-span means nothing. Seventy years is but a moment in seven hundred million years. Here indeed we find ourselves a speck of dust in eternity and glimpse a vastness beyond our comprehension.

The people who live always in this presence are different from the rest of us. All humans have an infinite ability for not allowing external conditions to overpower the mind and to be able to live on without thinking out the meaning of their existence. But the people of this Western world are touched by the very grandeur of the Wild and are no longer just human units but each has to be recognised as an individual man.

∗   ∗   ∗

I was married during my research years at Great Ormond Street to a beautiful girl I had got to know on my first journey to Baltimore.

She came from Fowey in Cornwall, one of those deep inlet harbours on the south coast packed with craft of all kinds. Phyllis possessed a fourteen-foot dinghy in which we sailed along the spectacular coast, running into coves by the Gribbon close to Menabilly, later made famous by Daphne du Maurier who at that time was a slim girl in jeans with whom we were on nodding terms, her father having been the eldest when I was one of the youngest cadets in the Guards cadet battalion.

At this time we lived in a little flat in Brunswick Square in Bloomsbury, a strangely beautiful enclave in that part of London. Our high-up window looked out not only on the Square but also on the Foundling Hospital site and Mecklenburg Square on the other side. There were great plane-trees of much grandeur in which many birds lived. It was only a minute's walk to the back gate of the hospital where my research laboratory was situated and I could therefore slip backwards and forwards during the day and night as the work required.

Here Dermot, my eldest son, was born. He was a most entrancing baby. Being very short of space we put him to sleep in the bathroom. There he used to stand while I shaved in the morning, all beaming smiles, gurgles and baby talk. One's first baby, while he is still in the natural stage, gives a relationship of joy to a father. At that time I worked all day and sometimes all night and I was a poor enough companion to my family but for me these years were full of creative work and without tension caused by uncertainty of mind.

Phyllis was content with the little time I could spend at home, and was happy with Dermot. But it came to an end when I went back to Ireland. The Georgian house in one of the famous Dublin squares which my father had given us was tall, cold and uncomfortable. To begin with we had hardly any money and prospects both inside and outside Ireland at that time were gloomy.

The following year our second son, Robert, was born. From the first he was a sensitive creature who cried if uncomfortable but quite rapidly grew into a well-organised child, mentally and physically.

During these early years I was not much use as a father. I got on with my own affairs and the lives of my sons did not impinge very much on my thoughts. I was a much better paediatrician to other people's children than to my own.

With Phyllis, it was the same. I got on with my work and left her very much to her own thought-life. She was very good to me. She never quarrelled or made scenes. She suffered much ill-health, characterised by blinding headaches which seemed to incapacitate her so that she had to lie down every afternoon. This and the fact that her mother came to live with us and enjoyed a decline, in the Victorian sense (which actually lasted for thirty-five years), prevented Phyllis from ever achieving a full life with me. In Dublin I filled my days with creative work and left my family without much thought, though when we went on holidays or into the country around, particularly in the lovely county of Wicklow, we had moments of great joy together.

We spent one very happy summer at Lough Dan, a lake hidden in the Wicklow mountains, surrounded by ancient, beautiful, mysterious woods and glens. One day at the upper end of the lake where a mountain stream of dark brown water forms a golden sand bar I bathed and lay down alone. On one side the dark water flowed silently; the sun striking it made it appear like a looking glass. On the other the black lake broken by white ripples glimmered in the sun which warmly comforted my bare back. A furze bush flamed yellow; small blue and golden wild flowers pin-pointed the grass.

Above the grey rocks the mountain crags towered, gaunt, but not
unkindly. Up the valley the hills sloped away in giant cupolas, one
behind the other, purple with heather. The spirit of the place seemed
to blaze out of the soil and to flow upwards around me. I turned
inwards so that I was filled with a feeling of oneness with the earth.
At that moment I felt a love in my heart for them all, Phyllis,
Dermot and Robert, and a completeness which was with me for days
afterwards.

That holiday was memorable for its expeditions into the glens
and forests around. On one such occasion with the boys I explored
a particularly overgrown glen through which a river crossed over a
number of falls or flowed through deep, dark pools between the rocks.
We fought our way up through the undergrowth, hot, wet with sweat
and pricked all over by thorns, and came at last to the main waterfall
below which was a deep pool of black water laced with white foam.
Here we stripped, as to cross the pool we would have to swim. It was
very dark and the rocks by the side were slippery. I let myself into
the water slowly and swam about the pool feeling the bottom where
possible. When I found a ledge which stretched across I called to the
boys to follow. For a moment they hesitated, then Robbie who had
learned to swim well let himself into the water and swam across
strongly, his fair head above the dark water, his eyes set on the rock
beyond, his little brown body gleaming through the golden water.
Then came Dermot, less skilfully. On reaching me he immediately
began to dramatise the scene, talking volubly. He opened his mouth
just too soon, failed to catch the rock and sank. He came up
spluttering and coughing and I hauled him out of the cold black
water. There we all stood, the sun coming between the trees drying
us. Our tiredness had gone; the freshness of the water had quickened
our senses. We were part of the forest, the earth breathed about us,
and the water gurgled and talked. I looked at my sons and was
content for a moment to be with them and part of the land of Ireland.

On other expeditions we often went on horseback. On one occasion
Robbie's horse, while passing along a narrow path in a glen through
which ran a stream, suddenly stumbled and slipped down the bank
into the river below leaving the boy suspended in a tree. Nobody
was hurt except for a little missing skin and we rode triumphantly
home where I subsequently wrote the following prose poem, catching, I hoped, the feeling of that day.

        'Cream cracker', not white, not yellow
        muddy cream, maybe.
        Mongolian they said

Robbie rode him
Like an elf
Drawn by Walt Disney
perched up with
A little straight back
Legs swinging out
At a funny angle,
Stirrups too short.
Dermot rode the pony
Loosely, lightly, with easy confidence
And I came along
On old Skite
Down the road
And up the hill
Through the woods
Over the mountain
Flaming gorse and
Crackling dead leaves
Young larch and
Old surly oak
Green new grass
And early wheat.
Then jogging home with the sun behind
Happy in an earth-like heaven
Robbie trotting like a yellow sprite
Dermot swinging free and long
Myself on Skite hammering behind
Bel-Air, Wicklow and spring in the air
The brothers, their father, Wough and Skite,
Phyllis waiting their return.
Happy peace and content of mind.

During all the years of my life I have found riding horses the one complete form of relaxation for mind and body. Every muscle is exercised. You sweat out all the toxins in your blood. Your mind rests from the unsolved problems as all your senses are concentrated on the next obstacle in a hunt. On the jog home afterwards your vision is enlarged and you see the beauty of the world around you: 'the winter trees trace out their twigs against the pearl grey sky'.

It was with the Bray hunt that I usually rode, because they were a drag hunt and pursued a dragged scent rather than that of a fox hunted to death. The idea of a creature being tortured to death by chasing it till it could run no more has always outraged my doctor mind and, although I have ridden sometimes with famous fox-hunting packs and enjoyed the wild thrill of the mad free gallop over country with unknown hazards, I have always felt a moment of guilt and personal pain in my consciousness, most particularly when I have been present when the animal was torn to pieces by the hounds. Then all the joy of the ride has gone out of me and I have ridden home miserably.

After returning to work in Ireland, I could only afford hunting at the cheapest rate. I obtained a number of inexpensive mounts from Jim, one of the Magee brothers. He and his brother Bill kept riding-schools. Jim used to say, 'We're twins, doctor. If you go I'll have to look out.' He died two years ago.

In those days he had a stable with a very odd selection of horses which he used to keep for members of the Bray hunt and hire out. The most outrageous of these horses he had bought on a spree for twenty-one pounds and called Skite.

Skite was very ugly, too long and too broad, but he stood about sixteen hands. Jim said he had 'great blood in him from some famous racehorse on his mother's side'. He did not look it, nor did he behave like it. He would kick in his stable and when ridden at hunts would refuse suddenly and then nothing would make him go again. He constantly got girth galls. However, from the first day I took him out we established a sort of understanding. I learned it was no use striking him if he refused to jump a certain bank or wall. Actually he knew a lot more about banks than most of his riders did. If he refused to take a particular obstacle it was usually because it was too difficult for him. After a time I would not ride any other horse but Skite. As soon as I had somewhere to stable him I bought him off Jim for forty pounds and rode him steadily for the next seen seasons.

* * *

Phyllis did not ride or share many sides of my life so that other people and other thoughts filled most of it. Once or twice when I fell in love with some entrancing young person I realised the danger that I was drifting towards. One thing, however, I always shared with Phyllis which ever brought us back together: her understanding and love of the creatures whom she brought into the fold of her family. We shared the companionship and earthly love of two unusual personal dogs. The first was a rough-haired Airedale whom Dermot christened Wow though we pronounced it Wough to rhyme with lough and be properly Irish.

Dermot said he had 'gleautiful' red eyes. He was an Airedale of the O'Shaughnessy–Fitzwilliam Square breed. We got him when he was

a puppy from Miss O'Shaughnessy whose father, like Sir John Moore, had outlived his generation. The old gentleman used to hire a fourwheeler cab every day and sit in it for an hour or two under the shade of the trees in Fitzwilliam Square. It was never clear whether he thought he was having carriage exercise as was customary for Masters of the Rolls and people of equal distinction in the society of his day, or whether he was just resting quietly in a cab whose musty ancientness gave him peace of mind. He had always had Airedales, Miss O'Shaughnessy said, though it was somebody else who said he sometimes took one of them along to the Bench, the dog sitting beside him and barking at the defendants. Wough, however, had no legal leanings and made a number of enemies. He scared the timorous lady who lived in the top flat of our house so that she was afraid to pass up the stairs. This got us into trouble with the lady's sister who was the wife of an important medical professor. If she met any of us in the street, with or without Wough, she would now cut us as if we were obstructing her view of some imaginary object immediately behind us. This used to infuriate Wough who would begin to bark at her in the O'Shaughnessy way.

Before the invention of antibiotics had revolutionised the treatment of infection Wough got bronchitis and could not bark. Phyllis treated him with inhalations of Friars Balsam in steam administered from a jug under a towel. To avoid further chills she dressed him in a female jumper with buttons down his front. He inhaled the balsam deeply and began to bark again soon afterwards.

It is said Airedales are very clever. Certainly Wough had a splendid memory, particularly for smells; even in his sleep you could imagine the dreams he was having by the way his nose worked and by the little whining noises he made if a particularly luscious smell floated up from the kitchen such as boiling rabbit. He never forgot the people he bit and would bite them again if the chance offered. He was devoted to the family but outside it he certainly did have enemies.

Rusty, who came after, was an Irish red setter and a great contrast. He was very magnificent with his dark red coat and splendid ruffles round his neck. Everybody fell in love with him on sight. People still ask after him though he is now gone more than a dozen years. For me he was the greatest joy. To see him galloping across country, leaping ditches and banks or stretching himself in great bounds over some green field was a picture of astonishing beauty.

Like all of his kind, he was a terrible wanderer and used to trek all over Dublin. This resulted in all sorts of difficult situations. On one occasion he was locked up by an irate lock-keeper's wife on the canal for jumping over the half-door into her kitchen and endeavouring to carry off half a fowl. On another we were nearly driven crazy after searching for him for three days. By this time all sorts of people knew him and we were rung up from all directions in the city, sometimes from more than one area at a time to say Rusty had been seen proceeding in such and such a direction with, usually, a lady friend, often of rather inferior pedigree. This time we had rushed in the direction of the maternity hospital at one end of Merrion Square, then driven almost up to the Phoenix Park at the other end of Dublin and back again without finding him. . . . The telephone rang again and I picked up the receiver with some irritation.

A raucous voice shouted. 'If you've been looking for the red wone he's with the black wone down the alley by University College.'

We rushed round to U.C.D. There, strolling along the pavement by Earlsfort Terrace was red Rusty accompanied by the most deplorable mangy black bitch. He looked pretty worn out to us. I gave my usual toot on the horn. He turned his head and shook it sadly. 'You see I can't leave her,' he seemed to say. 'Oh come on,' I said, tooting a bit louder and opening the back door of the car. He rounded his head again. Then suddenly he turned away from his black companion and lightly sprang into the back of the car and lay down on the back seat at full length and closed his eyes. On reaching home he slept without waking for nearly forty-eight hours. In some mysterious way the black bitch discovered that he lived in Fitzwilliam Square and came and sat on our steps but he was not interested any more.

CHAPTER 11

WRITING

Whenever life has been particularly difficult or my fortunes at stake, I have always taken to the pen. So it was in the early thirties. I had written a number of descriptions of Rugby football and I first thought of writing a book primarily about the game as I had played it. But I found as I began to write that I was really writing a young man's autobiography. I wasn't sure what to do so I took the bones of the manuscript down to Mayo one Christmas time, to a cottage owned by the Burkes of North Mayo, above Lough Conn between Pontoon and Lahadoun under Mount Nephin. There sitting by a turf fire between the snow-capped mountain and the forest around the lake below I sorted things out and *The Silver Fleece* was born.

When it was finished it was accepted for publication by L. A. G. Strong who was working for Nelson at that time and the following year it was published.

The same urge had hit my two brothers, unknown to each other, at the same moment. So it happened that Maurice Collis published *Siamese White* in March, getting the English Book Society award. I published *Silver Fleece* in April, getting an American book award, and John Stewart Collis, *Farewell to Argument* in May. Jack was the only one of us who was a professional writer at that time. He had already published a remarkable work on Bernard Shaw written when he was twenty-two.

The Silver Fleece received the most flattering notices in England, Ireland and America. E. A. Montague gave me a tremendous leg-up by his notice in the Manchester *Guardian*. It was much too kind. My love of the country of Ireland bound up in my Mayo experiences must have shone out from its pages and touched some cord in the hearts of most Irish readers from Brendan Behan who read it in Borstal to Horsey Brown the Irish wing-forward and threw open a new world of Irish people to me.

I began to meet the leaders of Irish literary thought such as Frank O'Connor and Sean O'Faoláin, the then young Cork writers who were to become world-famous. They are the élite among Irish writers of this century. Frank O'Connor, whose real name was Michael O'Donovan (nobody ever discovered why with his own name, O'Donovan, he had to invent the pen name O'Connor), said to me one day that when he was writing he was 'ever trying to reach the last output in himself'. That only when in grand exaltation, sometimes walking up and down crying out and even weeping as he wrote, was he sure he had reached his goal.

Sean O'Faoláin said that sometimes the very reverse from what you had thought appeared as you wrote, opening up new avenues of thought, or a completely new outlook. He agreed that novel writing was like a tunnel in which you saw the start and the end, both in daylight, but between you groped forward in the dark.

I also met and became close friends with a number of the contemporary Anglo-Irishmen of literary distinction such as L. A. G. Strong, Cecil Day Lewis and Frank Pakenham, now Lord Longford.

I began to dine once a week with George O'Brien and Edmund Curtis, professors at University College and Trinity. I got to know Robert Barton, signatory of the Treaty, who with David Robinson carrying nine wounds from World War I, represented the Anglo-Irish Protestant supporters of de Valera's Republican régime. I also became friends with Erskine Childers, son of the elder Erskine Childers, who had been shot by the Free Staters after Michael Collins had been killed in the Civil War.

The comparative fame which publication of my book gave me in high circles lent me above all a platform from which to attack the social evils of contemporary Dublin. At that moment the plight of the poor in the city was appalling. Ninety thousand people lived in one-roomed tenements mostly in old battered eighteenth-century houses without proper water supply and only with communal washing arrangements. Ten thousand of them existed in basement cellar rooms, or old wine cellars. The dirt, the smell, the awful squalor that the people lived in was terrible and wrung the heart of any feeling person. But few in the upper classes knew or really cared. It seemed to be accepted that if you were born into the poor working class your job in life was to work for almost nothing in order to support the other upper section of society in comfort, if not luxury. Diseases such as tuberculosis which killed thousands a year had no scientific treatment, and the poor just died in extreme discomfort. One scene has always remained in my mind. On the foot of a bed three old men were playing poker in a sort of home for the dying near the opening of the main Dublin sewerage system, where the air was full of the smell of sewage. The three old men were hopeless cases of tuberculosis with cavities in their lungs. They continually coughed up horrible blood-stained sputum. In the bed beyond them lay a boy, ten years old, dying of tuberculous meningitis. The old man dealt out the cards, coughed and spat. The boy lay unconscious beside them, his eyes turned up. I stood silently watching. Nobody looked up; nobody spoke.

At this time I met Father Canavan, the Jesuit, through my friendship with Robert Barton and he inspired me to try and rouse the people of Dublin to the filthy degraded state of the poor sections of their beautiful city. The Irish Press, under the then American-trained editor, took up the scandal of the slums. In an article I wrote for the Press I said: 'If you go up into the hills outside Dublin and look down you will see the red roofs of new houses ringing the city and spreading out into the country. Something is being done there. The "Old Lady" is being bought a new cloak. Yet nobody has attempted to treat her sores because they stink too much of vested interest.'

This did not make me popular. I was attacked by every gombeen man in the city. I was called a lot of bad names, from 'self-advertiser' by my medical colleagues to a 'capitalist' by the communists, and a 'communist' by the 'capitalists'.

In the medical world my position after my failure in the Irish M.R.C.P. examination was now fortunately restored. The two ancient men who had examined me the year before were dead and when I took the examination the second time I found Professor Abrahamson as examiner and all was well. I passed the first part and was allowed the second part on presenting a thesis on my rheumatic fever work including my seven papers on the subject. Then at the same moment I was elected a Fellow of the London College of Physicians along with Sheldon and Moncrieff, an honour seldom given at our age.

With Father Canavan, we formed a committee called the Citizens' Housing Council. This Council brought together a group of Dubliners of the most diverse backgrounds. Father Canavan was a chairman of the greatest ability and vision. He was immensely intelligent and could feel his way back to the source of the problem and see through plausible arguments. In those days he sometimes spent a few days at Glendalough House, Robert Barton's place in County Wicklow. It was here we planned the Citizens' Housing Council. In the end it contained such different personalities as the Protestant Archbishop, Dr Gregg, Professor Theo Dillon, the best of the Dillon family, Miss

Louise Benett, one of the Irish women of her day, beloved by the working women of the city, Robert Childers, another son of the executed Erskine Childers, a young man of integrity and ability, and Stoirin Barton as secretary.

The Council worked hard for several years and drew up a number of reports on the housing problems of Dublin and the appalling conditions of the slums which were then among the worst in Europe. These reports were the basis of its work; they helped to produce an informed public opinion.

As well as this academic approach the Council organised public meetings to rouse the people of Dublin to the plight of the poorer citizens. One such meeting was held in the big hall of the Mansion House which was lent by Alfie Byrne, the Lord Mayor of Dublin. Father Canavan did not like Alfie. He saw through his facile façade all too clearly. Alfie was too glib at saying the right thing to please whatever audience he was addressing. He sometimes attended as many as half a dozen functions in one day from the Rotary Club to a sale of work in aid of some orphanage. He almost took the place of royalty in Dublin. In his own gay incorrigible way he won the hearts of the people who kept on re-electing him over and over again. He must have shaken hands with almost everybody in the city by the end of his career. On this particular occasion as Father Canavan was the chief speaker he did not appear. Father Canavan made a powerful attack on the apathy of the well-to-do and was outspoken in his criticism of the Dublin Corporation whose lack of initiative and mediocrity he despised. When he had finished and one of the leading gentlemen of the city was making a detailed defence of the city-fathers and their policy, one of those Dublin scenes took place which used to delight Sean O'Casey and which he not unusually incorporated in his plays. A tall person arose from the back of the hall and called out in the most exaggerated Dublin drawl:

'Mr Chairman, as a Dublin-maun to a Dublin-maun I waunt to ask Mr X won question.'

'Sit down,' I shouted.

He sat down but was up again in a minute.

'Mr Chairman! Mr Chairman! as a Dublin-Maun . . .'

'Sit down!' This went on until at last I said 'All right—ONE question.'

'As a Dublin-Maun to a Dublin-maun I want to ask Mr X what he did with the funds of the Drumcondra Football Club.'

'Throw him out!' They threw him out, but Mr X's defence of the Corporation was lost in the tumult which followed.

The meeting went on, however, until after midnight. Finally when

Father Canavan and I were walking out we came upon a woman with two sleeping children near the back of the hall.

I recognised her as one of the mothers from the National Children's Hospital.

'Ah, Father and Doctor,' she said, 'why wouldn't I be coming to hear you?'

'But how are you going to get home? The trams have now all stopped,' I said.

'Oh, some way. We can walk!' she smiled. Father Canavan said, 'Doctor, let's take her home.'

So they all packed into the back of my car and we drove them back to their tenement house on the north side of the city.

There Mrs Brennan got out carrying one of the children who was asleep in her arms, the other holding her skirt. They stood in the battered doorway of their old Georgian tenement house. The clocks struck one. Father Canavan raised his hand. Mrs Brennan bent her head while he blessed them. Then I drove him back through the now almost silent city to the Jesuit College on the south side of the city. He was one of the loneliest men I ever knew.

*　　*

One day Frank O'Connor, who had become one of the directors of the Abbey Theatre, said to me, 'If you feel so strongly about the Dublin slums why don't you write us a play about them?'

At the same time Rachel Ryan, E. A. Montague's sister, said to me, 'What are you, a doctor or a writer? Anyway if you write any more, make it objective next time, something that has nothing to do with Bob Collis!'

'All right,' I thought, 'I'll write them a play.'

I thought a bit and collected material and planned out a plot. Then a lot of other work crowded in and I had to leave the play for six months. I suppose it must have been forming itself in my subconscious because a very curious thing happened to me when I again took up my pen to write.

I sat down to write one evening about ten o'clock and gradually became immersed in the lives of the people I was creating. The story was that of a country girl from the West who comes to Dublin, marries a Dublin man and has a baby who dies. She is destroyed by the slums of Dublin.

After writing for some hours, and midnight was past, it seemed as if my room was filled with people—the girl, her mother, her weak Dublin husband, friends and relations. I wrote as fast as I could; I wrote all night. At last as the dawn began to lighten the sky I found that the story of the play was finished. I went to bed and lay tossing. This is the only time in my life that I have experienced something completely outside myself containing emotions and other factors of which I had no previous conscious knowledge.

It was only the bones of the play, later called *Marrow Bone Lane*, and a great deal had to be done to make it actable. In this I received great help from my literary and artistic friends though their views did not always correspond. Lennox Robinson, the producer of the Abbey Theatre, and Sean O'Faoláin gave me diametrically opposed advice about one scene where some money was stolen, Sean saying it was too petty to include and Lennox saying it made the scene dramatically.

At the last moment the Abbey decided not to put the play on. Robert Spaight had come to Dublin to act Beckett in *Murder in the Cathedral*. His beautiful and talented Welsh wife had us all in the palm of her hand and finally ran off with Frank O'Connor. The immediate result was that Frank O'Connor had to resign from the Abbey directorate. This seemed a horrible blow to me at the time but was a blessing in disguise for the play was now accepted by the Gate Theatre and Micheál Mac Liammóir and Hilton Edwards, by far the most talented pair of actor-producers in Dublin, or indeed in Europe, accepted it. Again, we worked over it. Now with their experience we succeeded in making it actable. The evening before the first night the dress rehearsal went on till four a.m. It did not seem possible to me that it could be produced the next evening. But such was the skill of the Gate players that in fact it went on on time the following night. Micheál Mac Liammóir himself only took the small part of the brother from the West in one scene but he was such a consummate actor that he stole all the male parts in the few minutes he was on the stage. I have only seen this done on one other occasion when Olivier came on as the 'button-moulder' in *Peer Gynt* and stole the play from everybody, including Ralph Richardson.

The star of the evening was Shelagh Richards, as the girl from the West. Shelagh is a very accomplished artist but on this occasion she rose to the height of a great tragedienne. As the final curtain came down on the scene when her baby dies, she had the audience in tears that first night. I was sitting somewhere in the audience and found myself almost in tears too. But when there were shouts of 'author, author', at the end and I struggled up on the stage I was completely unable to say a word. I felt a fool as I opened and shut my mouth without any sound coming out. Finally somebody laughed and the tension broke.

On another occasion, when the play was being acted at the

Olympia Theatre, which originally had been a tough garrison musical hall and had retained some of its toughness, I tried to get in at the stage door but was thrown out by the doorman who was clearly an ex-prize fighter. He took me for just another opportunist male. But I went round and sat in the pit alone. In the second interval while the orchestra was playing a symposium of Tom Moore's airs I heard two gentlemen sitting directly behind me in loud argument.

'Lookit,' said one, 'look at the band playing those Tommy Moore tunes written in the drawing-rooms of London and this play written out of the bones of the people of Dublin.'

I remembered my strange night's experience, wondering where it had all come from. These people and their story were utterly foreign to my ordinary thought. To this day *Marrow Bone Lane* is a mystery to me and I can hardly be sure I wrote it.

I suppose I am a Dubliner born and bred. My father was a Dubliner and his father and his father's father. For generations we have walked her streets till the house fronts of the Georgian brick red-yellow or grey with smoke, the Irish sky above, the glimpses of green hills between high buildings, the smells of the back streets, the cries of the children are so imprinted on the cells of my brain that they are part of me, while other cities, even those I know well, are alien to my mind. Here I am forever turning a corner and finding what I knew I would find, I enter a room I know I have never seen before but it is not strange. Or I pause for a moment by the river and look at the water lapping in the moonlight against the quay before the eighteenth-century Custom House and some old memory stirs within my mind.

Even more deeply imprinted than Dublin views have been moments in the Children's Hospital Clinic. A mother and child brought in, she is dirty; the child smells.

'What's wrong?'

'He's been vomiting all night and I've been after walkin' up and down between the beds comforting him and him keening since four this morning.'

As she speaks I see in my mind a room with two beds and a cot. In one bed are the father and two boys, in the other two girls. The air is heavy, the smell of dirty clothes and sweat fills the air. The child cries as they undress him, his hoarse screams tear at the ear-drums and sear the senses. But I feel relaxed. The sound, the smell, the pain are in some way gathered together and suddenly as I examine the child I know what to do. These are the people whom I love, Dublin people. So perhaps in some transcendental way they wrote the play.

CHAPTER 12

WORLD WAR II

If you were Anglo-Irish, you were unlikely to be able to hold an independent position before the onset of World War II, but this the Collis brothers achieved each in his own way. Maurice found himself part of the British Raj in the Indian-Burmese embroglio after World War I. In Burma he learned to understand and love the people and in his famous books, such as *Trials in Burma*, he stood up for them against the stupidity and arrogance of British Imperialism of the old style. Later by his historical works he made the Burmese people known to the rest of the world.

My twin brother Jack has lived in England since he grew up, remaining true to his ambition to become a writer. This he has proved in a number of beautiful books finding in Dorset the same experience of the infinite which he saw in Wicklow when a boy.

For my part, after a period as a student and a young doctor in English and foreign clinics, I came back to work in the medical Dublin of my forbears my foreign training allowing me to view the Irish scene objectively, not through brainwashed Irish protestant, English or Celtic Irish eyes. I found myself on the side of the poor on whose bones much of the wealth and power of both Great Britain and the United States had been built during the last hundred years. I found them the most lovable people who called forth from me an immense affection. As the thirties wore on and the tensions began to boil up again in Europe it was not at all easy to know what to think. Remembering 'the corpse factory' Hun propaganda and the patriotic enthusiasms of 1914 and the millions of young men's graves, many of us were wary of the politicians in 1939. We were rather inclined to sympathise with so-called appeasers who were trying to avoid condemning another generation of young men to death. We did not realise yet that evil was loose in the world again. We did not yet know what Nazism meant although we didn't like

96

what we heard. We disliked anti-semitism but were apt to put it on one side, even to be a little influenced by anti-Jew propaganda, though we did not admit it. Gradually the real beastliness and cruelty of Hitler became apparent and it was clear that he and his Nazis were the real enemies of mankind.

Then the great stand of Churchill and the English after the fall of France called forth our highest admiration. And to a man the Anglo-Irish backed the English in their stand. For the Celtic Irish it was not so simple. Few people had ever suffered more at the hands of others than the Celts at the hands of the Anglo-Saxons. For them England's difficulty was still Ireland's opportunity and the new German war merely another example. Fortunately Ireland was led by de Valera at this moment in her history and he was able to hold the country together. He had been in over ten British prisons, condemned to death and had had a long time in the political wilderness, but like Kenyatta and other leaders of their peoples he possessed no bitterness. He was able to steer Ireland along an officially neutral course while allowing those who wished to volunteer and back the Allied cause either through support of England or hatred of the Nazis or simply through love of adventure.

*   *   *

As the war proceeded I became more and more uncertain as to what I should do myself. As a children's physician there was no point in becoming a regimental doctor or, worse, a physician in some base hospital looking after wounded adults while all my knowledge was how to look after sick children. So I carried on in Dublin while writing another play and several works on medicine.

I belonged to a number of committees in London, however, and went there whenever I could and thus saw the astonishing scene which London presented during the war years.

On one occasion during the blitz period I heard that a woman, who as a young girl had become paralysed was having a very bad time in a London suburb during the raids. The house next door had been bombed and she had to be dragged out into an Anderson shelter in the back garden every night. I decided to fetch her back with me to Ireland. I spent the first night in the Strand Palace Hotel in London which had been hit the night before. I saw the people in the Tube at Charing Cross. Their extraordinary calmness was what struck me most. Quite a lot of them had been bombed out but they were completely compensated mentally. Sleeping on the platform was uncomfortable but that was all. One stout Cockney lady took me for some sort of supervisor.

'Oh, it ain't so bad,' she said, 'if it wasn't for Mrs Smif over there.'

'What's wrong with Mrs Smith?'

'She keeps stuffin' 'er baby that 'orrid! All night, sir. Now I don't like to say nothing to 'er but I don't like 'er going on stuffin' that kid!'

Their house had been blown up. There she was with her own children, away down sleeping on a Tube platform with a couple of rugs. But it was only Mrs Smith who worried her—not Hitler.

In the Royal College of Physicians the same Englishness was apparent. We sat in rather a stuffy room as the usual hall was draughty due to the bombing. For two hours I sat between Newman and Lawrence, two men of astonishing knowledge and wit.

Lawrence was not only a diabetic himself but the world authority on the treatment of the disease. The meeting was being held to discuss the form the British Health Service should take after the war and Lord Dawson of Penn was arguing with Lord Horder that the adjective 'perfect' in front of the noun 'health' lessened its force and should be omitted in the draft proposals. In a diary I was keeping at the time I made an entry describing the scene in the Royal College and putting under it: 'This is why England lost/won the war.' It wasn't for another four years that I was able to cross out 'lost'.

I visited Jack on his farm in Kent above which the Battle of Britain had been fought, aeroplanes diving into the ground around him and bombs falling everywhere.

I picked up the paralysed girl during a day-light raid on Bromley and got her to Euston. This was difficult enough as she was no lightweight and had to be carried in and out of cars which was made particularly awkward for me as one of my fingers had gone septic and was extremely painful.

We reached Euston and got on to the Irish Mail train but it got no further than Rugby as this was one of the nights the full German air fleet was bombing the Midlands.

There we had to spend the night. I rang up the School where I knew the doctor and got us both put up in the school sanatorium. He looked at my finger which was now desperately painful and swollen. 'Must do something,' he said. 'Can't just leave you to get blood poisoning.' So he opened it without an anaesthetic. This was a most painful experience. I turned my head away as the scalpel cut into the inflamed flesh like a hot iron. At that moment the main German air fleet were passing overhead on their way to blow up Coventry. The pain in some way fixed that sound in my subconscious so that if I hear the high drone of planes at night, even now I can feel that finger.

Another time the sirens went just as I was leaving the Hospital for Sick Children. I jumped into a taxi. A French lady jumped in through the opposite door at the same moment. She wanted to go to King's Cross Railway terminus and I to Euston. 'Orlright,' said the taximan, 'we've just time for both.' So we rushed the French lady to her train. Then he took me to mine. By then everything was blacked out and the guns were roaring and the bombs falling.

When the lights came on again I found I was sitting opposite a young man in the railway carriage. He turned out to be called Doherty, from Donegal, a flyer, one of the Battle of Britain boys.

We spent the night together in that carriage. He was on his way to fly out to the Second Army in Egypt. He told me he loved his job. Fighting away up in the clean heavens was 'gorgeous', he said. He was shot to pieces at twenty thousand feet, dived through the German planes, pulled out his parachute late and came down in the sea, was picked up and was fighting again the same day. He had been flying behind Fanucane, the Irish ace, at the Dieppe raid when the latter had been shot down into the sea. Just before he dived into the waves Fanucane called to him on the inter-phone, 'Goodbye now Johnny!' and dived into the sea.

Doherty told me he'd been married that day. Later I contacted his girl. He survived the war.

During the flying-bomb period I found myself on a committee planning medical aid for the civilian populations of Europe after the invasion which was about to take place. I got to know the Free French at that time, General König and his men, and the Red Cross, British, Irish and International. It was very difficult to get anything settled during that period: everybody got completely tired out as the bombing went on continuously day and night for weeks. During the day everybody carried on as if nothing was happening though at its height a loud explosion would occur every few minutes. It was at night, however, that the pilotless bomb-planes were at their worst. The propeller-jet from their tails showed up as a bright flame moving across the sky at night. They had a mesmerising affect if you went up on to a roof and watched them coming in. If they seemed to be coming directly for you, and if they suddenly disappeared and their drone stopped you knew they were falling and you left your look-out very rapidly and got under the stairs in the house as quickly as possible.

On one occasion I had been lunching with some prospective medical-team people and had just got a taxi when a flying bomb literally flew down Piccadilly. It exploded at Hyde Park Corner. Everybody had thrown themselves flat and were getting up as we approached. I saw a very respectable gentleman in a bowler hat handing a pretty young lady up out of the gutter. Where the bomb had actually exploded there was simply a pool of blood and a human hand. The rest of the person had disappeared.

The percussion of these explosions often had the strange effect of blowing off all your clothes. This happened to a Cockney girl I met that afternoon. 'I got in one of them shelters,' she said, 'quick-like, seeing it coming after me up the street. It 'it the shelter, see, and when I came out stark naked I thought I was dead, sir, till I saw one of them firewatchers looking at me.'

At this time I met a number of Europeans who were planning their return to their own countries as soon as possible, French, Dutch, Czech. Among these was Jan Masaryk whom I met at lunch one day with my Rugby School friend Frank Roberts of the Foreign Office, later to become British Ambassador at Moscow and Bonn. Masaryk drove me back after lunch but an air raid supervened and during our forced sheltering from the storm above we became firm friends as sometimes happens in life when external circumstances throw two kindred spirits together in such a way that the usual barriers of reticence are down and each can see into the other's soul without hindrance. So it was that blitzy afternoon with Jan Masaryk and me. We became part of each other for ever though we were only to meet twice again, once more for a few minutes in London, and then our last sad meeting in that bedroom of his in the Czernin Palace in Prague where he was murdered shortly afterwards by the Communists.

During that afternoon in 1944 Jan told me how his father had created Czechoslovakia out of World War I, and of the history of his country. He told me something of his personal and family life and I told him of Ireland.

CHAPTER 13

BELSEN

Towards the end of the war early in 1945 I eventually found myself in the Red Cross with three other Irish doctors, a famous surgeon, a general practitioner and Patrick MacClancy, my companion paediatrician at the Rotunda Hospital. We had taken Lady Limerick's advice and joined the British Red Cross and St John's Ambulance Brigade as the most likely group to get us quickly to Europe.

At that moment Holland above the Rhine was still held by a German garrison. Many of the people there were literally starving. At last the Germans allowed several shiploads of Dutch children to be taken out to England. We met them at Tilbury and organised a number of mobile medical units to go into North Holland as soon as the war would end and it would be possible to cross the Rhine. Under this plan I found myself in Tilburg in Brabant in April 1945. The Red Cross headquarters were in a convent in the town and our mobile units camped down there. Then the war suddenly ended. There was wild jubilation in Holland. The Dutch lost their customary reserve and danced in their streets. I managed to cross the pontoon bridge at Arnhem and reach Utrecht on a reconnoitring expedition to find out how best we could help. There I met a British colonel (retired) who was a senior officer in the British Red Cross. 'Look, Collis,' he said, 'the Dutch have plenty of doctors and nurses. They only want supplies. Your doctors can't speak Dutch and don't know the conditions here. Do you think you will be of any use to them?'

'Doesn't sound like it,' I said.

'Well,' he said, 'look at this.' He produced a dispatch about Belsen concentration camp in Germany which had been uncovered by the advancing Second British Army.

I read it—thousands dying of starvation and typhus, a hospital being formed for some eighteen thousand displaced persons including quite a lot of children. They had now only about one nurse to every five hundred patients and a handful of army doctors.

It didn't sound possible to me. But the war was over and there could be no propaganda value in inventing such a horror now.

'Well,' I said, 'it doesn't sound sense, but if it is anything like this we could be much more use there than in well organised Holland.'

'Go and see for yourself,' he said.

'Thanks,' I said, and next morning I took a fifteen-hundredweight truck and an Army driver and set out for Belsen some hundreds of miles away in the British Zone of Germany, near Hanover.

It took two days to get there along battered roads and bombed cities but my Red Cross cap and rankless battle dress got me through everywhere. I was recognised as a doctor and now that the motif of destruction and death to the enemy was over, men's minds swung to the opposite extreme, the healing of wounds. Everybody was exceedingly nice to me—British, American, French, Dutch army personnel, and Germans of all kinds. The roads were crowded with haggard released prisoners who walked trudging along towards the West. They smiled and waved as we drove past them. We gave them all our chocolate and any supplies we had. On the afternoon of the second day we went through the German town of Celle in a southerly direction. After driving for some time we became aware of a disquieting aroma which came to us in wafts and gradually filled the air in the truck around us. It was the Belsen smell of death and decay.

Finally we came along a straight road and stopped at the closed gate of a vast compound. We were directed by the British sentry to the commandant's office and passed into a large military camp with numerous blocks stretching away in every direction—it was like Aldershot. The British Commander, Colonel Johnston, had been doing a splendid job since the liberation of the concentration camp with a number of Army hospitals, some hundred medical students from London, teams of international Red Cross personnel from Switzerland, and other volunteers. He was, he told me, desperately short of doctors and nurses. The inmates of the camp had been starved during the last winter and now their malnutrition was accentuated by an epidemic of typhus carried by lice, and every form of enteritis including typhoid fever was rife. He calculated that they had been dying at the rate of a thousand a day when the camp was opened by the British Army. Any help our Irish doctors could bring would be more than welcome.

'Would you like to see the Horror Camp, now?' he asked. They took me down the road into the concentration camp area. This consisted of a large number of long wooden army huts enclosed by a formidable barbed-wire fence in which were numerous watch towers raised some fifty feet above the ground.

Johnston's men had been emptying the camp as fast as possible but as every person there had to have the lice washed off and be disinfected before passing out into the clean area there were still many huts to be emptied. I was taken to a number of barracks which had not been evacuated, and some which had but which had not been cleaned. In one of these the human excreta covered the floor about six inches deep. One of the medical students told me that when he had gone into the hut to take the people out the smell had made him vomit every time he tried to enter.

I went into a hut which had been partially cleaned. It contained some sixty persons and was supervised by two splendid young medical students. The inhabitants were mostly lying in bunks one above the other. As I walked down the room a strange noise arose.

'They are clapping you,' the medical student said. Outside I saw a few corpses lying on the ground. They had been pushed out of one of the huts recently and had not been collected as yet that day. When the British arrived, I was told, the piles of dead had been ten feet high in places. These corpses appeared strange, shrivelled, dried-up remnants of mankind, terrifying to look at. Even more gruesome were some of the inmates who were walking around. Their subcutaneous tissues had apparently been completely used up during their long starvation. The skin hung on their bones in folds. Their eyes were sunken into the sockets giving their faces a gaunt bird-like appearance. They no longer looked human but seemed to belong to some sub-human species. This is exactly what the Nazis had been aiming at: to make the Jews appear an inferior race who had no place in a well organised world and might as well be put down like vermin.

Indeed this was their greatest crime. Murder, torture, violent death have been meted out by hundreds of conquerors to their opponents down the years in every part of the world, including our Western islands. But it was left to the mid-twentieth century for one of our Western ethnic groups to attempt to degrade another whole ethnic group among whom were some of the world's most cultured and charming people. In these camps, apart from mass murder, was perpetrated a system of degradation of the inmates. In Belsen there were no latrines. The resultant filth and smell can be imagined. There was no hygiene of any kind. It was impossible for a refined woman to keep herself clean. All were chronically starved so that they lost all interest in life or fought each other for a morsel of bread. If they showed spirit and disobeyed any of the rules they were cruelly beaten, sometimes to such extent that their prominent bones would come out through the flesh and sepsis would set in so that they died horribly. They were forced to perform awful tasks such as shovelling the gassed corpses of their companions into the crematoria.

The 'final solution of the Jewish problem', as the Nazis called this crime, has sickened the conscience of the world. But the crime was at least partly ours as well. There is not a single people, Christian, Moslem or other, who have not worshipped Kali, the god of violence and destruction. Love and compassion have been mocked in every age throughout the world.

'Well,' said Colonel Johnston when I got back from the Horror Camp, 'what do you think of that?'

'I'd better go and collect my Irish doctors and anybody else available, and come and help you,' I replied.

'Be as quick as you can,' he said.

I sat up till after midnight in his tent writing an article for the British Medical Journal to tell the medical people at home what was happening in Germany. After four hours' sleep I set off on a ten-hour drive to Brussels to see the top brass there and get leave to move the Red Cross teams from Holland to Belsen. In Brussels I met a couple of generals who told me the war wasn't over till the Japanese were defeated and that I couldn't have any further Army doctors or nurses. My article, too, was held up by the censor—'so as not to cause alarm or the diversion of the effort needed to end the business'. However, they said I could move any Irish doctors and Red Cross personnel from Holland to Belsen if I liked, and allowed me to raise any other volunteers I could. I drove straight back to Tilburg getting there at supper time.

When I arrived I found them all having a party in the convent hall, with a number of the Dutch underground who had come in and joined them.

I saw two girls and a group of husky young Dutchmen at the lower end of the long table.

'Hello,' everybody called, 'What luck? Where and when are we moving? What are we going to do?'

I told them how I had been to Utrecht, and about the Dutch situation. Then I told them what I had seen in Belsen.

'This is something new in the history of the world,' I said, 'something none of us really guessed or believed possible even when we heard something about these German concentration camps. I feel that we should go and help immediately without any delay. Will those who wish to accompany me please hold up their hands?'

Everybody, including the Dutch contingent, raised their hands.

'All right, we start first thing tomorrow morning.'

I walked down the hall and was introduced to the Dutch. The men were driver mechanics I was told and would look after our transport. 'I am Annie Bonsel,' one of the girls said. She was rather stout and had an open smiling face. 'I've had some nursing experience. And this is Han Hogerzeil.' She introduced the other girl. 'She is a lawyer and speaks five languages. She has been looking after a house full of Jews to save them from the German concentration camps.' I looked at the slight girl who got up from the table and gave me her hand. She seemed the reincarnation of Rogier van der Weyden's fifteenth-century portrait of his young wife, Elisabeth.

'May I come?' she said in perfect English without a trace of foreign accent.

Next day on our way to Germany we reached the floating bridge at Arnhem. Han suddenly pointed down the Rhine. 'Over there,' she said, 'is Oosterbeek, the village where we lived. Our house was destroyed in the battle and everything we had. My mother and brother were in the cellar with the village doctor for ten days and nights and were captured several times by both sides.'

We turned left at Arnhem and drove down to Oosterbeek so as to allow her to see her home again. The old village had been killed. There was nobody there; the houses were dead, just gaping walls and open holes where the windows had been. We walked down a magnificent tree-lined road. Some of the houses had been shattered by shell-fire and lay at queer angles. We came to a house standing in grounds stretching across a little valley that ran down to the Rhine. The front wall had fallen out across the lawn. The house itself was a burnt-out shell. A great sequoia tree had been hit by a shell and its broken trunk lay across the garden. We stood in silence. 'My home,' Han said, stuffing a leaf from one of the trees into her handbag.

I touched her shoulder; we turned and walked back to the others, got into our trucks and drove to Belsen.

*   *   *

When we arrived at Belsen we plunged into work. The Irish doctors took on different jobs. Nigel Kinnear, our surgeon, immediately contacted the surgeons in the proper hospital which was part of the German military camp. MacClancy took over the women's maternity block which was a busy department working under high pressure.

I took on two blocks, one of which contained a large number of orphan children of whom the majority were recovering from malnutrition and the unhygienic conditions they had been exposed

to. Only a few were seriously ill. The second block we rapidly transformed into a children's hospital. The team which formed for the
job was a most remarkable and unusual group. There were a
number of English nursing sisters and V.A.D.s, the very best of
whom was Mrs Burroughs who emanated a loving kindness and
efficiency which was so infectious that she had us all working with a
smile, even the Hungarian cooks who were a little inclined to use
knives if criticised. There were Hermina Krantz and Luba Triszynska
who had been responsible for saving the lives of the orphans in the
camp by using every and any means with the Germans. Neither they
nor their children looked starved. Luba was Russian and Hermina
Czech. Both were Jewish by religion but their appearance did not
seem an ethnic matter. Hermina had the typical Czech dumpling
appearance, she was of the people, a great feminine motherly creature,
devoted to children, and like all the Czechs loyal. Luba was from
White Russian peasant stock—indefatigable, physically strong,
mentally stronger. She belonged to those people who had beaten the
German machine at Stalingrad and marched all the way to Berlin
where in the end they had killed Hitler. Luba and Hermina both
held their children's block inviolable in the middle of the Horror
Camp at Belsen and, when at last the relieving British soldiers had
arrived, had come out and denounced Kramer, the Camp Commander, and the SS guards to the English privates so convincingly
that the latter had killed quite a few of the SS with their fists before
the arrival of a staff officer who had stopped their awful rage at the
spectacle of mass murder which the camp presented when it was
opened up.

Luba and Hermina were given special rooms in the block. Luba
turned hers into an apartment where she now entertained Russian
liaison officers. And, of course, we had Bonsel and Han, whose
knowledge of English and French, German, Dutch and Yiddish was
invaluable as we had children from nine nationalities, mostly Jews,
except for seventeen splendid Russian children who had a dormitory
of their own with red flags and a portrait of Stalin.

We all got down on our hands and knees and scrubbed out the
second block, borrowed, stole or in some way procured blankets,
sheets and all other necessities and had a number of hospital wards
ready in a couple of days.

These were rapidly filled while we prepared others for the five
hundred-odd children in the camp. The British soldiers ran up a
half-circle of large army tents into which we removed the convalescent children who had recovered extraordinarily rapidly in the
open air with the marvellous food which Mrs Burroughs and her

cooks were now producing with the help of more than ten thousand Red Cross parcels which we discovered in the German ports and with which we were able to revolutionise the commissariat of the whole camp.

On my way round the children's hospital one morning I came into a small ward. Here I found Han with the most entrancing scrap of humanity in her arms. He appeared one great smile. There was very little else of him. The fever (typhus) had just left him. His body was wasted.

'What have you got there?'

'Zoltan,' she said, rubbing her cheek against his, 'my boy.'

The child in the next bed was unconscious and all swollen up.

'Aladar, mein Bruder,' Zoltan said. Han asked me how he was. I examined him. 'Pretty desperate,' I replied. 'We might give him a blood transfusion. It's about the only thing that might pull him round.'

'There is a sister, also,' Han said, 'she's all right in the "well" block. Their father was a Slovak Jew but their mother was a Seventh Day Adventist from Hungary. She wouldn't give the father up so they were all taken here. Their small baby died in the cattle trucks on the way and the mother on the day of the liberation of the camp. They'd already murdered the father.'

'Let me look at him,' I said. Han undressed Zoltan. I found he had a left-sided pleurisy which later proved by X-ray to be secondary to a severe primary tuberculosis.

'He has a chance,' I said, 'a good deal better than his brother.' We were setting up the blood bank at that moment and collecting blood from ourselves and the British soldiers who very willingly gave their blood to save the sick children. Aladar rallied for a day or two after his transfusion but starvation had gone too far and he couldn't digest anything and sank once more into a coma and died. Zoltan, on good food, rest and regularity, got over the acute stage of his condition and although far from well was in no immediate danger.

Of the other children a certain few remain clearly in my memory. Tibor and Susie came of cultured Jewish-Hungarian stock. All of their family had been murdered by the Nazis. The murder of the Hungarian Jews is one of the most ghastly deeds of the Third Reich. It is said that twenty-five thousand were murdered during one weekend in a Polish concentration camp. So many at a time were lined up to be killed that the gas chambers couldn't accommodate the numbers, and thousands had to be shot in the back of the head by SS executioners and thrown into a pit.

Suppose an English or American leader suddenly decided that the

TO BE A PILGRIM

only thing to do was to murder all Irishmen wherever we were in the world because of our bad characteristics, many of which are probably worse than those of the Semitic peoples. The incomprehensible thing about the Germans and the Jews was that the German people as a whole swallowed the propaganda that the Jews were inferior, wicked men who were better 'put down' like vermin. We like to think that had a Hitler arisen among us with the same paranoid attitude we would have behaved differently. Would we? Would we have risked our lives, particularly in wartime, knowing the fate that we would have suffered if we failed like Von Stauffenberg's co-conspirators who were hung up on meat hooks when the plot to kill Hitler failed? It is hard to say. Maybe we wouldn't have followed a British, American or French Hitler. The awful fact is that a mad Hitler established himself as the undisputed leader of one of our greatest Christian Western nations in this century and was able to ravage vast tracts of Europe and murder millions of people in cold blood. This was what was driven into our minds in Belsen in 1945. We put all the blame on the wicked Germans. The Germans salved their own conscience by putting it all down to the wicked Nazis. The Germans either said they didn't know anything about what went on in concentration camps or, if that was obviously untrue, as for instance in the cases of actual German camp guards, they excused themselves by saying they were acting under orders in the same way as if they had been soldiers in a firing squad at an execution.

For us who lived with this horror through the whole summer of 1945 it was impossible to put it on one side, out of mind, forget it and go on with life as if it had not happened.

On the day we burned down the Horror Camp with flame-throwers, a cloud of smoke and mist hung over the scene giving the spectacle of the jets of flying flames a diabolical appearance so that we felt the wickedness of that place existed as positive Evil, that in fact positive Evil really exists in the world and that the old concept of the Devil may be true.

Susie was very weak after typhus and only just alive. Tibor was a splendid little male. He was only five but he nursed her and literally would not let her die. He fed her with a spoon. He got into bed with her every afternoon and put a brotherly arm round her so that she used to fall asleep in the crook of his arm content and secure.

Zoltan, his sister Edit, Tibor and Susie became my special children. One day Zoltan, who was always making statements such as 'My brother Aladar wouldn't eat and therefore he died,' said, 'Mein Vater ist gestorben und jetzt ist der Arzt mein Vater.'

'What does he say?' I asked.

'They have killed my father, now the doctor is my father,' Han translated. 'What are you going to do about that?'

'Well,' I said, 'Zoltan, you'd better come home with me and bring your friends and relations.' From that moment it was assumed by everybody that Zoltan and Edit, Tibor and Susie, if nobody turned up to claim them, would eventually be looked after by me.

Among the other children who became my special cases were two little girls, Mariana Baumöhl and Ludmilla Rosenzweig. They both came from Slovakia in the mountainous Carpathian country where centuries ago certain Jewish families had emigrated from the Hanover direction. They both had their mothers with them. Mrs Rosenzweig was a woman of enormous vitality and resource but her mind was filled with all sorts of queer superstitions often twisted into fantastic ideas which seemed so absurd to us that we didn't realise that she was undefeatable. Mrs Baumöhl had quite a different background. She could only be described as a 'lady' and her daughter was like her. Ludmilla and Mariana were very sick with primary tuberculosis contracted from one of the open cases of consumption which were common in the camp.

As time went on they both improved and when transport was arranged to bring the Czech internees back to Prague they were considered well enough to travel in one of our ambulances along with their mothers.

One of our functions had become to repatriate the children to their different countries as soon as they were well enough to travel, and Luba took her sixty-five Dutch children back to Holland where she was thanked by the Queen.

When the transport for Prague was being arranged it was decided that the vast majority of Czechoslovak Jewish children should travel in a special train but we were asked to take the sick ones in our ambulances.

I felt that a doctor must accompany the children as some of them were still very sick. So I said I would go myself and take Han as well to help with the mothers.

It was a long and desperate journey, first through the British, then the American, and finally the Russian Zone.

Ludmilla and Mariana did not stand the journey well and were very weak and sick when we reached Pilsen inside Czechoslovakia. We therefore thought it wise to leave them there in the local hospital with their mothers. At the time the modern anti-tuberculosis drugs were not yet available and I thought I was leaving them there to die.

This journey was an experience in international ways of thought. The British, particularly the English Cockney privates one saw walking about the roads of the Germany they had conquered, did not appear arrogant in any way. They seemed to wear a puzzled humorous look on their faces. They were kind. This was a revelation to me who had been trained for a crack fighting unit as a killer in World War I and had experienced the violent Black and Tan irregulars in Ireland after the war.

I particularly remember one evening when the British garrison at Belsen gave a great party to the convalescent internees. It included a dance in an open square with two army bands. The English soldiers danced with the thin convalescent Jewish girls, who had been degraded and made to run naked before the SS guards, with such gentleness and courtesy that they restored my belief in ultimate goodness which I had almost lost.

I remember also that night a Canadian sergeant dancing in a circle with my bigger children with a smile of absolute happiness on his young face and the children crying out with joy around him.

The American Army was quite different. They were not Europeans. They didn't know what it was all about. They didn't know why they were there. They had won—of course they had won—they'd always won if it came to a fight. They were young, like boys, strong, good or bad, savage or kind, very friendly. Unlike the Europeans they spoke English but otherwise they were farther off from us than, say, the Dutch or the French.

We met a charming group of young Americans at the frontier between Germany and Czechoslovakia. We were very tired and travel-stained at that moment and our sick children were in poor shape. The American boys carried them out of the ambulances, washed them, fed them on marvellous food, joked with us and behaved like a bunch of gay cousins of ours whom we'd met before. We forgot we were doctors and they soldiers, we Europeans and they Americans, and for a moment we were all just happy humans.

The Russians were quite different again. In Prague they had their crack troops—very correct, but rather distant, curious but suspicious of us, the first Westerners they had met.

We travelled back to Belsen by a different route, through Leipzig and Eastern Germany, some of which the Americans were now evacuating to the Russians for reasons of higher policy. The German inhabitants were terrified and on several occasions seeing the Western markings on our vehicles begged us for help, kneeling in the road with their hands upraised. There were stories of rape everywhere. This was the only crime which the Germans seemed to have omitted from their war behaviour as far as their invasion of the West was concerned. To us the Russians seemed generally to behave well but they continually made passes at our women and suggested exchanging girls to me. In the end I was forced to seek the assistance of a Russian general to get us out of their Zone as our passes were regarded with suspicion by the junior officers who all appeared to have been brainwashed into believing that all Westerners were capitalists and essentially enemies of their way of life. They kept us waiting in many places hour after hour and were anything but cordial. The Russian general was a contrast; he was smartly dressed, very polite to us, giving us coffee and Russian cigarettes. He didn't appear to like his commissar who sat scowling, unshaven and obviously doing the proletarian act for our benefit. The general gave me a special personal pass through the Russian Zone and could not have been kinder, though a Russian firing squad shooting Germans outside made us jump while these pleasantries were going on. The general and his staff gave us our first experience of Russian charm which we have met many times since, finding their human quality always disarming even when their system seemed a prison to us.

Hermina who had accompanied us on this journey to Prague refused to stay and came back with us. She didn't like the atmosphere in Prague. She didn't trust the Russians which was not surprising because her ample curves seemed to appeal to the Russian soldiers who continually made passes at her, sometimes not too gently.

Also the German anti-Jewish propaganda depicting the Jews as clever cheats had affected everybody whether they realised it or not. In a sense the Germans by their 'final solution' had only brought years of persecution of the Jews by Christians to its logical conclusion. We had taken over the Jewish religion as our own. Their prophets were recognised as messengers of our God. The greatest messenger was Jesus. True, He was murdered by their establishment but it differed little from all our establishments down to the present day. We made Him and His mother into immortals along Greek lines of thought, forgot or wilfully set aside His main message, and commandment—'love one another'—we persecuted and tortured each other to death in His name. And the Jews who insisted on going on living with their own traditional religion, the worship of the Universal God, were in most countries denied the right to own land and were forced to be shopkeepers. Being more sharp-witted than most other ethnic groups, they were good at trade. This meant being quick enough to get there first which left the second-comer with a sense of grievance. But the main sin of the Jews has always been their insistence to be different from the peoples in whose country they have lived. This, combined with their talent for making money has always led to jealousy and often hatred of the people around them.

The mad Nazis exploited this feeling everywhere. In the Eastern provinces of Czechoslovakia there were said to have been one hundred and twenty thousand Jews. The Germans murdered a hundred thousand of them. To do this they had to persuade themselves and the local inhabitants that what they were doing was destroying a bad people. The necessary propaganda to put this across was organised by Goebbels so well that it affected people everywhere even where the Germans themselves were hated. So by 1945 there were few countries where the Jews were regarded as worthy of love or respect. The new Russians although they deny the old Russian ways have always regarded the Jews with suspicion. For in Russia unless you adopt their Communist religion you can never have a place in their established order.

In the few days that Hermina was in Prague she felt the anti-Jewish tension and she didn't like it. She came back with us. As we approached Belsen again she called out she was 'home'. When we drove into the camp and Luba ran out to meet us Hermina jumped off her ambulance and flung herself into Luba's arms sobbing with joy. All the Czech Jews we knew felt the same and most of them have subsequently managed to escape to Israel or America.

Dr Berger is a good example. One day Han found a gaunt, haggard looking man standing outside our children's hospital in Belsen.

'Schwester,' he said in a low voice. She stopped and asked him if she could help him. He told her he had been a doctor in Czechoslovakia but because he was a Jew the Germans had taken him and his wife and transported them to a concentration camp. As he was a doctor he had perhaps been treated better than others and was not gassed but when the Eastern camps had been evacuated he and his wife had been taken to Belsen where she had died and he very nearly, from typhus just before the liberation. He had lost heart when his wife died; the typhus had reduced him physically so that he could hardly feel any more—'I was once a doctor,' he said.

Han called me. 'May I introduce Dr Berger,' she said.

'Tell him we'd be glad if he'd join our staff.' Han translated. Berger, who had been looking at the ground, raised his head. I held out my hand and took him into the ward and immediately put him to examining a group of children. I didn't stay to watch lest I embarrassed him. In a few days he was a regular member of the paediatric department. Long afterwards he wrote me a charming letter in which he said we had restored his human dignity and given him back his will to live. He has ever since remained our friend and we hear from him regularly. He escaped from the Russian world at the time of the Czech crisis and now lives in West Berlin. In the end Hermina, Mariana, Ludmilla and their families managed to escape to Israel, and Luba went to America.

*　　*　　*

It was now July 1945. Bernadotte, the famous Swede, had visited us and offered to take all our remaining convalescents to Sweden for rehabilitation and sorting out, and his offer was accepted. This meant that we had to wind up our work. This raised considerable difficulties as our remaining children were either still sick or had no one belonging to them left alive. These children had become our special care, they trusted us completely and we loved them. Han and Bonsel had a regular family, the Zynns and the Molnars being perhaps the most beloved. 'We can't let them go by themselves,' Han said.

'All right,' I said, 'we'll go with them to Sweden and later I'll take Zoltan and his sister to Ireland and Tibor and Susie and any others for whom a home cannot be found.'

When all was ready for the evacuation of the children from Belsen to Sweden, lists completed, final examinations made and only a few weeks left, Han said 'I haven't seen my family since six months before the end of the war. I have heard they are in Friesland in the north of Holland. Can I have a week's leave?' 'All right,' I said, 'I'll take a week off too and drive you home.'

So we set off through the north German plain in my captured Opel. We came to Leeuwarden, the capital of Friesland amid its many lakes, and drove up to a house which looked like one out of an old Dutch landscape. Out ran Han's mother and aunt. They laughed and cried with happiness, for they had not known what had happened to one another in those last months when the north of Holland was still held as one of the last fortresses of Hitler's breaking empire.

'Can you take me home?' Han's stepfather, the old doctor of Oosterbeek, asked me.

'Of course.' So next day we set off for Arnhem and Oosterbeek with Dr Brevée. We arrived there about midday. The scene had completely changed since last we were there at the end of hostilities. Then it was all silent, its battered shell-holed houses glowering at us from dead eyes. Now it was all bustle. The people were coming home, rebuilding their broken homes and picking up their shattered lives.

The sun was shining with full summer splendour as we drove down the main street. Suddenly somebody recognised the old doctor.

He took off his hat and called out so that the others heard and a rumour spread immediately that the 'old doctor' was home. During the battle of Arnhem his eighteenth-century house had been destroyed over his head while he looked after thirty people in its cellars. Shot through and through, the old house had fallen in heaps as the young men of the opposing armies had struggled and died for the possession of the rubble.

Dr Brevée had served the villagers as family doctor for forty-five years. He had healed their sores, cured their pains, listened to them pour out their troubles and comforted them. They had thought him dead but now here he was alive and coming back home. Everybody bowed, some cheered, some cried. He stood up in the back of the open car, took off his hat and bowed back. His grey hair and beard were blown back by the wind. I drove on slowly, feeling like the chauffeur of a royal personage on some great occasion.

We stayed a few days in the village. Han was welcomed by every-body, doctors, shopmen, friends and relations. I explored the battle-ground where ten thousand British and Polish men had fought for ten days against the German armour, one-third being killed, one-third captured, and one-third escaping back across the Rhine out of the Oosterbeek woods in the night.

On the Oosterbeek-Arnhem side of the Rhine the hills rise a few hundred feet clothed in magnificent forests of splendid trees, elm and beech, oak and silver birch. In those days they were very silent; here and there lay a broken army vehicle or a tree whose trunk had been shattered by a shell. It was very mysterious, almost frightening, to walk there alone.

One day I passed down a path where tall beech and elm-trees met overhead so that when you looked upwards it was like standing in a cathedral nave, so high and so stately were the branches. The sun glinted on the coloured leaves and shone down in shafts of light between the avenue of trees. Suddenly I saw a movement on the ground to my right. From behind a beech trunk appeared a red squirrel. For a moment he did not see me. He hopped along un-concernedly to the trunk of an elm. Then, sensing me, he dis-appeared behind it. Curiosity, however, overcame him and at the first fork I saw his head appear for a moment. Then he was gone only to appear again at the next diversion in the trunk above. There he paused for quite a long time looking me over. I stood quite still for several minutes. As I did not move, he thought he had better, so he ran along a thin high-up bough which swayed dangerously under his small weight, and then sprang, sailing through the air like a bird, to the next beech-tree and was lost for a moment among the green and russet leaves which were falling around. I followed the direction he had taken and came to a large woodland pond upon which floated two immaculate swans, one propelling himself with one foot while keeping the other black web folded between his damask wings.

The swans stretched out their necks in my direction but having no swan refreshment about me and occupied in my mind with following the squirrel, I passed on up into a little glade through which a small brook ran to enter the pond. Here the tree-trunks were black fir but the ground was completely carpeted with golden leaves which were floating in from the taller beech-trees bordering the glade. It was quite still. I looked up and there again passing effortlessly from one high branch to another was the red squirrel. For a moment I was back in my room at Kilmore watching one of the squirrels of my childhood leaping from branch to branch in the copper-beech-trees in the garden. Then a breath of wind stirred the trees around. A cloud of leaves came floating down, making patterns in the air around. A deep sigh filled the air and suddenly the forest was alive with ghosts. I looked at the carpeted ground around me and remembered that it was here that the last stand had been made that day and night when the rear guard of British and Polish paratroops had retreated down the wooded slopes and tried to recross the Rhine, many dying on this very ground.

The squirrel who had brought me to this spot was now gone and I was alone and yet not alone as I stood amid the falling leaves and heard the sighing wind rustle through the trees.

*   *   *

After less than a week in Holland I got a signal from Belsen that the evacuation of the displaced persons to Sweden was proceeding faster than expected and that the last transport in a week's time had been reserved for the children. We raced back to Belsen, getting there just in time to get our things together for final evacuation so as to be able to accompany the children.

The day of the final evacuation of the children was one of great excitement. They had heard fabulous tales of the Northern heaven they were going to and when a complete German train, little green engine and all, was provided for them they went wild and ran up and down the platform in gangs. The children's train eventually started and chugged along at about twenty m.p.h. through the darkening German forests as the evening wore on. It was some sort of troop-train with bunks in the carriages and a dining-car and kitchen. Our celebrated cooks prepared a final meal on the train. The children laughed and shouted. The noise was colossal; the boys almost went mad. Finally, they settled down, sinking onto the bunks and falling instantly asleep. It was late summer and darkness was very slow in coming. At last Han and I passed down the train to see all was well. The children were lying on their bunks in the strangest positions, having been suddenly overcome by sleep after their excitement. As usual Tibor had Susie in the crook of his arm. Zoltan lay, his round face upturned with tight-shut eyes and a tell-tale flush on his cheek bone. Han and I stood and looked down on him silently. Outside the dark German forests, the haunts of their hobgoblins and in some way perhaps the basis of their aberrations, slipped by, first in the fading light and then more sinister still in the pale white moonlight.

Next day we found an even greater excitement—a children's ship. The Swedes had provided a spotless Red Cross ship at Lübeck to bring us across the Baltic to Malmö. Everybody was washed and deloused, first by extremely humourless Swedes who mixed up English nursing sisters and Polish men, having taken everybody's clothes away. In the end we sailed out into the Baltic cleaner than we had ever been before. It was a sparkling moment in every sense. The sun shone from a cloudless blue sky on a calm expanse of the bluest sea we'd ever seen. The blue and gold Swedish flag flew from our mast head. Beauty and peace reigned supreme. We felt a great release in our minds. The children gathered on the foredeck with Luba and Hermina. Luba, her fair hair blowing back from her face in the warm breeze, began to sing a Russian song and the children joined in. Han and I coming upon the scene from aft of the vessel were entranced by the beauty that shone about us. For a moment we were in heaven, a blue heaven. We had come together out of hell, out of hatred, dirty deeds and despair; out of the worst that the senses could comprehend, smelly death and slow torture. We had found and brought these children out with us and here they were singing in the sunshine. Hate had gone and love had come back.

We stood very close together side by side. We turned and looked into each other's eyes. We didn't speak but we both knew that life had changed for us and that it would never be the same again. We knew we loved each other, not only with the fever of love, but with the understanding that the sharing of the meaning of life and death can bring to two mortals.

* * *

In the autumn of 1945 I returned to Belsen for the trials of the German guards. Every day we drove from Belsen to Lüneburg where the trials were taking place. The main trials of the war criminals were, of course, at Nuremberg where the Nazi leaders had to explain their ideology and its crazy results. At Lüneburg we were merely dealing with the actual men and women who had carried out the murders planned by Hitler and his group.

As we sat and listened to the story unfolding itself before us both in the planning and the execution of the plan, it seemed scarcely credible.

The tensions which produced World War I were not new. They had grown out of the tribal struggle for dominance which had included the super-race theory, expounded first by Napoleon, then in Bismarck's creation of modern Germany out of a welter of princely states, and finally the last fling of the dynasts, the German-speaking emperors in 1914. For the defeat in 1918 the Germans had to find a scapegoat. The mad, demagogue orator, Hitler, put the blame on the Jews. His able lieutenant Goebbels managed by his astonishing propaganda to make most people believe that the Jews were evil. It is extraordinary how an entirely untrue assertion can get general credibility. We have seen this happen again and again, as for instance the propaganda of genocide in the recent Biafran war. Goebbels was particularly successful because he believed in his own lies completely, even to the extent of murdering his own children before shooting himself in Hitler's bunker in Berlin.

Never before has a group of men sat down in committee and worked out a plan to destroy a complete race. Hitler decreed that not only were all German Jews to be 'eliminated', but Jews everywhere, men, women and children. When his conquering armies swept over Europe his police and SS troops rooted out the Jews from Holland to Poland and murdered them. The 'final solution of the Jewish problem' as worked out by the committee involved the murder of millions of perfectly innocent, ordinary people.

Such an undertaking was no simple matter and they had a very difficult job. Under the able chairmanship of Himmler, however, their highly efficient police chief, it was carried out. At first nasty problems were produced by the machine-gunning of large numbers of people, as after the fall of the Warsaw ghetto. This was a very gruesome business and the SS chief had even to tell Himmler 'to brace up' and not show weakness of feelings when the victims screamed, fell down, got up, ran wildly about and had to be shot over again before they were properly dead. Then a certain professor told the committee that if hydrocyanic acid gas was introduced into a humid atmosphere it would volatilise and anybody inhaling the subsequent air and gas mixture would be quite silently dead in less than three minutes.

An experimental gas-chamber was constructed in one of the Polish concentration camps. It was arranged to appear like a wash-room with showers. This had several advantages; the people could be persuaded to enter quietly, thinking they were going to have a bath; the running water moistened the air so that the powder which was dropped in from above volatilised at once; the people left their clothes outside and the corpses did not have to be stripped afterwards.

The experiment was a splendid success. All the Jews who were put into the gas-chamber were dead, as the professor said they would be, in three minutes and Himmler and the others looking on through the sealed glass windows were more than satisfied. Subsequently gas-chambers were established at all the main concentration camps. The problem of the disposal of the corpses was overcome by the somewhat crude method of burning them in specially constructed crematoria which belched human smoke day and night for months at a time.

Now we sat, day after day, in the Lüneburg courtroom and heard an incredible story. Most of our own Belsen concentration camp guards had been previously in Polish elimination camps such as Auschwitz or Treblinka where millions of Jews had been murdered.

Trainloads of Jews would turn up every day from the conquered territories. The first selection would be made on the platform; those old, infirm or sick were immediately gassed, those looking fit were put to work in war slave factories on rations small and bad enough in time to reduce them to starvation level, when they would be gassed and their places filled by a new influx.

Belsen itself was not an elimination centre but had originally been intended merely as a transit camp. But as the Eastern front broke and the Russians overran Poland the inmates of the Polish concentration camp were moved into Germany, and Belsen, designed to hold about six thousand people, in the end accommodated nearly sixty thousand. They were not gassed but merely starved, and typhus was allowed to reduce their numbers so that when the British at last arrived they were dying at the rate of nearly a thousand a day and there were some thirteen thousand corpses on the ground.

The court heard all this with what might be described as British phlegm. True, the other Allies were represented on the Bench and everything was translated by the interpreters, but the prosecutor was English and the whole atmosphere of the court was very British. The chief defendants were Kramer and Irma Greese, the male and female commandants. Both of them had previously been at Auschwitz and other camps.

'Do you believe in God?' the prosecutor asked Kramer. He replied 'Ja'. The interpreters said 'Yes,' 'Oui,' 'Da.' The interrogation lasted

Killiney Bay

The author's last game of rugger

(*from left to right*) Tibor, Susie, Edit and Evelyn, four of the Belsen children who came to Ireland

Sean, with Potts

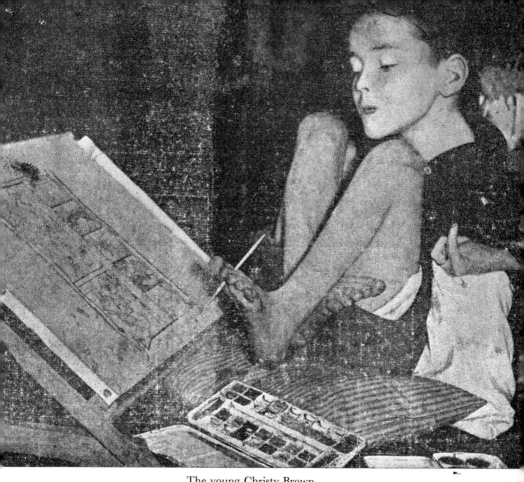

The young Christy Brown

Mrs Brown with Christy, her daughter and grandchild

The author and research team in Nigeria

The author with the Provost of Trinity College Dublin at the opening of the medical school in Lagos

Abubakar Tafewa Balewa, first Prime Minister of Nigeria

The author at Bo-Island, with Henry and Old Mike

Opposite: The author and Ha

for weeks. The evidence piled up. On one occasion the prosecutor asked Kramer if he had 'turned on the gas' on a certain day.

'Yes.'

'Why?'

'I had a chit from Herr Himmler for fifty corpses.'

'Well?'

'I collected fifty Jews and brought them to the gas-house. When I got there I found the gas-man was out at his lunch. So I put them in the chamber and turned on the gas myself.'

'Why?'

'If you got a chit from Himmler, sir, you jumped to it!'

'I see. Well, what did you do then?'

'I sent the corpses to the University on lorries.'

'Which department in the University?'

'I didn't ask, sir.'

Kramer's defence was simple. He was a professional executioner like Mr Pierrepont doing his duty without asking questions, obeying orders.

Irma Greese, like Kramer, said she was just doing her duty. She turned out to be the daughter of an anti-Nazi father and had been brainwashed in the Hitler Youth organisation. She looked like a lost soul in Hell standing there in the dock with the shadow of the hangman's noose behind her.

The trial went on. More and more terrible deeds were revealed.

We looked into a world where ordinary decent values had completely disappeared and where positive evil had ruled supreme. So devastating was the impact of these revelations that never again have we been able to accept the comfortable shibboleths of ordinary society.

The principle of the Court was that an order by a higher authority to commit a crime was not a valid excuse for a person actually to commit it, even if by disobeying the order he exposed himself to the wrath of his superiors. Under such circumstances a man must face the ultimate value of his soul which transcends death and must face the consequences whatever they are.

Han and I were no ordinary observers at the trial. We knew the evil falsity of the propaganda that had led up to these appalling deeds. We had found the Jewish people perhaps the most lovable we had ever met in the world. Our special children were splendid youngsters that any parent or group would be proud of. Their mothers were sweet persons. Yet they had been called foul names by these mad Nazis, tortured, degraded and murdered.

More than ever these weeks brought our minds together so that we found ourselves conscious pilgrims on a road that seemed to lead through a jungle.

We decided we must try and put down our experiences on paper and tell the story of the rescue of the people at Belsen and of our children. We started to write then and there, and even decided on the title. On our journeys through Europe, from Prague to Arnhem, we had often been at a loss to find our way and had had to ask for directions from the people—Germans, Dutch, Poles, Czechs. In that German-speaking world they would cry, 'Links, rechts, gerade aus.' 'Gerade aus' had become a sort of motto to us. So we decided to call our book *Straight On.**

On my way back through London I had an interesting meeting with the people who were planning the United Nations secretariat. When I told David Owen about the Belsen experiences and how Han Hogerzeil had interpreted for me there with her extraordinary command of European languages and with her law training he immediately decided to invite her to take part in the original U.N. Preparatory Commission who were then centred at Church House, Westminster, before making for New York.

Before Han was transferred to New York on the Commission for Refugees we seized an opportunity and slipped over to Sweden to visit our Belsen children again and make arrangements for those I had promised to look after personally to be transferred to Ireland.

We found our special children at a home in South Sweden. Tibor was his usual small-mannish person, Suzie had recovered and was all dimpled smiles. A little German-Jewish girl called Evelyn Schwarz was added and arrangements made also to take a child whom we had called Franz Berlin because he had been picked up unconscious in the street in Berlin and brought to our hospital in Belsen. We never discovered who he was. And of course Zoltan and Edit. But the very day we arrived it was discovered that Zoltan had developed tuberculosis of the spine. There he lay in his cot, pale and sweating. A great smile enveloped his face when he saw us. He held out his arms and put them round Han's neck. He was bent forward as he sat. My hands felt a little knob rising out of the spine between the shoulder blades, high up. They showed me his X-rays. There was no doubt, he had Pott's disease, tuberculosis of the bodies of certain vertebrae of the spine; these had softened and were now tending to collapse.

The outlook was very serious. If the lesion progressed rapidly pressure on the spinal cord with subsequent paralysis might develop. Abscess formation was common, with coincident fever. Spread of the

* Methuen, 1947

tuberculous focus was to be expected. In fact things looked very bad.

What was I to do? I had promised not only to take him to Ireland but to adopt him personally into my own family, give him my name, educate him and be ultimately responsible for him. And now here he was with this serious and complicated condition.

At the back of my mind also was the thought that here was a responsibility which would bind me, more particularly as a children's physician, if I accepted it. It would make it still more improbable that the longing of my heart could ever be satisfied.

My hesitation must have shown on my face. As Zoltan rubbed his cheek against Han's she said 'You will take him?' I looked into her eyes. I looked into his eyes.

'Yes,' I said.

The Swedish Red Cross were all cooperation. 'You must take him to your Fairy Hospital,' the Head Lady said. 'We will fly them all over to you accompanied by one of our nurses.'

So it was settled.

Han flew to New York where I gave her an introduction to Kate Davison who let her live on the Davison estate on Long Island.

*   *   *

I went back to Ireland and made preparations for the reception of the children at Fairy Hill, a beautiful little open-air hospital on the Hill of Howth outside Dublin. They arrived in a few weeks, safely accompanied by a fair Swedish nurse. They had made a plaster-cast for Zoltan which kept his back rigid. But he was very sick. His temperature was swinging up to 103°F every night, and he was pale and very weak. He lay in the open air at Fairy Hill and just kept alive but week after week the fever wracked him. Slowly an abscess developed around the affected vertebrae and the pus crept along an intercostal nerve between the ribs, eventually forming a large, round, 'cold' abscess swelling at their edge. This we had to aspirate again and again with wide thick needles which hurt as they were pushed through the skin. Zoltan, being an extrovert, yelled wildly when it hurt but didn't hold it against us afterwards.

Towards the end of the year his condition was desperate. The fever had persisted and he had wasted away. He looked as if he was going to die. Then one day Sir Alexander Fleming, the discoverer of penicillin, came to Dublin and in some way was invited to Fairy Hill and introduced to Zoltan. He had a pre-streptomycin treatment for tuberculosis which he was working on at the time. He gave me all he had with him. This entailed more painful injections and poor Zoltan yelled. His cries scared the other children, made things difficult for the nurses and horrible for me who had to give the injections. But his temperature at last came down to normal and he began to pick up and his famous smile was now a well-known part of the beauty of Fairy Hill. Soon he had greatly improved but his back was badly hunched and to lessen the deformity it was decided that he should go to the Orthopaedic Hospital and have compensatory curve put into his back.

All went well there for some time and he continued to improve generally and put on weight. Then quite suddenly one afternoon the matron of the hospital rang me up.

'I think Zoltan is very sick,' she said. 'His temperature has shot up to 104.3°F this morning. He says he has a very bad headache. His neck is stiff and he's holding himself backwards in a strange way.'

'It sounds like meningitis,' I said. 'I'll come straight away.'

The diagnosis was obvious when I saw him. In all probability the focus in the bone of his back had spread through the membranes and he was down with tuberculous meningitis.

I did a lumbar puncture immediately and collected a specimen of cerebro-spinal fluid (the fluid which surrounds the brain and spinal cord) and confirmed the diagnosis.

So far, out of hundreds, I'd never seen a case of tuberculous meningitis recover. But only a matter of ten days before I had received a consignment of streptomycin, the then new cure for tuberculosis. I did not know how to use it, whether to give it direct into the fluid around the brain, into a vein or into a muscle. I didn't know the dangers or the safe dose. Actually hundreds of cases of meningitis who recovered after treatment with streptomycin given intra-thecally in those early days were subsequently found to be deaf. In Zoltan's case his astonishing luck held. He had objected so much when I had to perform the diagnostic lumbar puncture that I decided that to attempt to use that route was literally not worth it in his case. So instead I gave him the drug, in probably excessively large doses, intramuscularly. It acted like a charm. All symptoms disappeared within a matter of days and in just four weeks his cerebro-spinal fluid had returned to normal. In his case we had started treatment much earlier than usual, probably in the first two days of the meningitis.

At the end of six weeks I stopped the injections altogether as they were causing him to panic at the sight of the needle to such an extent that I feared the consequences of the mental trauma.

But he never relapsed, and the streptomycin treatment seemed to have stopped the tuberculous infection everywhere else in his body as well, and now, except for the slight hump in his back and the fibrosis of the original focus in his lung, he appeared to have got over the primary infection and its secondary spread. He put on weight, got up and began to lead a normal life. Schooling was arranged and he showed no hint that further trouble might be expected in years to come.

CHAPTER 14

TROUBLED PEOPLES

After an initial period at the U.N. headquarters in New York, Han was transferred to the Inter-Governmental Commission for Refugees in London which at that moment was dealing with the most complex problems of population displacement which had occurred during the war.

One of the strangest of these cases was that of the Mennonites, a religious sect with very strict beliefs and customs who had originated in Friesland in north Holland in the early sixteenth century among the small farmers. They had suffered religious persecution and had therefore moved into north-west Germany and later to the neighbour-hood of Danzig. There they became experts at draining marshes and in the eighteenth century they moved again into the basin of the Volga at the invitation of Catherine the Great. Wherever they went they maintained their strict religious life, their language and their peculiar dress (for instance no buttons on their clothes). They did not intermarry with the peoples they lived with and thus tended to be looked at askance or actively persecuted wherever they went.

When World War II carried the German armies into the basin of the Volga they found the Mennonites who had refused to take part in military service on religious grounds. When the Germans started their great retreat out of Russia the Mennonites accompanied them fearing reprisals from the Soviets when the latter came back. And now here they were in camps in Germany when the war ended—some ten thousand of them. Nobody knew what to do about them. They could not stay where they were in Germany; they could not go back to Russia. Then Paraguay in South America said they could go there. But in the post-war settlement there was no international provision for German refugees and, unless they could be proved to be of Dutch and not of German origin, the International Refugee

Organisation could not pay for them. The ships were at Hamburg waiting to take them but apparently nothing could be done.

Han had herself come of a Dutch Mennonite family and the Commission's Director turned to her and asked her if she would produce proof that the Mennonites were really Dutch.

She set out for Holland and made every sort of enquiry without getting much further. Then quite suddenly she found a pile of books in an abandoned library in the belfry of the main old Mennonite church in Amsterdam. She looked at the piles of dusty volumes which littered the floor, without a catalogue, with a feeling of despair at the hopelessness of finding any help there. She walked across the room between the piles of books. A crumpled leaflet caught her eye. She picked it up and opened it.

It was a volume which contained the names of all the original Dutch Mennonites. She compared this list with the nominal roll of those now waiting to board the ships at Hamburg—the Mennonites who had come out of Russia after two hundred years. They were all of the same names, but one.

Han caught the night plane to London. The Commission were now satisfied that the Mennonites were really Dutch. A wire was dispatched immediately to Hamburg and the Mennonites solemnly boarded the waiting ships for South America.

On the gangway the Chief Elder paused when he was accosted by a journalist.

'Aren't you very pleased at your unexpected escape?' asked the man.

'Not at all,' replied the Elder, 'we have been on our knees in prayer to our God for the last three days. We knew this would happen.'

This Mennonite rescue carried Han back into the middle of the whole refugee problem in Europe and she was in a position to find out whatever information might be available about individual families who had been in the German concentration camps. She heard that Zoltan's grandmother was still alive in the foothills of the Tatra Mountains, part of the great Carpathian mountain barrier in northern Slovakia bordering on Poland. As we were able to find out little else about the family I decided that I must try and discover the family circumstances before legally adopting him and his sister.

Suddenly Jan Masaryk came to London to a meeting in the Albert Hall. Han and I went and when it was over we came round behind the stage and found Jan. He was just the same charming, unassuming person whom I had met that afternoon during the blitz. We told him about the children and that we didn't quite know what to do.

125

'You'd better come and see for yourselves,' he said. 'When you get to Prague, come and see me and I will arrange everything for you. You'll find my Ministry in the Czernin Palace on the hill above the river.'

Some months later we flew to Prague where we spent a week with the refugee committee, the children's hospital staff and a number of other medical people. The professor of paediatrics was one of the Fanconi–Wallgren group and was very glad to see me. I saw a number of cases with local doctors. Recently, a quarter of a century later, I received a letter from the parent of a child I saw then:

'Years, years ago—some hundred at least, as it seems to me, but actually in 1946, a doctor of your name was visiting Prague and was introduced to us by Dr Aul and spent the afternoon with us, the memory of which is cherished in our family. It is difficult for me to describe the effect of this visit of the first foreigner we had since the war.

'It was not unlike a biblical story, for you were the first one to say to our seriously sick eleven-year-old son, Martin, who had been in bed for over a year following an attack of pancarditis [acute heart trouble] "Rise up and walk!" You took him for a walk in the neighbourhood hilly park. From that moment Martin returned to the happy world of sound childhood—we will never forget this event.'

The memory of this little boy has completely passed out of my mind and I cannot recall what I thought or what I said. I must have found his heart quite compensated and decided that he was better up than lying in bed. It illustrates rather frighteningly the power doctors possess over the destinies of people whom we may only see for a moment of time and forget—a sobering thought when one remembers the many occasions when one may have been less right.

As invited, we went up to the Czernin Palace to see Jan. It was a sunny day and Prague was shining like a jewel, its great palaces rising above the Charles Bridge across the Moldau with the many statues of ancient Bohemian heroes and kings along its balustrades. But the streets were full of a very unroyal mob. Street-marching in those days was a new form of public expression and as yet had not become a daily event as now when young people march for any cause from Biafra to free contraceptives. The streets of Prague were full of grim-faced men and women. The predominant colour was red—red scarves, red banners—red everywhere. The Russians were not in evidence then but they had indoctrinated the Czech proletariat during their occupation after the rout of the hated Germans. And now the Czech Communists with Russian support were planning a takeover of the dictatorship, proletariat-type. Beneš was still

President of the democratic state created by Jan's father after World War I, but the Nazis had destroyed this little island of freedom which had arisen out of the old kingdoms of Bohemia, Moravia and Slovakia so thoroughly that though Beneš and Jan had come back after the war they found little left of the great Masaryk dream.

All they could do was to compromise and hope that something would turn up to save them, an all too common Czech defence when oppressors loom up. But with Russians behind the scenes the Czech Communists had the ball at their feet.

It did not look at all pleasant—the mob animal was loose. It was sniffing the air for blood. One remembered Madame Lefarge and the 'sans culottes' around the guillotine.

Jan was his usual gentle self. He met us just inside the door.

'Come let me show you round this place,' he said, 'the old Austrians did themselves pretty well.' He led us through gorgeous reception rooms into a vast empty hall, an arena really. 'This is the place where I keep my toothbrush!' he said. 'The renowned Austrian Lippizaner horses used to perform here.' Then we went upstairs to a little room overlooking a stone courtyard below. 'Come in,' he said, 'only in my bedroom can we talk safely.' He sat down on the couch bed.

'I could go,' he said, 'indeed they have made all sorts of plans for me to fly to America but I can't go and leave my people. They trust me . . . and my father would have me stay if he were here, I know.' He looked out of the window. He bowed his head, 'I may ride out the storm,' he said. 'If not . . .' I remembered that window afterwards.

He made all the necessary plans for us to fly to Kosiče in Slovakia where a driver with a car would meet us and take us up to the Tatra. The local people had been told to welcome us as guests of the nation. He thought we would have no difficulty even if the Russians were about, for people who had opened the German concentration camps were very much persona grata in that part of the world which had suffered terribly from Nazi occupation.

And so it proved. Our arrival was broadcast from Bratislava and wherever we went we were met with open arms by the Czechs, the Slovaks and of course our old friends from Belsen. At Kosiče we were received by the local Communist committee who gave us a lunch. They were a little put out when Hermina suddenly turned up and embraced Han and joined in. She wasn't quite right class for a Communist lunch, being a Jewess!

There was an excellent up-to-date hospital in the town built, I heard, before the war by the Rockefeller Foundation. It was like an isolated island in the Communist Slovak world. We met doctors there who were not at all part of that world, among whom was an English wife, a beautiful looking, fair girl who seemed like a lost soul in that strange place. We would have liked to have asked her a lot of questions but this was obviously not the time or place so after much comradely hand-shaking we drove off with our driver who seemed to be well in with 'the right people'.

We drove north through a charming countryside, first low-lying and containing many vineyards, then as we climbed after hours of driving we found ourselves approaching great mountains that seemed to rise up towards the sky.

We had heard that Mrs Baumöhl and Mariana were home again in a village not far from our destination. On entering the village we suggested to our driver that we would like to see if we could find the Baumöhl home. He stopped and asked a tall thin man with prominent features. The man took off his hat and bowed low to us.

'You must be our doctor,' he said to me, 'they said on the radio that you were coming—I was in Belsen too.'

We found Mrs Baumöhl happy with Mariana well again and looking a very beautiful young girl. They brought us into their home with all the charming manners of their ancient race. Mrs Baumöhl told us she planned to get somehow to Israel where perhaps she could be 'free'. We heard this word 'free' again and again then though as yet we did not realise the height of the prison walls that were closing round Czechoslovakia, Poland and the other Iron Curtain countries at the time.

We came to Kezmarok and found our Zinn grandmother, an aunt and an uncle by marriage. They were all very badly off and had barely enough to eat. The uncle who had been the local schoolmaster had lost his job under the new régime. Indeed the grandmother, whose husband was dead, seemed to have no visible income. When I told her how sick Zoltan had been and still was she said, 'You must keep the children, doctor, only you can cure him and look after him. What can I do? The Germans have killed their mother and father and the Russians have taken everything else.'

CHAPTER 15

THE INNER CIRCLE

Back in Dublin I was soon again plunged into the medical scene. The fund associated with my play *Marrow Bone Lane* opened up all sorts of paediatric fields to me, including Fairy Hill Hospital run by a remarkable group of people and it also helped to start the National Association for Cerebral Palsy.

The work for the newborn in the Rotunda Hospital took on a new social significance. The Dublin Corporation asked us to supervise all children born on the Rotunda service for one year from birth. As this would have entailed looking after all the children born on the rapidly expanding north side of the city the numbers would have been too great. We compromised by looking after all normal babies for six weeks and all neonatal problems as long as was necessary. They built us a beautiful little neonatal unit in the grounds of the hospital for dealing with the latter, including many surgical emergencies. It was one of the first in these islands. Now this work is recognised as one of the most important aspects of paediatrics all over the world. At this time its significance was only just being realised and the prevention of physical handicap caused by birth trauma had not yet come into prominence as it has in subsequent years. But the preliminary work was very exciting and absorbing and filled much of my mind at that time.

At home, Phyllis, Dermot and Robert welcomed me. I tried to tell Phyllis what had happened to me; she was very kind. She did not utter one word of reproach. Naturally she thought I was suffering from the extreme mental trauma I had been through and that Han was a wartime romance and our love like a thousand others which had been brought about by the stress of war. I was very tired out at first and could not sleep but the beauty of Bo-Island and the creatures there soothed my mind and made it possible to go on.

Edit and Zoltan were accepted into my family and they also found peace and contentment in the Wicklow mountains.

On one occasion in May when the gorse was flaming everywhere and the world seemed to be born again Leo, our farmhand, came into the house and woke Edit who was sleeping on a camp-bed by the big cottage fireplace.

'Come quick,' he said. She followed him and he led her into the near field where the blue and white cow had just calved and was licking a small, all white calf. The mother cow had that particular maternal expression of completeness, satisfaction and mother love which the act of reproduction produces, perhaps not more in cows than in other mothers but certainly always very clearly to be seen in their large brown eyes.

'What shall we call her?' Leo said.

'Snow White, of course,' Edit cried.

I stood behind in the fragrant meadow in the early sunshine. The mountains towered behind the tall trees. It was a picture—the mother cow and her calf, and the small Czech girl holding Irish Leo's big hand—a long way from Belsen.

Some years before I had acquired Bo-Island, a cottage in the Wicklow mountains with farm land, a little wood, a river, a bog and a gorse-covered hill, for little or nothing, when we needed somewhere outside the city to get a breath of fresh air. One day when riding over the hills with Robbie we saw a little cottage in a beam of sunlight. We rode over and found it for sale. Its story was very Irish, almost Somerville and Ross. It had been owned by a horseman who had ridden a great young horse in the local Calary race. The horse had been bought by a visitor from the East who had been brought to see the wild Irish ride, and the rider and the horse had gone with him to India where he had won many famous races. Eventually when fifteen years old the horse was sent back home with a pension from his princely owner and lived till he was twenty-seven. The horseman had lived in one end of the house and the horse in the other. Now both were dead. I turned the horse's stable into a study and knocked a great hole in the thick old loose stone wall so that my window looks out through the wood at Djouse, the rounded Wicklow mountain behind. Immediately below the window Dermot dug a pond over which presides a Buddha which Maurice brought back from South-East Asia.

We have always had a strange collection of horses at Bo-Island over the years. At that time there was old Mike, the Clydesdale, who had come with the place when we bought it. Skite, my wicked hunter, had been gathered to his ancestors one sad wintry day, but

Bridget had mothered a beautiful foal by a famous thoroughbred. We called the baby foal Henry and he was the joy of our lives for years to come. Then I had acquired for a song the best hunter I have ever had. We called him Tim. He was a 'rig'. That is, he was really a stallion having an undescended testes inside his abdomen. He was perfect to ride but, like many stallions, dangerous in the stable, and when I found him carrying the stable boy around in his teeth, holding him by the back of his breeches and shaking him, lion-like, I felt something must be done, so I got the professor of veterinary surgery to come and operate on him. I gave the horse an anaesthetic in an open field by fixing a bag of chloroform over his nose. To begin with, he circled on a rope around us but soon began to stagger and eventually fell down. We rushed over to him and I pulled off the bag and continued the anaesthetic with more chloroform. The veterinary surgeon's assistant chained up his tremendous legs so that he could not kick. The surgeon then opened the abdomen with a wide incision, put in his arm up to the elbow and brought out the testicle which was clamped and cut off.

Tim never bit anybody again. With the loss of his testicle, he seemed to lose his male animus but this did not affect his joy when galloping across country or jumping great banks and I rode him with several of the famous packs around Dublin and forgot everything else in the glory of his flying strength over stone walls, double banks, dykes and small rivers. I even rode him in a point-to-point.

Both my mother and father died during this period. My father's leave-taking as I have told was quite characteristic of his independent, determined, Victorian character.

My mother went shortly afterwards. She had been suffering for a long time with a slowly progressing cancer. She was now eighty-seven and, after numerous trials in different nursing homes when it became necessary to remove her from Kilmore where she could no longer be looked after, she came to rest in a very kind and efficient home run by Roman Catholic sisters. They were very loving to her.

I had always promised to be with her when she died, and, as a matter of fact, had returned several times to what proved false alarms. Now, however, came a week in which she was clearly going. Actually she was immensely strong physically in spite of her imagined delicacy and although she no longer ate or drank for several days she went down very slowly. Towards the end of the week, I thought she was sinking so I stayed with her from eight o'clock onwards. She was breathing with difficulty and apparently unconscious. At just after midnight she rallied and seemed to become conscious of my presence. She opened her eyes and smiled at me for a moment. In that smile she conveyed recognition and a kind of eternal message of love for me. She then closed her eyes and rapidly sank into deep unconsciousness and after about an hour stopped breathing.

I got up stiffly and went back to my Dublin house, collected Rusty, the Irish red setter and drove out to Killiney, walked along the shore in the dark, climbed the White Rock and sat there with Rusty's head on my knee as the sun came up slowly over the sea and lightened up the sweep of Killiney Bay and the circle of the Wicklow Mountains behind.

It was a tryst, if ever there was one, and I felt the presence of the spirit that had left almost beside me. I had no anguish but only a glimpse of the meaning of death which I could not put into words. I did not try to analyse why she had loved me too much and Jack too little. I only breathed in the beauty of the sea and the sky about me, felt the soft trust of the creature at my side and glimpsed into eternity. Later I went up to Kilmore, now deserted, and collected a great bunch of early May flowers and brought them in to her.

*   *   *

Of all my experiences of Dublin, medical or literary, my association with Christy Brown was, and is, the most vivid and complete.

At a huge Christmas children's party given in one of the Dublin theatres with the aid of the Marrow Bone Fund, I saw a small elfish figure with a strange fey face, balanced on the back of a big brother as the children were noisily streaming out of their seats. 'Who's that?' I asked. 'Christy Brown,' one of the Social Workers replied. 'He's a very badly handicapped boy but his big brothers bring him everywhere!' I looked again and saw the boy on his man-horse trotting through the crowd who called to him, and he seemed to answer back jerkily to them. His face was completely arresting with a boy-childish Michelangelo aura of beauty.

I never forgot this scene of Christy and his brother. Years afterwards my sister-in-law, the late Eirene Collis, having worked during the war with Phelps at the Johns Hopkins in Maryland on his new therapy for cerebral palsy, set up one of the first clinics for treating these handicapped children in the Children's Hospital, Carshalton, in south London. She came to Dublin and persuaded me to start a clinic there also. I remembered the scene in the theatre, for the strange impression Christy's face had made remained in my mind. Now I asked everybody who might know where I could find Christy Brown. I was told in Kimmage, a vast new suburban Dublin dormitory area.

After some weeks' search I heard of a Brown family living in a long row of similar, small, semi-detached houses on an endless road. I set out for Stanaway Road and at last located number 54. I knocked at the door and was admitted by a young girl and led into the main room which took up most of the ground floor, serving as kitchen and general living-room. I cannot remember how many of the family were present at that moment but it seemed that the room was crowded. I remember particularly the smiling face of the woman of the house who was standing by the fireplace. She held out her hand as I said I was a doctor who had come to see Christy. I followed her gaze, and turning saw behind me a boy who looked about twelve years old, half-propped up against the back wall of the room.

'Hello, Christy!' I said. He made an unrecognisable sound and waved a naked foot in obvious greeting while his hands flung out in uncontrollable involuntary movements. As I looked at him I recognised the strange child I had glimpsed more than five years before, and again something stirred deep in my consciousness—an ancient memory, or a premonition if you like. I knew what I had to do immediately. I sat down and told him and his mother that we had started a new clinic in Dublin for the treatment of cases of cerebral palsy and that I had come to arrange for Christy to attend.

The daily transport of a heavy adolescent who could not even sit comfortably required a good deal of organisation and for the next few weeks I was constantly in the Brown household. During this time I gradually learned 'the family history' as we call the medical background of a patient.

Mrs Brown had had twenty-two pregnancies and now had fourteen living children of very varying ages, from small children to adults. Christy was the ninth. He had had a very difficult birth in the Rotunda Maternity Hospital. He had been a blue, asphyxiated infant who had not breathed properly at once and had thus received considerable brain damage which had resulted in an athetoid cerebral palsy condition caused by a lesion in the mid-brain which had left his intelligence intact but made proper coordinated movement impossible in almost every muscle group in his body, so that he could not walk or even stand, or talk. When he tried his movements would be wild and he would fling his limbs around and contort the muscles of speech to such an extent that the voice sounds produced were quite unrecognisable to the ordinary person. So bad had he been as a small child that he had been generally thought to be a hopeless physical case, and also mentally deficient due to the fact that he could not communicate with those about him. Neighbours and other people sympathetic with the burdens which Mrs Brown's immense unwieldy family pressed on her advised that Christy be 'put away'. But Mrs Brown would not let him go. She knew, she said, that underneath, behind somewhere, was a conscious, thinking, living, lovable child who needed her. She held on year after year, bearing more children yet holding her whole family together. One day when Christy was about five years old he was half-lying on the floor of the kitchen and his small sister was playing beside him with a slate and a chalk. Suddenly the chalk broke and Christy leaned across and picked up one of the broken ends with his left foot, holding the chalk between his big and second toes. He made a scribble on the slate. At that moment his mother was passing behind him bringing in the tea. She paused, put down the tray and came and knelt down beside him. 'Christy,' she said in a firm voice, 'I'll show you what to do!' She took the other end of the broken chalk and drew the letter A on the kitchen floor. 'Copy that,' she said. Christy looked at her with comprehension in his eyes. He took the broken end of the chalk between the toes of his left foot. She held up the slate for him. With determination he drew one straight line, then the other upright of the letter A. The chalk broke again but with a still smaller piece he managed to complete the letter with a wobbly cross line. While this was going on the other members of the family had silently gathered round and when the letter was completed a cheer went up and his father who had come in in brick-laying clothes picked him up onto his shoulder. Now they all knew that he understood what had been said and that he was not mentally affected however badly handicapped he might otherwise be. From that moment on his remarkable mother taught him to read and write through the medium of his left foot which was not only unaffected by the brain damage but seemed to be able to take on the functions of a right hand in a normal person. Indeed so proficient did he become that at the age of twelve he won a children's painting competition organised by one of the Dublin evening papers.

Down the years his family had rallied round him. His brothers and sisters had taken him out in a wheelchair round the neighbourhood and on all sorts of expeditions. His father had been kind and helpful to him though he was a strange mixture of passionate violence and imagination. He had been one of Padraig Pearse's volunteers in the 1916 Rising in Dublin in which the Irish Republic was born. He had impregnated his wife twenty-two times. He was often drunk. But he had a queer sensitivity and was a great worker in the building trade. But it was the mother who released Christy from the imprisonment inside his body. It was she who with all her other household duties found time and patience to teach him to write with his left foot and to read turning over the pages with his toes.

Now we started to try and use all the brain cells and nerve paths in his body that had not been affected by the asphyxia at his birth. He was taught to sit up well and even to walk very unsteadily if his elbows were supported from behind. He was given much speech therapy so that now he could be understood if one did not look at his twisting mouth as he spoke, but only listened to the voice sounds. (One does not realise ordinarily how much one normally lip-reads.) Nothing that we could do, however, enabled him to use his hands for the more he tried the worse the uncoordinated movements threw him about. Eirene Collis came over specially to see him and forbade him to use his left foot so as to pressurise him to use his hands. But some weeks later when I came to see him I found his whole condition had deteriorated and the tragic expression in his eyes was like that of a man in solitary confinement. It was clear to me that this was the wrong approach in his case and that he must be allowed to free his mind by expression through his left foot. So I released the foot once more. Immediately his whole appearance changed. Unknown to me then he had started to write with his left foot though it was nearly a year later that I suddenly received a telegram from him. 'Am writing my autobiography please come and help.' I hurried round to 54 Stanaway Road. It was some time since I had been in the house but all was the same. Mrs Brown entertained me to tea in her inimitable way with stories of Dublin and Christy produced a file of school exercise-books filled with ragged but legible writing. I glanced at them and realised that I was in the presence of a great endeavour which I must try to understand. I said nothing immediately but took the notebooks home to read carefully when undisturbed. I sat down that evening and opened notebook after notebook reading here and there. Most of it seemed impossible, unreal, full of Dickensian clichés of one sort or another. Then suddenly I came upon two pages of what seemed to me pure gold. It was Christy's own description of the letter A episode when his family had discovered that he was not mentally defective. So I came back to him and gave him a lecture about writing. I told him particularly how the cliché can destroy good descriptive writing. I asked him to rewrite the letter A scene fully. He couldn't speak at that time so he couldn't answer back. He just listened. I do not know whether what I said really sank in but I think everybody will agree who has now studied his work that the cliché plays no part in his writing—perhaps he has gone a little far in the opposite direction! Anyway he now produced a little master-piece which I sent to Maevis McIntosh, my New York literary agent, who immediately wired back two hundred pounds as an advance on the American rights of the book when published. And so Christy Brown the author was born. The subsequent book *My Left Foot* was an immediate success. It was simply written in longhand (or longfoot). At that time he did not have the electric typewriter which he has now and on which he types like lightning with the big and little toes of his left foot. People said I must have written the book but the truth is I merely corrected the manuscript so that it could be typed, it is very difficult to correct writing done with your foot—you are too far away from the paper to read the words and then correct them as required. But the writing and production of the book brought us very close together so that a friendship was created which has lasted down the years and has taught both of us much about our different worlds. This has been both an inspiration and a relaxation to our minds and we have had great fun together on all sorts of occasions as when Secker & Warburg, our British publisher, gave a party to celebrate the launching of *My Left Foot*. It was held at the Irish Club in Eaton Square and all sorts of distinguished people were invited as well as cohorts of Browns.

I had to leave just after it started to attend a B.B.C. dramatisation taking place at the same time. When the latter finished I hurried back to the party. By now it might be said to have reached its Celtic peak. Nobody recognised me when I came in. Two waiters with trays laden with glasses of neat Irish whiskey were walking up and down and suggesting to the guests loudly that they might have another 'Sup of the craythure!' Secker & Warburg were calling loudly 'Shut the bar.' Mrs Brown was apparently sitting on the knee of Cecil Day Lewis, or was it Lord Longford's? Everybody was very happy. In the end the only way I could get one of Christy's brick-laying brothers to bed was to pretend he was a dog and take him upstairs on an imaginary lead, barking!

*   *   *

All seemed to be going well at this time with Zoltan until suddenly one day he brought up a pint of blood in one of the main streets in Dublin. It appeared that the original tuberculous focus had broken down forming a large cavity in his left lung. We put him to bed and gave him all the latest remedies for tuberculosis which were now freely available, but though the infection seemed completely overcome the cavity remained enormous and would not close. After three months I felt something further must be done. It is impossible to walk about with a cavity in a lung for any length of time without getting a haemorrhage, and in Zoltan's case having had one already another was only too likely. So I took him across to London to Mr Price

Thomas, the best chest surgeon at the London Chest Hospital in the Brompton Road. Price Thomas had him admitted to the hospital and fully investigated. While this was going on he became the regular hospital mascot. Everybody had heard his story, including Burl Ives the famous American folk singer. Ives had once been thought suitable for the part of Blind Raftery, the Irish poet, by John Huston, the producer, and sent over to me in Ireland. Unfortunately Burl was sixteen stone, while Blind Raftery had been only a wisp of a man. Burl looked like a German troubadour and Raftery like a leprechaun. It didn't work, but Burl had met Zoltan in Ireland and now, while he was singing at the Café de Paris in London, he heard that the boy was in the Brompton Hospital and with his usual generosity and big-heartedness he came round and sat on Zoltan's bed and sang. The whole staff used to gather round to listen.

After about ten days Price Thomas came to me and said: 'Look there's only one thing I can do really to cure him and allow him a full life. We must remove the cavity surgically.'

'What does that entail?' I asked.

'A pretty desperate operation in his case. We shall have to remove half of the left lung probably,' he said.

'What are the chances?'

'About fifty-fifty. Do you think he can take it?'

'Yes, I think so.'

'Right then, let him live properly.'

So it was arranged. The big day came. Everybody in the hospital seemed to know what was going to happen.

Price Thomas' surgical list was due to start at 1.30 p.m. He expected to take two hours on Zoltan. Next on the list was a British colonel who also had to have a formidable chest operation. The best anaesthetist was in attendance. Enough blood was brought into the theatre to cope with any eventuality. Zoltan went off to sleep without a sound. I stood beside Price Thomas. The incision was a very long one across his chest wall and the opening of the chest cavity between the ribs left only the right lung working. When the ribs were prised apart the full problem was revealed. The whole left side of the chest was filled with adhesions between the pleural lining of the lung and the heart sac. Price Thomas now had to strip these adhesions back carefully so as not to tear the tissues below. This was very tedious and took a long time. After about two hours he got down to the great vessels running from the heart to the lung, the pulmonary artery and its branches. Suddenly one of the main branches was punctured by the knife and the chest cavity seemed to fill rapidly with blood.

137

'He's going to die on the table,' Price Thomas said to me, 'unless I just clamp off the lung and stop.'

'He'll die afterwards then,' I said, 'but he's not going to die on the table—go on.'

He went on. After another hour he said, 'But he'll die on the table.'

'He won't,' I said, 'it's not in his fate!' But I wasn't sure—I saw myself carrying all that was left of Zoltan back to Ireland in a box.

Price Thomas went on. The anaesthetist ran in three pints of blood to replace the loss. At the end of another hour Price Thomas said: 'That's that!' He handed the now separated lobe of the left lung to his assistant. 'Take it away!' he said. 'I'm going to sew up the pulmonary artery now.' And stitch by stitch he sewed up the rent in the vessel. He took off the clamps. It held. The remaining sewing up and repair took another hour. The anaesthetist brought Zoltan round as the last stitch went in. 'I'm on fire,' the child cried before he passed into deep sleep with an injection of morphia.

Price Thomas and I walked back into the surgeons' room and sat down. It was 6.30 p.m. He had been operating for five hours. Neither of us spoke. We were soaked through with sweat. We were utterly exhausted. The colonel who was to be done next had been wheeled into the anaesthetic room.

'I can't. I just can't do a thing more today,' Price Thomas said.

'Is the little feller all right?' the colonel asked. 'Don't mind about me, I can wait!'

For the next forty hours Zoltan's life hung by a thread but his Karma was to live out a lifetime in this world and so he gradually came round. He was nursed in a ward with five other patients, grown men. They were Cockneys.

During his critical days these men took it in turns to sit beside Zoltan's bed all the time. When he improved Burl Ives appeared again and now his songs had a ring of triumph. Everybody crowded round the door of the ward—matron, sisters, nurses, wardmaids, even other patients. When Zoltan sat up for the first time it was hospital news. When he actually got up it was a gala day for all.

He recovered rapidly and was able to return to school some months later. His operation was a complete success. The diseased part of the lung had been completely removed and the intensive course of chemotherapy which had preceded the operation had apparently eliminated any other tuberculous focus which might still have been present in glands or bone. From that day to this he has never had any recurrence of tuberculous infection anywhere in his body.

*   *   *

It was some six weeks after Zoltan's operation when I was back in London again that Han told me she thought she might be pregnant. I examined her and found that she was.

'I have dreamed about him for a long time and I know his face,' she said. I was equally glad. It never occurred to either of us to turn back. But it complicated my life and the medical course she was now following. What was she to do? What was I to do?

We knew that what had happened was our fate, the meaning of our meeting and of our love. For Han the complications were terrifyingly difficult to surmount. For us it meant the end of the unreal life I had been living these last years. It meant I must find some new work, some change of scene, as it would be impossible to join up with Han and continue to work in Ireland. That made the distant future very insecure but it was the immediate future which had to be managed first. With complete fortitude Han continued her medical course until she was some five months' pregnant. Then I arranged for her to come to the south of Ireland, first to stay with some friends of mine in County Limerick and then to have the baby under the Professor of Obstetrics in Cork.

The Limerick family were very unusual even for Ireland. I had met Peggy first at a dance when the London Irish were playing Rugby football against Limerick. She was the daughter of one of the Irish rebels in the Troubles who had been badly beaten by the Black and Tans. When the Troubles ended and her mother died he had married again and now Peggy wanted to get away. She came for a time as Dermot's nurse when I was working at Great Ormond Street. Later she became a hospital nurse, emigrated to Rhodesia and married a South African doctor she had met in the hospital. He was killed hunting leopards. Peggy then married Franz, an Austrian baron. During World War II he joined the British side leaving Peggy to run the tobacco farm in Rhodesia. When the war was over she had amassed a fortune from the farm. She brought Franz to Ireland where they acquired a Cromwellian house in County Limerick and there settled down with their three remarkable sons. (One of Franz's tremendous Catholic titled Austrian aunts chopped Cromwell's head off the bottom of the wooden stairrail where it had been carved.)

The boys went to the best Catholic school in the country and Franz acquired a number of splendid horses and hunted with the local hard-riding gentlemen of the county.

Han went to stay with them for her last three months. They were completely kind if somewhat eccentric. Father and sons not uncommonly would ride full gallop up to the steps in front of the hall door, take these together in one tremendous leap stopping with a clang and a bang of iron hooves before the front door or, if it was open, actually in the hall.

Once an Englishman who lived next door brought their car back which he had borrowed. Unfortunately he left a whiskey bottle in it which the maid carried into the house and placed on the drink tray. Later one of the boys, returned from school and thinking he needed a little pep up, took a swig out of what he thought was his father's whiskey. Some hours later he became very ill with vomiting and purging. When he had owned up the bottle was found to have written in pencil on its label: 'Arsenical'. The gentleman friend was contacted. He was most upset when he heard what had happened and told them the bottle contained sheep-dip, not whiskey. By this time the boy was very ill, so they rang me up in Dublin. I discovered that sheep-dip consists of a solution of twenty per cent sodium arsenic and I told them I would come down immediately with the antidote and in the meantime to have his stomach washed out.

When I arrived some three and a half hours later I found the boy with a very dilated heart, collapsed and cold. We filled him up with BAL, the antidote for arsenical poisoning, and he recovered gradually. Fortunately nobody else, including Han, had taken any of the mixture which had been handed round with the other drinks before dinner the previous evening.

On the strength of this the family have been my friends ever since, particularly the boy who still writes to me from different parts of the world. Franz being that sort of person they naturally went bankrupt fairly soon after this and had to go back to Africa where I met them all once more in Rhodesia.

Life in Limerick County was at least never dull and the time passed pleasantly enough until Han had to move into the nursing home in Cork.

The confinement was complicated and difficult. Finally after hours of struggle, the Professor of Obstetrics said to me about 5 a.m., 'She has done all she can. If we are to get the baby out alive I'll have to help her.' This he did, but even so it was touch and go. Han was completely exhausted when finally the child was extracted. The Professor handed me a blue baby which was not breathing. He said over his shoulder to me, 'The mother has stopped breathing.' While he worked to resuscitate Han, I worked mechanically, without conscious thought of what might happen, to save the baby.

After a minute the Professor said, 'She breathes.' At the same moment the baby gave a convulsive gasp and began to breathe also. Soon both had lost their livid blue appearance and were once more pink. I looked at the small boy in my arms. Sean seemed to me the most beautiful baby I'd ever seen. But again the same day a plug of mucus caught in his windpipe and he became asphyxiated once more but I was present and was again able to free his airway and get him breathing quickly again. When Han saw him she said, 'But he is exactly the baby I dreamed about!' Together they looked very beautiful and all those in the nursing home who saw them loved them.

They both recovered quickly and were soon able to travel. They flew back to London where for a few weeks they went to stay with my great friend Cecil Day Lewis and his beautiful and charming wife Jill Balcon. Then my twin brother Jack, and his wife Eirene, volunteered to look after them at their house in Ewell in the southern outskirts of London. Han moved there. For three months she looked after Sean herself. Then she placed him with the Dutch wife of an Englishman who lived nearby and went on with her medical course of which she still had some two years to complete. Each evening she came back from London and sat with Sean for an hour and played with him and told him stories. Each weekend he came to her at my brother's house. 'I was very happy then,' she later said. 'We really got to know each other.' He was a very easy baby and showed great affection. Even as a baby before he could walk he would crawl up to her and catch and kiss her hand. Han treated him with respect even when he was quite small, always explained the reasons for everything and he always responded with surprising understanding. This rare quality became one of his characteristics as he grew older so that there never was any friction between him and us. He and Han formed a remarkable friendship, not very usual for a not too young mother and a small baby under such difficult circumstances. He enjoyed life very much. He loved going places, the train, the under-ground, the zoo. His dazzling smile would light up a whole railway carriage of dull ordinary people and make them smile too.

It now became clear to me that I could not go on any longer living a double life. I knew I loved Han, and I realised Sean who knew me as father must be given a proper security and future. Dermot and Robbie were nearing the end of adolescence and were both at university age. But to change my life would mean leaving Ireland if I was to marry Han and give her and Sean a real home. So I began consciously to look around and see how it could be done.

Just before World War II I had had a young Nigerian assistant doctor called Ade Majekodunmi who had written a particularly good M.D. thesis on the premature baby while working with me at the Rotunda Hospital.

He had always wanted me to come out and help to start paediatrics in Nigeria. Now he suddenly appeared in London where he was taking a higher medical degree. He introduced me to Abubakar Tafewa Balewa then a Northern Minister in the recently formed Nigerian administration, later to become Prime Minister of the Nigerian Federation. I was immensely struck with his erudition, charming speaking voice, and gentle manner, and I spent the whole afternoon with him discussing Nigeria. We became friends at once and so remained to the end of his life, I being actually the last friend to see him the night he was murdered some ten years later.

I decided on the spot to go to Nigeria, and some months later the matter was finally settled. A young Great Ormond Street doctor friend of mine introduced me to an enormous man, Professor Lawson, the then Dean of the Medical Faculty at Ibadan. He told me that some five million pounds were being spent on the creation of a new medical school there, the first in English-speaking West Africa. He showed me photographs of one of the most beautiful hospital buildings I had ever seen.

'Will you come and build up the paediatric department?' he said. 'We're under London University and we have therefore no Chair in paediatrics but you can be director of a new paediatric department, and you will have a whole floor in the new hospital and your own out-patients' department similar to adult medicine, obstetrics and surgery.'

'Very well,' I said, 'I'll come.' It was then January and he asked me to come to Ibadan for the next academic year, starting the following October. I agreed.

I went back to Ireland and made all the necessary arrangements to enable me to get away for the following year. I did not then resign my appointments or go into further personal explanations as I did not know what I would find at Ibadan or whether it would be possible to remain in Nigeria. But I knew in my heart the decision had been made and it seemed to me that I must make the break complete. As the moment of leaving approached the parting became more and more painful. Phyllis who sensed the inevitable was kindness itself to me. Dermot and Robbie, now that I was going, seemed to fill a much larger part of my life than ever before and my creatures tore at my heart. I rode Tim, the ex-stallion, in a point-to-point race. I took Rusty, the red setter, everywhere with me. He would stretch out on the back seat of the car and wait patiently for me for any length of time, rising and greeting me with his beautiful eyes and a wagging of his great tail when I returned. He always slept on the end of Phyllis' bed.

The last week came. I rode Tim for the last time over the hill of Bo-Island early in the morning. I said goodbye to him drawing his great head into my arms. All the family saw me off at the airport in Dublin. I saw Han for a moment in London and said farewell to her also at the air-terminal at Victoria Station. I arrived at Heathrow completely numb and finally walked out to the waiting plane like a man going to the scaffold.

As it turned out Han and I were to be separated for two years. Then Phyllis with great generosity made it possible for me to marry Han, recognise Sean and bring them both out to Africa. But I was not to know that then.

CHAPTER 16

NIGERIA

I obtained a seat by the window on the left side of the plane. To begin with the journey was like all other flights in those days in propellor-driven planes before the smooth days of swift jets. We flew on and on, south, south through the night. I took some sedative, I think, and fell into a deep sleep. Hours later I awoke with a start. A small beam of light was striking my face from the window. I looked out. There on the horizon half a red ball seemed to be rising out of the East. With extraordinary speed the sun rose up out of the curve of the earth's edge like a lantern being pulled up on a pulley to a mast-head. As it did so the world beneath lightened up. There below us stretched away endlessly the brown-grey Sahara desert dry and empty. It was like a moonscape. Half mesmerised I looked at the new world below. Soon we began to lose height and some vegetation could be seen here and there. Before long we could make out single trees and dry water-courses. As we approached Kano the desert became savannah. We circled and came down, landing on a long runway, turned and taxied up to the airport buildings.

We got out stiffly and walked down the steps out of the plane. Immediately the African air was around us—hot and dry. It smelled different from any air I had known. A camel was standing in front of the air terminal building. The faces of the attendants were ebony black. As I stepped out of the plane my loneliness left me. I had entered a new world; I was in Africa. Something stirred within me, a prevision, a knowledge of what was before me. I no longer had a feeling of loss nor did the place I had come to seem strange though I did not have that feeling one sometimes encounters on visiting a place for the first time that one has been there before. Rather I knew I was in the right place at the right time with a purpose, part of the karma of this time of mine in the world.

*   *   *

From the moment I reached Lagos and clasped Ade Majekodunmi's outstretched hand time began to race so fast that often I was
only just able to think coherently. However I kept notes of the daily
happenings around me and formed them into two books down the
years. The first, *A Doctor's Nigeria* (English) or *African Encounter*
(American), and the second, *Nigeria in Conflict*, were written on the
spot and contained all the advantages and disadvantages of works
composed when the author is involved up to the neck in events
around him. The Nigerians are a people intensely human and warm
to whom it is impossible to be indifferent and hard enough to regard
objectively as many expatriates discovered during the civil war days
when Europeans found themselves passionately partisan, either for
or against the Ibos (Biafrans). This was particularly noticeable
amongst the missionaries, such as the Holy Ghost Fathers, who
became among the best exponents of the Biafran cause. I myself was
able to see the wood for the trees as, having become one of the senior
doctors in the country, particularly as a children's doctor, I found
myself the confidant of most of the Nigerian leaders when I was
looking after their children and one by one events overtook them and
they were ruined or murdered.

Awolowo and Dr Azikiwi (Zik), premiers of the Eastern and
Western Regions respectively when I arrived in Nigeria, both became
friends of mine. I looked after one of the Awolowo children in the
University Hospital at Ibadan when he was seriously ill and came to
like the father for his modesty and lack of formality so that I grieved
for him personally when he was impeached and cruelly locked up
when his administration was broken by the Federal Government.
Zik was personally frank with me. When he was the first Nigerian
Governor-General he said to me one evening at the State House in
Lagos when he had been showing a movie of Dick Tiger, the
Nigerian boxing champion, 'Collis, you'll understand, when I was
a poor student in America I partly worked my way through college
by being a professional boxer!' And when in the end the civil war was
over and the Ibos had been defeated and I met him again he took
my hand in both of his with a gesture of real friendship.

Balewa remained my friend down my years in Nigeria from the
time when I visited him at his home in Bauchi shortly after coming
out, to that last terrible night of assassination when at the start of
the first coup the Ibo junta foully murdered him.

Ironsi, who became supreme commander of the Ibo junta after
the first coup, had a very fat daughter about whom he asked my
advice. He became very friendly and I often saw him, before the
second coup, when he was captured by the young Northern officers

who are said to have hung him up by the legs in the forest outside Ibadan until he confessed that he knew about Balewa's murder, when they shot him. He may have known but if you are hung up by the legs I guess you may confess anything your tormentors want.

Yakubu Gowon was the only leader whom I knew well who did not fall foul of opponents, maybe because he is so absolutely honest, or, to use an old-fashioned word, 'good', or perhaps it was because his bodyguard was exceptionally efficient and tough.

My positions while in Nigeria—first as Director of Paediatrics at the University of Ibadan, then Professor at the University of Lagos and Director of the Institute of Child Health, and finally as Professor and Clinical Dean of Ahmadu Bello University in Northern Nigeria and for a time chairman of the West African Physicians—gave me a position of responsibility in non-political affairs which enabled me to know what was happening behind the scenes on both sides and see through the war of words which confused the issues of the Nigerian civil war almost everywhere in the world. Indeed, due to the splendid case put forward by the advertising agency employed at great expense by Ojukwu, the Biafran leader, even now many people still believe that the Biafrans were a poor put-upon Christian people who were brutally assaulted by the cruel Moslem Nigerians urged on by a policy of genocide. The truth is almost the complete opposite. The Ibos tried to seize power in the first coup by killing all the leaders of the other tribes and the army men who wouldn't join in with them; when their plans were defeated in the second coup by the younger Northern officers they tried to secede, taking with them the oil which lay just outside their area, and were only stopped with the greatest difficulty after a protracted civil war. The whole business for us Westerners was thoroughly disreputable including the propaganda advertising campaign, the white, highly paid mercenaries, the diverse oil interests and the armament manufacturers who managed to market vast quantities of ammunition which was becoming out of date.

*   *   *

The general Nigerian scene when I first arrived in the fifties was somewhat similar to the last days of the British Raj as described by Maurice Collis in *Trials in Burma* some twenty-five years before. Similarly now I met the best and the worst of the Raj. The former was epitomised by the last British Governor-General, a Scot whom I had met in my rugger days as a fierce member of an Edinburgh side, and after him the first two British High Commissioners and their wives, Lord Head and his wife who assisted me to establish the best paediatric unit in West Africa with the help of the Wolfson Foundation, and later the Cumming-Bruces. He was an old Trinity, Cambridge, graduate, like myself, and she an artist. In their house I met many distinguished Englishmen including Lord Mountbatten, Group Captain Cheshire, and Malcolm MacDonald. The worst of the dying Raj were men like the commercial gentleman I met in his cups sitting at one of the few white bars left in the country. 'The great thing here,' he said, 'is that you haven't got to meet the bloody blacks.'

However, when I got to Ibadan I had hardly time to notice what was happening outside medical circles for I was immediately thrown into the maelstrom which every medical man encounters in Nigeria where in a population of sixty million there is only about one doctor to twenty thousand people, in some places only one to fifty or even one hundred thousand. Among the uneducated the child death rate (children dying before they grow up) is fifty per cent in many places so that any doctor dealing with children is permanently overworked to breaking point. I discovered this on my second day in Ibadan when I took the children's general out-patient clinic in the old town hospital, and saw ninety-two sick children. 'Saw' is the operative word. Really all I could do with the help of a Nigerian nurse was to sort out the very sick or actually dying from the less sick. We worked on while the temperature gradually rose to 90° when my vitality had receded to a level that made it impossible to continue. I was soaked through with sweat and utterly exhausted mentally and physically and could only go back to my house in the University and lie down. This overwork was the general picture which medicine presented then and even now still exists. I remember one young African at a conference who was the only doctor in a town of a hundred thousand people. He had been sent there to start preventive medicine. 'But,' he said, 'what am I to do with people who insist on dying in my garden?' The chairman who believed in prevention rather than cure ruled him out of order. I might have been altogether submerged by medical work like most of the doctors in Nigeria if it had not been for Majekodunmi who was secretary of the Nigerian Medical Association when I arrived and afterwards became the first Federal Minister of Health after Independence.

After a few weeks at Ibadan it was clear to me that in southern Nigeria the most important underlying cause of child death was malnutrition, particularly a virulent type of protein malnutrition which has been called kwashiorkor by Cecily Williams whom I had first known at King's College Hospital in London after World War I, and who now was generally considered a world authority on the condition. Kwashiorkor is a Ghanaian word meaning 'the sickness of the first-born when the second child comes' and is due to the mother taking the first child off the breast which in many African countries is the only source of milk among the poor. When I put this view to Majekodunmi he immediately arranged a nutrition conference, inviting as speakers Cecily Williams, and Professor Emmett Holt, the well known American nutritionist, who had been the Associate Professor of Paediatrics when I was at the Johns Hopkins Hospital in the twenties. The Conference was the first of its kind after the medical school at Ibadan moved into the beautiful new five-million-pound hospital presented to Nigeria by Great Britain as a teaching centre for the new medical school. The Conference was an outstanding success.

Following it the United Africa Company, one of the great West African trading concerns, informed me that they proposed to make a donation of over a hundred thousand pounds to Nigeria to celebrate its independence, due to occur shortly. They asked me how best they could give it to help the Nigerian children. I put forward a plan for an Institute of Child Health for the whole country. When this was accepted I then approached the Rockefeller Foundation with a proposal for a wide scheme of research into the whole problem of malnutrition in the different parts of Nigeria with special emphasis on kwashiorkor. The Rockefeller Foundation welcomed the project enthusiastically and gave us immediate support in the most generous manner. These two approaches completely changed life for me and saved me from a hopeless daily drudgery of simply struggling to cope with a queue of dying children (in one day six children died waiting at the children's out-patients in Ibadan). I found myself engaged in the most fascinating investigation. We discovered that the children of the educated and better off mothers in Ibadan were six inches taller by three and a half years of age than the children of uneducated poor mothers. These and other findings in Nigeria when published caused me to be known as an international paediatric nutritionist and involved me in conferences and meetings all over the world during my time in Nigeria. On one occasion I was rung up from New York and asked to fly immediately to a conference at Cali at the Pacific side of the Andes in Colombia in South America. I flew off and picked up Emmett Holt in New York. Except for a little difficulty with a local revolution in Bogota we arrived safely at Cali, and spent a week there discussing kwashiorkor with all the world experts on protein nutrition. From then on I was a regular member of these conferences on nutrition as well as numerous paediatric meetings which took place in North America,

India, the Near East, Douala in the French Cameroons, Addis Ababa in Ethiopia, Nairobi and Kampala in East Africa, and Cape Town. And the fact that we still were required to take two months' leave yearly from West Africa for health reasons enabled me also to visit Italy, Greece, Egypt and Israel on our way to and from Europe, and to get to know Africa as a whole and to glimpse God's creation other than man. In my previous books I have described the Nigerian scene and conflict and here will only touch on events as they affected my life.

*   *   *

On Han's arrival I took the opportunity of visiting different parts of Nigeria with her. During this journey we stopped at Bauchi one day when Balewa was staying in his mother's house. It was perhaps the most revealing glimpse of that gentle and charming man that I had. On reaching the town I stopped in the main street bordered by houses built in the Arabic tradition with flat roofs, ornamented fronts and courtyards behind, and asked someone where Balewa lived. A happy smile of welcome at once spread over the man's face and not content with telling me where the house was he insisted on coming with us and showing us the way with a courtesy like that of the people in the West of Ireland. He brought us to a house bigger than most of the others. I left Han in the car and spoke to the door-man. He did not understand English but led me into a large reception room with thick mud walls. It was cool and the shade comforted my eyes tired with driving in the sun's glare. Balewa immediately appeared and came to me with hands outstretched, his face wreathed in a welcoming smile. He spoke with the charming accent of the educated Englishman, introduced me to his mother and to one of his wives. Han was brought in. When we were leaving he came out to the car and bade us a charming 'God speed'.

As he stood bare-headed in the wide Bauchi street, where horsemen and camels were passing, an air of sadness seemed to hang over him, almost like an intimation of the fate which lay ahead of him.'Good-bye,' he said, 'come and see me in Lagos—I wish I could go back and be just a schoolmaster again, instead of having to be a politician.'

On the same journey we visited the Cameroons, where the chiefs are called Fons and are celebrated for the numbers of wives they keep. The Fon at Bafut was said to have seventy-five. All the wives of a Fon are not sexually active at the same time or he could hardly survive. When a Fon dies his son inherits his father's wives, including, one supposes, his own mother. These ladies of the previous generation are only 'wife' by protocol, but even so a Fon has a pretty busy time and finds it difficult to satisfy all the girls, as an anthropological American lady found in her Ph.D. thesis on the subject.

When we arrived at Bafut we found the Fon was up in the mountains conducting a 'second burial' of one of his chiefs. The people of these parts believe in an after-life not unlike this one. In consequence in the old days it was common practice when an important man died to send one or two of his slaves along with him to look after him where he was going. At the ceremony we attended there was no human sacrifice, Bafut being now part of the British Commonwealth, though they still felt that if they wanted really to please the 'great spirit' of the next world then some sacrifice, a bloody one if possible, was necessary. On this occasion they merely cut a goat's throat as a sacrifice. This was horrible enough, the poor animal having its head bent backwards while a knife was thrust in behind its windpipe and great vessels in the neck and then brought out forwards severing the structures so that the creature panted out its life through the slit windpipe while its blood spurted on the coiling roots of the juju tree. 'Second burials' are very noisy affairs as it is important for the spirits in the next world to be impressed with the importance of the spirit now joining them. Noise is thought a good way of attracting them, so now there was a lot of firing of old flint-lock guns.

When the ceremony was over we drove back to Bafut with the Fon and his favourite wife, a very good-looking girl dressed in a pretty blouse and skirt. She spoke some English and showed me round the palace. It covered a considerable area as might be expected with all the ladies who had to be fitted in. There was a mausoleum where the Fon's father was buried and a wives' 'waiting house'. The latter contained three or four young women. It had been explained to me previously that one of the other Fons finding it too expensive to keep his wives supplied with the latest fashions had introduced a 'Fon-wife fashion'—no clothes at all. All the other Fons had taken this up enthusiastically as a splendid economy.

The Fon waved a friendly greeting to the girls in the 'waiting house' as we passed. They waved back in the most seductive manner. I thought our dressed wife looked at them venomously. On completing our tour of the palace we were regaled with warm beer mixed with palm wine in a kind of throne room where the Fon was seated on a chair covered with a leopard skin.

I said something about Gerald Durrell. The Fon smiled benevolently. 'Ah, my friend, Durrell,' he said in broad pidgin English. 'He drank all my whisky.' Then turning to me he said, 'Doctor, I want your advice . . . you know the English. The Resident has been here again. He says the time has come before Independence when democracy must be introduced into the Cameroons. Everybody—men and women over twenty-one—must have a vote. This might be very awkward here,'—he made a sweeping gesture to include all his wives—'what do you say to my having the polling booth in my palace? I think if we did it would be possible to control matters and prevent me from being out-voted at home.'

I agreed heartily as a palace wife revolution would obviously be misunderstood in the Cameroon mountains. But the whole thing ended very badly. When Independence eventually loomed up the British Cameroon area was given a choice of remaining as part of Nigeria or joining up with the French Cameroons. They voted to join the French area and form part of a new African nation. Whether this decision was influenced by bribery or inspired by the hatred of the British Cameroon people for the Nigerians is hard to say—probably both. Certainly the Ibos who had come to the Cameroons had become very unpopular even if they were Black African brothers, and the people on the whole preferred the white British outsiders. The idea of independence under the Ibos did not appeal to them at all. So they voted to join up with the French Cameroons.

Recently when at the Palais Wilson in Geneva I happened to turn up as the champagne was being handed round after one of those splendid international compromises had been successfully achieved. In the new medical school for the now United Cameroons it had been agreed that the first two years of studies should be in English and the second two years in French. Everybody in Geneva was delighted, another peace formula had been devised. How exactly a poor Cameroon medical student was to master text-books in two foreign languages written by foreign professors with as different outlooks as London and Paris was not mentioned in the congratulatory speeches.

*   *   *

To begin with our life at Ibadan was not very happy. By the time Han reached me I was already caught up in Nigerian affairs to an extent even more absorbing than that in Ireland previously. Africa has the capacity of involving you almost subconsciously so that you become altogether part of its life down the years as most Europeans have found. Apart from the great names such as Livingstone, Burton, Lugard and Mary Slessor, the ordinary expatriate who stays in Africa any length of time becomes enthralled, so that he can never escape her nostalgia again.

At first Han found my uncomfortable hot house on the University campus at Ibadan where she had to live while I was often away was almost more than she could bear. Having discovered the enthralling joy of being a doctor during her post-graduate years in hospital before coming out, it was very hard for her to become a housewife. After qualification at King's College Hospital in London, she had done her internship and post-graduate years at the Jewish Hospital in the East End of London. Having had so much contact with Jewish people during and after the war, she felt very contented there though it was highly Orthodox Jewish and she had to get used to their customs. The honorary staff of the hospital were a particularly distinguished group and she was able to acquire a first-class experience of medicine. She learned Yiddish with her exceptional capacity for learning languages and was very happy with the patients. Now she became pregnant again and had a very unpleasant complicated pregnancy which resulted later in a poor little handicapped baby being born prematurely.

Sean was always our link and our salvation throughout those difficult times. And Han's brother, who had come out to Nigeria in the leprosy service, was now the chief doctor at Uzuakoli in the Eastern Region at which famous hospital Davey and Browne had done much of the research which has led to the modern treatment of the disease. The number of cases in their area had already fallen from thirty-five thousand to less than five thousand. We spent every Christmas *en famille* there and these visits were amongst the happiest of our days in Nigeria. We got to know and love the Ibo patients in the hospital. During the civil war it was tragically destroyed.

It was the place more than any other where I felt our Western world had given of its best to the people of Africa. Here these Europeans had come with all the knowledge of modern scientific man in their brains, carrying in their hearts at the same time the love of God. The result was not only a tremendous advance in the treatment of this historic, fearful disease but a complete change of attitude so that the ancient fear of the horrible appearance associated with the condition was banished and replaced by loving kindness. Actually leprosy has a very slight infectivity rate and healthy staff working in leprosy settlements very seldom contract the disease which now can usually be cured if diagnosed early. But fear generally dies slowly and although the rule that affected persons must ring a bell in public has been abolished, at that time the horror behind its diagnosis in the individual patient had by no means gone.

Inside the settlement, however, all was hope and peace. Always on Christmas Eve a midnight service was held in the Ibo language. To kneel with a hundred lepers, in the church which they had built themselves, on Christmas morning was an experience of transcendental beauty when one could feel in the presence of God. Looking up in the dimly lit church nave and seeing the dark bowed faces on every side with hope and love all around, you felt humble and proud at the same time.

On the Sunday after Christmas there was a particularly moving ceremony when those cured received their certificates. On one such occasion Lykle (Han's brother) persuaded Han to present these. All the friends and relations of the lucky ones turned up from their villages dressed in their best and stood in a circle behind. This time there was one now elderly man who had been very resistant to treatment but who at last was clear after twenty-two years. His whole village had come to welcome and receive him back. He hobbled up to Han, bowed low, took the certificate roll in his deformed old hand and danced back waving it to his people drawn up behind. He nearly fell because he had no feeling in his feet, but when he righted himself a cheer went up from all present as he staggered into the group of his people and was triumphantly carried away with them.

Most moving of all was a scene I witnessed on one of our visits. Han was wheeling Niall, our small son, along a path through the settlement. He was now one and a half years old and, though handicapped, was a lovely baby with fair waving hair. They were a little ahead of me when they met an elderly woman who had been in the settlement a long time. They stopped and she bent down over the child. A bright smile lit up her face as he looked up into her poor, black disfigured old visage now wreathed in an expression of loving joy. She stretched out a puckered hand towards his fair hair. Han standing behind the push chair, smiled and greeted the woman in Ibo. It was a moment of beauty in a world torn by fear.

After three years at Ibadan I retired from the directorship of the University of Ibadan Paediatric Department and became head of the Institute of Child Health for the whole country. After a lot of chopping and changing of residences we moved into the most perfect flat on the top floor of the new Institute at Ibadan. Here we had ample space for the whole family and Han was able to create a beautiful home. We had a balcony looking out over a little valley with a stream at the bottom. There was a profusion of flowers on the balcony, anthuriums, morning glory, geraniums and Cape violets. We would sit there in the cool of the evening, very content. Suddenly, however, Han had to have a serious operation. She had a difficult convalescence but gradually recovered and was allowed home to the flat. That morning Sean and I got up early, went out and

picked great bunches of flowers—frangipani, zinnias, and bougainvillaea. We settled them round the room. They looked very beautiful
before the mirrors and the white walls of her room, particularly the
red bougainvillaea on her dressing-table. We turned on the air-
conditioning to cool the air. Then I fetched her. Slowly, slowly I
helped her up the three flights of stairs. She was weak but as we
entered the flat she cried out 'Oh, how lovely!' when she saw the
flowers. Then one by one the staff of the Institute came up to
welcome her home till the room was filled with black smiling faces.
Gilbert and Mama Yabo, Goodlucky, Lewis, Yabo, Moneygirl,
Timothy and Mamma Chizom, Chizom, James and Joseph. Then
Esther came in with Niall. He climbed into Han's arms, his baby
face and blue eyes all smiles. When they had all gone we took out a
bottle of Italian wine and Han, Sean and I drank the health of our
family, to Africa, to the journey we had come upon and to the future.

*   *   *

During this period Nigeria celebrated her Independence. Balewa
became Prime Minister of the Federation of Nigeria and made
Majekodunmi Federal Minister of Health in Lagos.

As soon as he was settled in he sent for me and told me he was
planning to create another medical school in Lagos, the Federal
Capital. He asked me to help and to come and be their first Professor
of Child Health and Paediatrics. I agreed enthusiastically and we
set about making plans and obtaining help from the outside, particularly from Toronto, and Trinity College, Dublin.

This meant that I had to divide myself between Ibadan and Lagos
which entailed an eighty-mile journey along one of the most
dangerous roads in the world. It first passed through thick dark
forest with many bends and corners and then ran into the Delta
around Lagos where it had to cross many water-ways and swamps
which were not uncommonly flooded in the rains. I had to drive up
and down it twice a week. I seldom did so without meeting a
motor wreck or some recent violent accident.

On one occasion on rounding a corner I saw two trucks collide
head-on. Each then careered into the bush on opposite sides of the
road. All four men in the front seats of the two lorries were flung
through their windscreens. I stopped and sorted them out. One was
scalped from nose to the back of his head, his skull bones showing
white below the severed tissues. The blood was spurting out of the
severed arteries with each heart beat. Another man was unconscious,
a third appeared to have a broken leg and the fourth had a missing
nose. I stopped a passing Yoruba lady with a huge head-dress. This

she unwound and I applied it as a rough tourniquet round the scalped head. At that moment another car was passing. I stopped it and asked a rather green-looking young Englishman if he would mind taking some of the wounded in his car. I took the rest and a very black policeman who had turned up. We all drove to the nearest government hospital about four miles away. It was Saturday afternoon, about four p.m. There was only one nurse on duty and she had only been there a week and did not know where the key of the emergency cupboard was. However with about three feet of cat-gut and two artery forceps I managed to stop the first man from bleeding to death. After about three-quarters of an hour another doctor arrived. He turned out to have been an old student of mine in Dublin and together we coped with the stricken field. I learned afterwards they all recovered. At the end I got up stiffly. I had started out completely in white—I looked at myself now as I emerged from the operating room. I was red all over.

On another occasion I saw a man lying by the side of the road. I stopped and raised his head. He was quite dead. So I replaced it gently and drove on. There was no point in wasting time under the circumstances. In Nigeria death was cheap, legal procedures lengthy and tedious, to be avoided at all costs!

*   *   *

During all my years in Nigeria, through all the tensions of personal life, medical struggle and external dissension and eventual civil war I was relaxed and comforted by a number of entrancing creatures which I acquired. Early after arrival at Ibadan I obtained the most beautiful half-bred Arab stallion for fifteen pounds at the Polo Club. He was bright chestnut, stood about fourteen hands and held himself like a prince of horses. He had thrown seven members of the club and was going to be shot when I took him over. I had a particularly good Hausa horse boy, called Shehu, who could ride any horse. I threw him into the saddle, Mulu went up in the air. Shehu stuck on and galloped him four times round the ground. I managed then to vault into the saddle and he took me round four times more. After that we found we could mount him if at the same moment he was offered a lump of sugar. While he lowered his neck to take the sugar I would get on to his back very quickly. Once on the field he knew the game of polo and behaved perfectly. He became the joy of my life. Almost every evening I used to ride him, either playing polo or on rides away into the forest which stretched for miles around Ibadan. I would sometimes get lost in the deep gloom of the trees but Mulu always knew the direction of home and given his head would find his way back, sometimes along paths quite unknown to me.

At this time I also acquired another creature companion. John Lawson, the big man who was largely responsible for my coming to Ibadan, invited me to dinner one evening. He told me that he had something for me which would make me look a lot less lonely. After dinner he presented me with a puppy which had been sired by his golden labrador, William, on a Gordon setter bitch. At that moment the puppy was all legs and stomach though even then he had a glossy black head in which were set two dark brown eyes. In these he conveyed more meaning than most humans can with speech. As time went on, he became my very close companion and the deep loving devotion of his gaze gave me reassurance in difficult moments. He had a white star on his chest; otherwise he was glossy black all over. While I was away once he was looked after by a young couple who christened him Spot. I thought they said 'Pot' which seemed appropriate because of his huge puppy stomach. My African steward thought I said 'Potts' and he retained of all unlikely names that of 'Mr Potts'. He became a regular personage on the University campus where Africans would call out 'Posh' as he went loping by. Soon I began to take him on my rides with Mulu into the forest hoping he would follow as Rusty had done in Ireland. The first day all went well for a time. He remained at heel and followed closely. Suddenly something in the forest attracted him. He shot off into the thick bush and disappeared. I called and called. He was gone. I knew there were no leopards in that part of the forest but I had met plenty of snakes, five at different times crossing my path in one day, and in the gloom of the trees I was full of apprehension. For what seemed an agonisingly long time I called and went a short distance into the thick forest from the path shouting his name. At last despairing and thinking I had lost him and might never see him again I turned my horse and was about to start for home. As I turned I called him once more 'POTTS!' Suddenly a black head appeared, almost under my horse's nose, out of an apparently impenetrable bush, followed by his black shining body. He wagged his tail when I swore at him and seemed to say 'Don't be fussy, I was only smelling around.' After this I took him on all my rides and he always disappeared into the forest but invariably returned to my call.

Sometimes I took him on exploring expeditions into the deep forest north of the University campus which then was completely uninhabited bush except for a few scattered villages which one came upon suddenly along some winding path. It was often very difficult to remember which direction one was going in as the sun in Nigeria is mostly overhead and does not help the traveller to tell the points of the compass.

On one such occasion I didn't know where I was. Potts did not seem to be able to help either as he usually did when I was lost, his homing instinct leading us back safely. After following a certain path for a long time I stopped at last, feeling that I must be going the wrong way. In some hesitation I threw the reins down on Mulu's neck and said to him, 'You get us out of this.' Mulu slowly turned round completely and started off briskly in the direction we had come from for about a mile, then branched off onto a path I had never seen before. Potts followed. After some time I began to recognise certain landmarks and knew we were right on the homeward path. It had grown curiously dark, however. Suddenly there was a bright flash and a clap of very loud thunder, directly overhead. Then the rain came down. When it rains in Nigeria it is not like the gentle rain in Ireland 'with no harm in it'. In Africa it comes down like water in a shower bath. It can rain an inch in less than an hour. On this occasion it was tremendous and I was soaked through in a moment. Potts looked like a large water rat, but my horse seemed to enjoy the cool it brought to the steaming forest. The University campus was bounded at that time by a little river which enclosed its Botanical Garden. Ordinarily, except in certain deep pools, it was easily fordable on foot if you did not mind your feet getting wet, and very simple on a horse. But now as we approached it we could hear the sound of rushing water and on reaching it we found that it had become a torrent. The water was visibly rising every minute so I saw the only course was to try and get through as it was impossible to stay where we were or go back into the forest. I leaned forward, pushed my heels into the horse's flanks and encouraged him with my bulala (hide whip). He stepped gallantly forward into the flood which soon reached girth height. At mid-stream for a moment his feet lost their hold on the bottom and he had to swim. He kept his head high and we reached the far side safely which had a sandy incline so that we were able to clamber out without difficulty. Potts had jumped in behind us. He was unafraid of water and could swim very well so as we plunged in I had called him to follow. Without hesitation he had leaped into the torrent and swam after us. As he reached the main current, however, he was swept away round the corner and I lost sight of him while endeavouring to manage the horse and remain in the saddle. As we climbed out I called him, fearing in my heart that he might have been swept away and drowned, but as soon as we reached the far shore he appeared from a little further down stream on the home bank shaking himself.

One day he limped into our house and collapsed at my feet. He had been run over by a taxi. Nigerian taxi drivers run over dogs if they can to propitiate by this animal sacrifice 'the God of Iron'. Potts had got home on three legs. He lay panting, his eyes full of pain. Every now and then he let out a little cry and looked up at me. I gave him a sedative, examined him and found a broken leg which I then X-rayed and set. He allowed me to do everything for him including assisting his hygiene, even holding his leg up when he needed to pass water. He recovered rapidly but was never able to gallop with the horses across country again.

These creatures of mine and the beautiful forests around Ibadan brought peace and beauty to me during my years in Nigeria, and the joy of riding Mulu or one of the other little stallions in some fierce polo encounter between Nigeria and Ghana or between the many Nigerian clubs was an absorbing ecstasy which drove all cares from my mind for days at a time.

*   *   *

During my years as Director of Paediatrics at Ibadan, Robbie, who had qualified as a doctor in Trinity College, Dublin, married another student in the University, a beautiful Chinese girl, and, having done a year's house jobs in Singapore, now joined me as a Senior House Officer at Ibadan Teaching Hospital. He did very well and later became attached to a visiting American psychiatric team. They eventually carried him off to the States where he became a psychiatrist of no mean stature. He now works for the World Health Organisation in different parts of the world from the Pacific to the Caribbean.

CHAPTER 17

GHANA

Ghana and Nigeria were both created by the same historical process of the expansion of the British Empire during the nineteenth century but before the British trade interests became paramount, the Portuguese and later the Dutch had established posts along the coast. With the expansion of British power these were pushed or bought out. Then as the British traders extended inland the full British Raj followed to protect the traders and police the territories. Ghana like Nigeria possessed all the disease-carrying insects which made settlement by Europeans impossible before the science of modern tropical medicine was born, and so the general development of both countries proceeded along the same lines.

I came over to Ghana for various reasons, academic, medical and athletic. These expeditions to Ghana taught me much about the tensions engendered by 'the winds of change' sweeping across Africa.

The first time I came was to play polo for Ibadan against Accra. We played on a ground by the side of the sea in brilliant sunshine, soothed by a cool breeze from the Atlantic. All the players on both sides were white. I had to mark a British major-general and my host that night was one of the Irish FitzGeralds. Later I often stayed in the University which, built on a hill outside the capital, rose tier upon tier towards the sky and was by far the most inspiring campus of any university I have known. There I used to stay with Conor Cruise O'Brien who was elected Vice-Chancellor of the University after becoming famous in the Congo. He is now one of the leading figures in our troubled Ireland. The story of his time in Ghana gives a vivid personal picture of what happened during these years which I was able to understand through my friendship with him and his wife.

To begin with, Nkrumah, the Ghanaian President, appeared to be a splendid statesman who had led his country well, created it really.

Then as time went on, if ever power corrupts, it corrupted him till he surrounded himself with fawning sycophants who called him 'Redeemer' and obeyed his every command, however ridiculous, without comment. Finally he became so intolerable that the Ghanaians who are a very intelligent people could not put up with him any more and managed a coup d'état while he was out of the country. I turned up a week later as Chairman of the West African Physicians, for a medical seminar. The satisfaction and jubilation of the intelligent people of Accra was very evident. They never let him come back and he died abroad. If ever one witnessed the fall of a dictator, pulled down by his own folly, it was Nkrumah.

On these journeys to Ghana I usually came by car which entailed going through the French-speaking African territories of Togo and Dahomey. They were passing then, and are still passing, through the coup d'état period which seems to affect all new African states. Several of their would-be dictators have already been killed in the process. Sometimes things were uncertain as you passed along the beautiful palm-tree-lined road by the coast on your way to or from Nigeria. On one such occasion I was stopped by a particularly ominous-looking and heavily armed group of black soldiers. They arrested my driver and it looked as if I might have to stay by the roadside all night. It was just getting dark and the moon was coming up, giving the scene a sinister undercurrent in the pale light. I just kept my head and remembered the extraordinary attraction American dollars have all over the black world. I drew out a ten-dollar bill which I fortunately had with me and presented it with a bow to the head black person holding a sub-machine-gun. Immediately a broad grin wreathed his face which became positively obsequious. He asked me in odd French if I had any more as his men 'loved dollars'. I gave them all I had and they released my driver whose eyes seemed to have completely turned upwards with fright, showing only the whites. We drove on very quickly before they had time to change their minds.

Apart from such unpleasant moments I saw into the life of Ghana past and present on several occasions which made me understand Africa and her peoples perhaps more vividly than anywhere else in the Continent.

The development of Ghana was fantastic. Each time I came back immense new advances into the modern world were apparent. The first time I saw that never to be forgotten sight in Accra, the unloading of ocean traders in the open sea into long boats driven through the waves by crews with painted canoe paddles. The boats raced each other out from the little jetty into the open sea, the warm spray shining on the crews' black skins beneath which their splendid muscles rolled. Each boat had its song which floated across in snatches through the wind and the waves. Huge bales and boxes were lowered with incredible skill from the ships into the tossing boats, which when full would be turned about by their crews and swept back to the harbour where each boat would be run up on the shore and its weighty cargo picked up and carried into the sheds. Nowhere in the world in no army or navy have I ever seen such splendid manhood. Here was a job demanding absolute fitness which has as its corollary that feeling of wellness which is almost a complete joy by itself for the male. Now that expression of life has gone, an artificial port has been built and the big ships can come alongside and be unloaded by ordinary stevedores with clanging derricks.

Travelling west along the coast from Accra you come to the Cape Coast, an enchanting neighbourhood containing one of the most interesting historical monuments in West Africa, the Elmina Castle. It was originally built by the Portuguese, then captured by the Dutch and eventually sold to the British. We came to it on a day when the sea was sparkling as it broke on the sandy beach of the cove to the side of the little headland which was the only anchorage that the ancient trading post possessed. Above rose the white walls of the main Elmina Castle and behind a second smaller castle, St George, on a little hill to landward. We explored the castle and found it still being used, now as a police headquarters. We saw the great hall where the slaves had been auctioned and the little room where the chiefs who were selling their fellow Africans to the white man could see out into the hall without being seen. We saw the spacious apartments where the governors used to live and the spy hole where they could observe the girl slaves and pick out those they desired. We saw the Christian chapel.

As I stood upon the Elmina battlement I could see in my imagination a black slaver lying at anchor in the quiet sea and a herd of chained black men and women being whipped into the boats to take them out to her. There they would be forced below into ghastly cramped quarters where a man had scarcely room to sit up, far less stand, between the crowded parallel decks.

The story of this slave trade is hard to understand in terms of human consciousness. How could the captains of these ships have so divided their minds that they could hold Christian services for their crews and read the Bible to them while leaving their captives chained, often dying of sea sickness or dysentery, stinking in their own filth in the foetid atmosphere of the decks below? It is told that the hymn so often sung with pleasure which commences 'How sweet the name of Jesus sounds' was written by the captain of a slaver, John Newton, while waiting for his consignment of slaves to arrive. There is to this story, however, a later sequel. This captain became a tremendous abolitionist, Wilberforce's right-hand man. But I suppose there is nothing very inexplicable in this psychologically, for it is by no means only torturers, executioners and butchers generally who can so divide their minds as to prevent the anguish and terror of their victims from affecting them. All of us almost daily shut out from our minds unpleasant thoughts such as abattoirs, of suffering man and beast about us.

If Elmina calls up the past of the Gold Coast and all its bitter memories of what the white man's civilisation meant in the old days, the Upper Volta Dam gives a glimpse into the possibilities being created now for the future of Africa by modern white man.

The main drive came from the Americans, the Kaiser group. The head engineer was then a Canadian, the main working party of the Dam itself Italian. Britain and Germany were contributing the electrical equipment, the pipes and so on. The work and the workmen were integrated at every grade. The Ghanaians worked like tigers alongside their white colleagues. They were paid well, not just the subsistence wage which is the general rule for black labour in West Africa. Overtime paid the truck drivers so well that it was hard to get them to stop working! Here work entailing all a man can give was recognised as something possessing a value in itself. The spirit here reminded me of the enthusiasm described by Rousseau and the pre-revolutionary Frenchmen of the eighteenth century, or that of the Russians whose mystique of work for work's sake they are always extolling. We are inclined to smile at this enthusiasm, as we are at all enthusiasms these days. We call it naïve. Here at the Upper Volta, however, it was extremely exhilarating to experience, after all the frustrations and usual difficulties of everyday life in West Africa.

CHAPTER 18

SOUTHERN AFRICA

During the years I spent helping to set up medical schools in West Africa I was often called to medical conferences on nutrition or paediatrics all over Africa from Cairo and Addis Ababa to the East African States of Uganda, Kenya or Tanzania, or South Africa. Although each one of these states is different in many ways they all are part of the mystique of Africa and during these expeditions I got to know many of the people of Africa, their cultures and tensions, hopes and fears, and also saw something of God's creations other than man, animate and inanimate.

Approaching Johannesburg on one of these journeys my mind flew back to my medical student days in London in the twenties when the London hospitals were full of South Africans, particularly in their rugger teams, for Rugby football has always been a traditional part of the student life in South Africa. (Guy's Hospital usually won the cup in those days and King's which I captained were sometimes the runners up.) I got to know a good many of the South Africans both on and off the field. Generally they were exceedingly tough, splendid athletes, rather lowbrow and aggressive, especially, we thought even then, in their attitude to 'niggers', a term they reserved for all races other than those of European origin.

Among these Afrikaners was a young Rhodes Scholar, Duval by name, who had come up to the London Hospital from Oxford. He was a man of slighter build than most of them and a brilliant student. He talked of 'The Farm' back home, bringing with him a whiff of open spaces under wide skies that was refreshing in the then dismal slums of London in which we all worked. Sometimes he was homesick for his own land, for the sunshine and the high veldt.

I did not see him or hear from him again for nearly forty years until one day he walked into my clinic in Dublin in the middle fifties.

I recognised him at once for he had changed surprisingly little. He had become Professor of Paediatrics in Pretoria, having acquired down the years the coveted Fellowships of both the Royal College of Physicians and the Royal College of Surgeons of London, and published many papers on his subject. In spite of his academic record he remained the essential countryman he had always been. Walking in the Irish hills with me he had told me his story. His father had owned thousands of acres of the high veldt—the family farm. Young Duval, however, found himself possessed of a desire for knowledge and a life of wider intellectual attainment than that of a Boer farmer. 'All right,' his father had said, 'I'll lend you the money to go to the university and become a doctor but you must pay back the debt to our farm when you are qualified.'

Duval took the loan, went to the university, got a Rhodes Scholarship, made good, paid back the loan and in the end succeeded in becoming a professor, but he still was a farmer in part of his mind and the Transvaal was his land, his soil.

When I tackled him on the subject of apartheid he was embarrassed, and a little evasive it seemed to me. When pressed he brought out the usual clichés about the superiority of the white man. He didn't like it when I pointed out that what he was saying was almost exactly what Hitler had said about the Jews, the same argument, only now presented in 'colour'.

Pressing him got me nowhere. His mind seemed closed on the subject or perhaps he was a little afraid to allow disturbing thoughts to enter it. After a while I desisted and we changed the subject to paediatrics and farming, upon both of which we could agree.

In the old days South Africa and its pseudo-Nazi ideology had seemed a long way off. Now, however, I had become personally involved in African affairs. I met a group of young South Africans at Ibadan who had had to flee their country, very much as the German Jews had had to flee Germany in the early Hitler days. These young men had been called 'coloured' because some progenitor of theirs had come from a country outside the European ethnic groups, whose colour had been brown or black. For this 'original sin' they were discriminated against in the most abominable way. They were disenfranchised, paid on a lower scale and segregated mentally in the most painful manner. As doctors they could not enter a 'white ward' or go to a 'white' post-mortem. In their own country they had no human rights; they had to live on a 'location'. In this dehumanised word the meaning of 'apartheid' and its degrading intent is epitomised.

These doctors in Ibadan were among the best we had. One has

become a professor and a recognised leader of his subject in Nigeria. Their bitterness made me face the issue seriously as this cancer in the far south of Africa seemed of vital importance to the whole future of the continent with its storm winds of change blowing across it from the Atlantic to the Indian Ocean. So I had set out to read as much as I could: Van der Post, Kruger, de Kiewiet, to know something real about South African history other than that which I had learned through British eyes.

Now I flew south and I began in my mind to go over what I had read so as to get it into focus before entering the Union.

As we circled down towards the landing ground over the great rubble hills of Johannesburg, the golden city, I wondered what I should find. Would my reading have proved false? Would I find that my sympathies lay with the Boers who had struggled so long and so gallantly for their place on earth, or would I find everything I had heard true, or would the scene be different as every other African scene had been from what I imagined?

*　　*　　*

Some years earlier I had considered spending a night in Johannesburg on my way to an international conference in Madagascar but I had decided against it as I had been accompanied by a Nigerian professor and I felt that it might have caused unpleasantness to use different washrooms in the airport. Partly because of this and partly because of what I had read of South Africa being a police state, I expected a certain amount of difficulty on coming to Johannesburg from Nigeria, a black country—but not at all. The arrangements at the airport were extremely efficient and all the officials friendly and courteous and not apparently in the least suspicious. There were no police about—very different from arriving in Moscow where you feel you are entering a real police state and every movement, every word you say even, seems under surveillance. On arrival I was met by Dr Wayburne, the well known white paediatrician. He drove me through the city, which immediately gave me a feeling of immense wealth and power.

Having some time to wait before meeting a group of the doctors of the city I bought a paper. There, across the front page, I saw in glaring headlines:

Bantu Bill legalises forced labour
Graff raps Botha
Sharp attack on Bantu laws Bills
Callousness over Bantu Bill

and below: 'It will profoundly affect the economic and domestic lives of millions of people. For countless Africans it will make normal married life impossible. It will destroy the security of tenure of even those Africans who were born in a white city. It will give the police power to arrest without warrant an African boy or girl of fifteen years for not being employed or at school, and such a child can be sent to another part of the country, without any stated obligation on the part of the authorities to inform the parents of the child . . . the majority of the white electorate are apparently callously indifferent to the harsh implications of the bill.'

Here was outspoken criticism in the Press, not at all what one would expect in a police state, and certainly not the sort of thing that would be tolerated for a moment in Ghana or many other of the newly 'free' African states. Nor was this an exceptional outburst for I was to find later that the Opposition papers in Durban and the Cape were just as outspoken. However this tolerated criticism came from a purely white opposition. It was not the vocal protest by the people really concerned, the dispossessed black and coloured man; that would be quite another thing. It was all right still to allow an intellectual white minority to argue which human rights should be retained by 'the natives', even to question apartheid itself, but quite another thing to allow the black man any real means of preventing proposed legislation which would still further curtail his liberty. The Government had a perfectly safe majority, and the best the small group of liberal opposition could hope for was merely an amendment here and there.

Still, it was something to have this freedom of the Press. The Bantu Bill was to enable the Magistrates to get rid of objectionable elements from the black townships in the first place but had been carefully drafted so that complete apartheid, the avowed policy of a section of extreme race segregationists, could legally be introduced later.

The next day I spent with Dr Wayburne chiefly in the Bagan-wanath Hospital for non-whites. It is an immense institution of some seven hundred and fifty beds built originally during the war as an army hospital on the usual army hutment plan. It was extremely well run—a great deal better than any Government hospital in independent Nigeria.

There were some three hundred and fifty children's beds in the paediatric department, excellently arranged and well equipped. The doctors were of different colours. The nurses and sisters were all non-white. I was particularly struck by the casualty department where I saw as many as twenty-three babies with enteritis being treated for loss of body fluid by a complicated procedure which was prescribed by a doctor but entirely carried out by one fully qualified nurse and one probationer. The procedure was one which was considered in Nigeria by our British-trained nursing staff (both white and black) as too complicated for nurses to do themselves. But here it had been mastered and was being carried out without fuss by nurses only. The general atmosphere in the wards was one of great friendliness between the children and their mothers on the one hand, and the nursing staff and doctors on the other. Everybody smiled at Dr Wayburne and he had a friendly word for them all. There were Zulu women in their traditional costume wearing many bangles around their necks, arms and legs. There were educated Bantu women and delicate looking Indians, and some charming coloureds.

I learned a number of techniques which I was able to bring back to Nigeria later with effect.

'Would you like to see the big Bantu township round here?' Dr Wayburne asked, 'as whites we are not really allowed inside without a permit, but if we go in wearing our doctors' white coats we won't be interfered with, I shouldn't think.'

The township started just outside the hospital and stretched for miles and miles in every direction. It was excellently laid out and the houses provided, if small, were decent and an enormous improvement on the ghastly housing conditions in the average Nigerian towns of the forest belt, and certainly more hygienic than those of the Hausa cities in Northern Nigeria.

Wherever I went in South Africa the governing white classes impressed on me again and again how much they had done for 'the natives'. Certainly millions have been spent on destroying the old slums and improving the awful conditions of the black workers in the Witwatersrand. But what about the other side of the question?

The township we visited was more than six miles from Johannesburg where the people had to work. They had to travel to the city in crowded transports every day, and had to be out of the city again by a certain time in the evening. They had to carry passes. A policeman could demand a pass at any time. If you were slow in producing it, he might get tough. If you had left your pass behind you were likely to be arrested. If the policeman did not like the look on your face he could throw the pass on the ground so that you had to bend down ignominiously and pick it up at his feet while he looked down disdainfully from his white superiority on your lowered black head. In Johannesburg with its gold, its riches, its white palaces inside, and vast, soul-destroying, endless townships outside, its utter inequality based on colour alone, the bitterness in the minds of the blacks seems to sour the very air, so that a person coming from the outside world feels an involuntary tightening of his face muscles, and an angry compassion for the black man so wilfully degraded.

Dr Wayburne took me back after dinner to my hotel. 'I advise you not to go for a stroll round the streets as you say you like doing in Lagos,' he said. 'You might be assaulted by a gang who would strip you of your money if not worse.'

Shortly after getting back to Nigeria, I got a letter from him about some medical treatment he had elaborated. He went on to say that shortly after I had left, he himself had been stopped in broad daylight by a black gang who had not only taken his money and his watch and some of his clothes, but had tried to throttle him as well, as dead men tell no tales. He had fought back and just escaped with his life. He stated the facts without bitterness or comment except to say he was shocked.

I hated Johannesburg more than any other city I have ever visited.

*   *   *

It is only a short bus journey from Johannesburg to Pretoria. At the bus stop there was Professor Duval waiting for me. He had changed not at all in the ten years since he visited me in Ireland, and little enough from the slim youth of our Rugby football days when we had first met. He held out his hand with a most friendly open smile lighting up his face. 'Come on,' he said, 'you have to give a lecture to our students in half an hour and we must get things ready.'

He introduced me to his students as an old Irish international rugger player rather than a professor. This produced a rousing response and my lecture on 'Protein Malnutrition as seen in Africa' went down very well. I spent the whole morning with them in the medical school attending a clinical seminar. They were as nice a bunch of students, enthusiastic, interested and full of life and fun, as I have met anywhere in Europe or America. Later Duval brought me round his wards which were divided into white and black, the latter being full to overcrowding, and the former with a good many vacant beds. This was the only glimpse I got the whole time I was in Pretoria of the black side of South Africa. Pretoria seemed completely a modern white town. If there were black Africans living there, they were kept out of sight.

That evening I climbed up to the Federal Parliament buildings which are used for half the year. During the other half, Parliament meets at Cape Town.

The buildings are set on the side of a rocky hill in the middle of the town. Leading up to them is a spacious park, consisting first of beautifully green lawns and then terraces, each with a different arrangement of flowers.

'They are kept by our pensioners, white pensioners,' Duval told me next day. As the sun was setting and the lights were coming out, I climbed the kopje behind the Parliament House and looked down on fair Pretoria, the heart of the Afrikaner world. I thought of Lord Roberts marching at the head of the British army, old Kruger fleeing to Holland, and the younger Boers rallying round Smuts, de Wet and Botha, carrying on the struggle. I remembered the Irishmen who had fought and died on Spion Kop, the Dublin Fusiliers on the British side. Roberts himself, if a British Field Marshal, had been born and brought up in Waterford, and carried with him on all his campaigns from Kabul to Kandahar a pot of shaving cream made especially for him by a Waterford chemist. I remembered the other Irishmen who had gone out and joined the Boers to fight for liberty and had been execrated by the English as traitors. And now where was I?

Which side was I on—the British or the Boer? Not the British. The Boer?—no, not the Boer either. What then, the Bantu? Would I advocate handing over these white South Africans, their white man's capital to the black man?

Next day Duval took me to his new farm close to Pretoria. It was quite lovely, the house modern with every labour-saving device, and beautifully arranged by his wife. The farm itself was full of fruit-trees, with grass lawns and flowers round the house.

He introduced me to the Zulus working on the farm. They came forward in the most friendly way and when he told them I came from Nigeria, a black man's country, they showed great interest and asked questions. There seemed a very friendly feeling between Duval and his men both inside and outside the house. He spoke with affection of them and they smiled back.

It was very puzzling. Under the law they were little better than serfs, yet these workers anyway were happy.

When I was leaving, Duval drove me to the airport bus.

'We are both getting on,' he said, 'we live in different worlds. Perhaps we shall not meet again.'

He held out his hand and again the same twisted, friendly smile lit up his face.

'Don't be too hard on us!' he said, and turned and walked away.

*　　*　　*

Natal was very different from the Transvaal, and British Durban from Dutch Pretoria.

The Professor of Paediatrics at Durban was a Scotsman, able, broad-minded, doing an excellent job teaching non-whites to be doctors. He met me and drove me to a hotel on the side of the hill overlooking the town. The vision from the balcony of my room was one of the most beautiful town views I have ever seen. Darkness was falling and the lights were coming out. Immediately below the famous race course supplied a large central green area. Around the city stretched red tiled roofs and gardens with flowers and many trees, so that the impression was of a town in a cultivated forest. Beyond the race course the skyscrapers of the business part of the city were silhouetted against the Indian Ocean behind. To the right I could see the great harbour with its ocean-going ships. The breeze was from the sea, soft like the winds of Ireland, and cool after the dry heat of Pretoria.

Here was a perfect man-made world—the creation of twentieth-century white man's imagination. True, it contained three ethnic groups, European, Asian and African, but the thought that had gone into it was European entirely. Neither the Indians nor the black Africans could have made this town or kept it so spotless and tidy. Indian towns, Bombay, Calcutta and even New Delhi, are untidy and dirty. There is plenty of cheap labour and it would be simple to keep them clean, but obviously the Indians do not care about this kind of appearance. You see refuse and loose stones lying about everywhere, even where the architecture, both old Indian and modern British, is as fine as anywhere on earth. Nor have I ever seen a clean, hygienic town built and kept by black Africans, ancient or modern.

It is necessary to emphasise this here if one is to understand the dilemma facing white minorities in countries with a black majority. Has the white man the right to suppress the black man? Has the black man, because he may outnumber the white man, a right to destroy the beauty that the white man has created?

Looking out on the beautiful city of Durban that evening, I felt this dilemma forcibly. During the following days it pursued me wherever I went. Professor Wallace showed me the medical school where non-whites are taught on non-white patients. He sent me to the McCurd Hospital, an American missionary foundation. Here I had lunch with a splendid group of young doctors of all colours. The atmosphere was one of complete friendliness and accord unlike anywhere else I had seen or was to see in South Africa. I gave a talk about Nigeria telling them of some of our problems and some of our victories, particularly that there colour feeling was almost non-existent so that we could work, play, dine or meet casually without thinking of the colour of our skins. I said that when this happened it seemed to add another dimension to life, each giving something to the other which he did not possess but needed.

After lunch I was taken to a new clinic in an African location. As I was leaving, one of the young black African doctors looked at me and I caught an extraordinary friendliness in his glance—glowing, warm, deeply moving.

On the way back from the Bantu township we passed through a new Indian township. This, I was told, was causing much hardship to many Indians who had done well in business or the professions, and were now, for apartheid reasons, being moved forcibly out of their nice houses in the main city into such segregated areas.

Wherever I went there was much complaint against the ideology of apartheid which seemed to the citizens of Durban generally likely to lead to their ruin in the end. As whites they had their own dilemma, as I have stated fairly above, and many feared Bantu dominance, but a minority were courageously outspoken.

That evening I was taken to the theatre in Durban where I saw an excellent dramatic production. The cast and audience were all white. Thinking of the wonderful productions such as *Porgy* in New York, or the outstanding acting of the present-day Nigerians, apartheid now seemed ridiculous as well as evil. In no other city have I encountered as much beauty, so much friendliness from all different races, and such despair.

*   *   *

The Indian Ocean coast of Natal and the Cape is beautiful. A warm stream flows down to the Cape of Good Hope where it meets the cold current from the Antarctic which flows up the west coast of South Africa. The warm current brings rain and a mild climate to Natal and the Eastern Cape, the cold one dryness and near desert to the west coast.

The Cape Province in consequence has a temperate climate where it is possible to grow anything from grapes to cereals. It is literally a land flowing with milk and honey, containing all the fruits of the earth. Looking down from the plane one sees an incomparable coast-line, blue mountains and a checker-board of cultivated fields like the best of lands in Europe, a graceful country where if anywhere on earth man should be in accord and at peace.

Cape Town itself is spectacular with its craggy Table Mountain, its great circular bay and the promontory of the Cape of Good Hope stretching out into the Southern seas, washed on one side by the warm Indian Ocean, on the other by the cold Atlantic. The town reminds one of an English city with its houses built by English architects of the nineteenth century, its great dock and the way the people talk and even walk.

Cape Town was now my next destination, for I had come to South Africa at Professor John Hansen's invitation. He and his wife, Joy, come of old South African Cape stock, English and Huguenot. These South Africans are different from the Dutch South Africans, not cramped in their thinking by an imprisoning race history, not prejudiced by class tensions, not prejudiced at all. They are born of the same pioneering ancestry that has made America great. They look out at the world bravely with their hearts vulnerable to injustice and cruelty. They know South Africa. They love her and her peoples intensely, fiercely. South Africa is their home, their meaning.

John Hansen was a brilliant young research professor of child health in the Cape Town medical school which is famous all over the world. Indeed, under the leadership of Brock, the Professor of Medicine, it is one of the leading schools. His wife Joy is dark, blue-eyed, carrying a flame, ready to battle and suffer for the right, but with it all feminine, the mother of two young sons.

They met me and took me to their home looking out on Table Mountain with its drifting white cap of cloud and the range of mountains beyond. There we talked and went on talking for the next days while they took me everywhere. First we went up Table Mountain and looked down on the smiling city and the vast seas. In the bay I saw an island lying at the entrance to the bay rather like Ellis Island outside New York.

'Is that an isolation station?' I said.

'Not in the sense you mean. That is where they keep the African political prisoners. Robert Sobukwe is still there although he has finished his three-year sentence.' (Mandela's trial was not then finished. He was to be sent there later.)

'Would you say apartheid was the same as the German super-race ideology?' I asked.

'No, not the same,' John Hansen said. 'In its essence it means "apart", separation of the races, not extermination of the weaker. But it is pressed forward with almost as much ruthlessness.'

They took me through Cape Town including the great docks, up to the site of the University on the side of the mountain with its superb view, and to the Rhodes memorial where his statue stands looking far north towards Rhodesia and beyond, for his dream was a 'Cape to Cairo' hegemony, all British. Perhaps he was the last real imperialist in the Roman tradition. Some think he did a lot of harm. Certainly his dream has not come true. Yet his idea of English-speaking peoples understanding each other, perpetuated by the scholarships for which he left his money, can be said to have been one of the more important factors which brought these peoples together to defeat the twentieth-century super-race dream of the Kaiser and Hitler.

They took me to the hospitals, again carefully segregated into black and white. Even in a children's hospital apartheid must be adhered to lest little black homo sapiens be cured or die beside little white homo sapiens.

The tragic thing is that the 'coloured' had full citizenship under the British for generations, but has now had it removed by the Boer federal majority, and this although the British defeated the Boers and the Boers belonged to the Commonwealth of Nations with all its mixed peoples for fifty years. One may talk of putting the clock back! This is turning Time upside down.

The extent of absurdity to which this way of thinking can lead was exemplified the next day. In the *Cape Times*, I saw a headline *Baxter Theatre 'Great Tragedy' Malan on All Race Proviso*. I read on: 'The Administrator of the Cape, Mr Malan, said yesterday that he would consider it a ('great tragedy') if the Cape Arts Board would not be able to make use of, or subsidise the proposed Baxter Theatre in Cape Town.' This was because of the proviso in the will of the late Mr William Duncan Baxter that the theatre should be open to mixed coloured audiences at all times. The great tragedy to Mr Malan was not that the Afrikaner Government did not understand that dramatic or any other art is not confined to those members of the human race who have white, or reddish white skins, but rather that the late Mr W. D. Baxter was so unapartheid-minded, so un-patriotic, as to put a shocking provision in his will. And the adminis-trator had to appeal to all decent minded people to subscribe so that they could have proper white dramatic *Kultur* uncontaminated by black or brown art of any kind—and naturally pure white audiences to appreciate it!

Before leaving, Professor Hansen suggested that I should see the other side of the question and arranged that I should be taken to the Afrikaner University of Stellenbosch, about an hour's drive from Cape Town.

My host there was a typical educated Afrikaner. He accepted the orthodox view that white men were superior to black, brown or coloured men, and that any mixing of blood would lower the civilisation of the white man. He did not bring up the view of the

South African Church that this was ordained by God. Perhaps he felt as a doctor that he was not on very firm scientific ground there and he wanted to talk as white man to white man, doctor to doctor, men with understanding of these things. Feeling that a direct negative would bring the conversation to an end I said nothing, but told him what an informed American had said to me, that perhaps partition was the only solution to the South African problem.

'Ah,' he said, 'you agree with Dr Verwoerd I see. He was such a kind man and very brave. When he was shot his first thought was for his wife.'

'No, I don't,' I said. 'We all admit that you South Afrikaners are brave and tough. I've played Rugby against you and I know. But there is a lot of difference between partition and apartheid even if the two words are inter-translatable. Apartheid seems to mean not merely white and black people living apart, but taking away from the blacks their normal human rights and beating them up if they object, apart from paying them less than whites for the same work and treating them as if they had no human dignity or could not feel the shame of being looked down upon without being able to hit back.'

He passed over this outburst very amicably. He was tolerant. As a peripatetic professor how could I know anything about this sort of thing? You had to be brought up in the country. How could you compare the average Bantu with a white man—ridiculous! His mind was closed on that score.

'All right,' I said. 'Leave that and let us discuss partition.'

'You do agree with Dr Verwoerd then,' he said.

'No,' I said. 'But leave him out of it for the moment and me too. The difficulty I see is that I don't believe you people would agree to any form of just partition.'

'Oh yes, we would,' he said vehemently.

'Would you give them enough good land?' I asked. 'Would you give a black state complete independence even in foreign policy? Would you give equal pay for equal work, equal opportunity for advancement founded on equal educational facilities for blacks and whites?'

'We have already given them a lot of good land,' he said.

'About a third of what they need, I am told,' I said.

'Well, I suppose we could give them more,' he said.

'And what about foreign policy?' I asked.

'If we give them control there, they might invite in a foreign power, don't you see,' he said. 'Russia!'

'Yes, I see,' I said. 'That's why I don't think you people are serious, can be serious if you like, about apartheid or you would agree to real partition.'

'If necessary we'll go down fighting,' he said.

'Not very pleasant for the women and children,' I said. 'Total war isn't a matter of a nice clean death on the field of battle.'

'Then what?' he said.

'I don't know,' I said, 'but I will not agree that this or any other problem should be left to be settled by the suppression of the human rights of one section of society by another.'

Stellenbosch reminded me of an old Dutch university town except for the surrounding mountains. The students looked the same—keen, clean, fine-looking young men and women.

The buildings were well planned and laid out, modest and of excellent line. The playing-fields, particularly the rugger ground, of course, were magnificent.

My host took me to his father's home. His father was a professor in the university, and had a small spotless house set in a lovely garden; he and his wife entertained me charmingly with the simple manners of cultured people, without ostentation. He talked of academic things, personal matters, the view, the sunshine, and I agreed that South Africa was heaven to look at. We didn't mention apartheid or any other burning problem of the day, one way or the other.

On the way back to Cape Town we became rather silent. There didn't seem anything more to say. But we parted in a friendly way for he had brought me to his home, showed me the garden he loved, introduced me to his parents, all with a charm and a simplicity which warmed the heart.

'Well, did you have a good day? What did they tell you?' the Hansens asked.

'He told me all the things his people had done for the Bantu—housing, employment, wages, hospitals and so on. He accepted the orthodox opinion that they were an inferior people, and therefore, that a superior people had the right, the duty in fact, to maintain their superior way of life even if it meant being harsh. But he did see the risk they were running,' I said.

Next morning, I bade them farewell sadly.

The hardest thing in the world is to be a moderate, to see both sides and yet to stand for the truth, alone if necessary.

*   *   *

In Rhodesia which I now visited I found no hope at all. The huge black hospital I saw in Salisbury had most of the drawbacks of the hospitals elsewhere in black Africa, overcrowding and shortage of staff. The treatment of the inferior blacks in Salisbury was not as good as that for superior whites.

The general attitude whether in Salisbury in a white club, or in the country outside, was depressing to a person such as myself coming from a country which, with all its failings, had at least overcome the colour bar. In the club your white host would say 'These black goons are liars and no-goods', while the black waiter was handing you the potatoes, as if the latter had no feeling or was deaf. The whites seemed to me to have no manners, to have a lowbrow-ness so extreme as to make reasonable conversation with most of them impossible. The owner of a farm of several thousands of acres which I visited, was making ten thousand pounds a year off his tobacco; he also kept a shop where he sold to his black labourers, who worked for him for a twentieth of what he would have been paying them in Europe, the necessities for their existence. I have never seen workers look at their employers with such cold hatred as the black men here at their white overseers. Here was a country where two hundred thousand fairly recently arrived whites had taken a beautiful fertile land with a good climate away from four million primitive black men and used the latter to produce vast wealth and beautiful towns for themselves. True, they had brought to the land electricity and all the appurtenances of a developed civilisation—roads, railways, not to speak of refrigerators and washing-machines, everything in fact except love of God for one's fellow man.

It is not surprising therefore that the civilised world, particularly the Christian world, has turned away sickened from all it has heard about Rhodesia, has tried by economic restrictions to show its loathing of Mr Smith and his incredibly selfish associates. But again, the money men from Wall Street to Johannesburg, not to mention the City of London, have kept alive this utterly unprincipled, immoral, white oligarchy.

CHAPTER 19

EAST AFRICA

My experiences in the black states of East Africa, Tanzania, Kenya, Uganda and Ethiopia, were chiefly in the medical field where their individual differences were of great scientific interest of a technical nature. But on my travels I was only able to glance at most of the sociological problems of East Africa which were and are potentially explosive. I had however a vivid moment on the spice island of Zanzibar one week before it went up in flaming revolution.

As we flew in we looked down on the coral island, the deep green of its million palm trees contrasting with the light green of the reefs and the golden sands. From the air the island looked like a haven of peace, but even as we flew over a sparkling lagoon I remembered that the waters around contained the world's most savage fish, the man-eating sharks, and one of the most awful of all the cold-blooded creatures, the stone fish with their sharp back spines containing a venom so terrible that men have died of pain after stepping upon one of them buried in the sand. The very thought sends a shudder of fear through one's whole body. From that moment I felt an unease, almost a menace, while on the island.

Having passed through the usual formalities, I stood uncertainly in the airport hall, at a loss what to do next. The clerks were all Indians. I approached one and told him I wanted to see the island. As I spoke, a man came up. He was an African. He said he had a car. He spoke excellent English.

'Go with him,' the Indian said. 'He knows the town.' He did.

As we drove in from the airport he gave me a few statistics.

'There are forty thousand Arabs,' he said, 'and a Sultan; twenty thousand Indians, two hundred and fifty thousand of us Africans and three hundred Englishmen.'

He drove me round the town. He showed me the old slave market, one of the great slave markets for the east coast of Africa where the

177

poor black people from the mainland had been put up for auction for the Arab world and then shipped away in dhows to the Arabian lands. The slave market had changed under the British, and on its site was now the Anglican cathedral. 'After their coming,' he said, 'the trade went underground, right up to the present day. Now of course, it's chiefly girls.'

We came to a house standing alone on which were two placards. One read 'No admittance', the other stated that this was the house from which Livingstone had planned his last journey. We passed through the Indian Bazaar where little brown men sat in open fronted rooms sewing or selling. It could have been a street in any city in India.

'They are the traders,' he said. 'The Indians buy and sell, the English manage everything, we Africans do all the work.'

'What about the Arabs?' I said. He smiled an African smile and then laughed an African laugh . . . the sort of laugh you see in a crowd of African men who have just watched a motor accident or a cow having its throat cut—not a funny laugh. We drove on. We came to an ancient fort built originally by the Portuguese. He showed me the great iron rings hanging from the walls to which he told me the Arabs had chained their prisoners. We stopped on the sea front and looked at the Sultan's white palace. It was like something out of the Arabian Nights. As we did so the Sultan himself drove out in a sports car waving as he passed. My companion made no comment. We came to the port and he parked the car. He did not get out but intimated that if I asked in the correct quarter I might get permission to look around. He pointed to a door. I knocked and entered a busy office. Here a large man, whom I took to be a Syrian of some kind, was talking in low tones to an enormous Sikh wearing a blue turban. I played my visiting professor card which I have found works like a charm all over Africa. (I once asked a very knowledgeable young Nigerian why professors were treated with such respect in Africa. 'Because you know everything,' he said, 'and we want to know.')

The Syrian stopped scowling when I said I was a professor, and said yes, he'd love to show me round the port. The Sikh came too. We entered a long shed on the quay. A heavy scent almost stifled one—cloves. Indeed the whole island smelt of cloves, its only legitimate trade. The long shed was piled with sacks of cloves in great heaps. As we walked along, a number of villainous characters approached and whispered in the ears of my companions who nodded at this pile of sacks, and that. I wondered what lay beneath for if ever I had felt myself in a den of thieves it was here. As quickly as possible, the Syrian gentleman and his friend passed me on to the manager of the clove-oil factory on the quay. He was a tall north-country Englishman with a twisted smile. The factory was old, the machinery decrepit but it was working away, and like all places where things are created it was fascinating to observe the hows and whys. It was situated right in the old Fort and looked out on the harbour crowded with dhows, some tied up, some coming in, some going out, their great lug sails hanging on their slanting masts, their navigation helped by long oars propelled by enormous black sailors pushing and pulling. Many of the ships seemed laden down almost to the gunwales. Many looked as old as history. They didn't seem seaworthy but one supposed they must have been designed for the Indian Ocean for even if their crews were expendable their cargoes, whatever they were, could not have been. All you actually saw were piles of clove sacks. 'There seems to be a lot of cloves,' I said. 'Yes,' he said, 'a lot of cloves,' and smiled. He was friendly. 'You see those fellas sitting there,' he said, 'the man in the middle is sharing out the dough. When I want a ship unloaded or something done, I bargain with him and he bargains with them. They work like fury and then I give him a handful of coins and he shares it out. There is a lot of talk but seldom any trouble. Though, of course, times are changing and I am told I must now do it all through some sort of trade union. Really, of course, it's a way of getting them to vote for the right side.'

'Patronage,' I said.

'Yes,' he said. 'Things have changed. Independence; democracy; the Arabs don't like us much and the Indians don't care much for us either. They feel we don't approve even if we haven't any power.'

'What about the others?' I asked.

He shrugged his shoulders as much as to say nobody has ever thought much about them.

'Are you staying on?' I asked.

'This is the end of the world,' he said, 'you can't go on and you can't go back.'

He smiled, strolled back to his essential oil factory and disappeared into a cloud of steam so impregnated with volatilised clove oil that the senses were intoxicated and he seemed to vanish into the scented air.

Back in the car I was driven around the island for another hour. My companion now was more silent. It seemed he felt he had said enough, perhaps too much, even to a sympathetic professor.

'It seems to me,' I said, as we neared the airport again, 'that all this won't last much longer, will it?'

'It might not,' he said.

I was glad to get into the plane again and fly away from this beautiful island around which the almost overpowering aroma of spices could not cloak the aura of cruelty and evil of its past or the threat of violence in the present.

A week later the explosion came. Some say four hundred Arabs were chopped up, some four thousand. A pro-Chinese communist régime was set up though the island is supposedly still working as part of Tanzania.

*　　*　　*

Man has still only a partial place in creation in Africa. The inanimate and animate 'wild' still commands our awe and wonder here more than in any other part of the earth. The vastness, silence and deadness of the Sahara's thousands of square miles, the incredible volume and length of the great African rivers, the Nile, the Niger, the Zambezi, with the utter violence of their great falls, produce a wonder in the human mind which drives out pettiness. Then the beauty of the young creatures, free in their original habitat, over-awes one at the thought of the Creator's 'mind' and makes one realise that man is not the only meaning of this planet.

The main difference between man and the other creations is in his individual consciousness. A man knows he is a man inside a world limited out of endlessness by space and time. He is able to try and think out what this means though he cannot understand Infinity. He cannot comprehend endlessness of time, having neither a beginning nor an end. Yet he reasons this must be so. He can speculate in abstract thought which the other creations, whether animate or inanimate, cannot do. They have a different kind of consciousness which does not require the human brain structure: the great mountains such as the Himalayas may be felt to be reflecting a conscious thought of their Creator inside our time-space world.

In the organic world the question of consciousness becomes more difficult to define. In the vegetable kingdom consciousness seems similar to that of the inanimate mountains but as we ascend the scale of animal creation we find a brain developing similar in fundamental respects to ours and which appears to be almost able to comprehend abstractions such as love and hate. A dog can die of grief for a lost master or an elephant can protect a wounded or elderly member of the herd. This is a similar type of consciousness to ours though we must not press the analogy too far and think that either the dog or the elephant are conscious in the same way as we would be under similar circumstances. In general the creatures obey the immutable rules of their species which may lead apparently to a savagery completely horrifying to us, as when a pack of wild dogs pick out a deer from the herd, chase it till it can run no more, and then, literally, eat it alive. We must be very careful when facing such phenomena not to indulge in human-thought transference and accuse the creatures of brutality. On the other hand when we see a herd of long-horned Fulani cattle who sensing the presence of a leopard suddenly form a hollow square with the hedge of their lowered horns outside and the calves within, we must not imagine that the cattle are nobly protecting their young by individual conscious thought. In both cases the creatures are obeying a herd instinct which has been imprinted on part of their brain through countless generations which under given circumstances will be acted upon reflexly without what we call conscious thought.

The animate world is evolving new creative forms and modifications of form all the time. The lizards are the best example. At one time the great lizards such as the ichthyosauri, weighing, it is said, some three hundred tons, with small heads and vast, elongated bodies, dominated the world for millions of years. Now except for a few small dragons, such as the iguanas, they have evolved themselves into creatures weighing a few ounces. This changing of themselves so as to be able to go on existing has been remarkable not only in regard to size but in other ways as well. They live by eating insects, often harmful, which are a nuisance to other animals including man, and they have become so scaly and dry as to be, themselves, almost inedible. They are not aggressive towards larger animals, either in offence or defence, like snakes for instance. They do not appear dirty or unpleasant in any way and are, therefore, tolerated, even liked. Particularly in the tropics, one finds them everywhere: special little grey house lizards that dart out from behind pictures, or orange, black and grey lizards which inhabit both town and country. They are completely independent of man though I have known a lonely doctor out in the bush who tamed a lizard family.

The creative urge behind life everywhere is easy to accept and partially understand but the enigma of man's consciousness remains. Why conscious unhappiness, or wickedness should appear inside Time as part of the plan of a Creator is difficult to comprehend. To say that positive goodness is impossible without positive badness or true love without hate may seem an answer satisfying for a moment but it does not explain the ultimate meaning of creation which still eludes our finite minds.

While living in the world of men, in what we call built-up areas, it is possible to put thoughts such as these out of our conscious minds and live busy lives from hour to hour and day to day. But if you stray into the Wild, that other creation, the question of what we are doing locked up in time and space, what was or is the Creator's idea —forces itself into our conscious minds. But meditate as we will we cannot unravel the mystery of infinity.

*   *   *

My first great experience of the African Wild was connected with the inanimate Victoria Falls. I had read of Livingstone's astonishment on coming on this extraordinary phenomenon after months of trekking through the African forest. How he had first seen the cloud of rising spray from many miles away and how the actual sight of the gigantic cascade had moved him. I had seen other celebrated waterfalls, including Niagara, and it was with no great enthusiasm that I delayed my departure from Southern Rhodesia so as to visit the Victoria Falls. But nothing I have ever met with in this world has had such an effect upon me as this inanimate demonstration of power. The Zambezi, which is the better part of a mile wide at this point and carries the most stupendous volume of water, suddenly falls into a gorge some three hundred and fifty feet deep and flows away at right angles at the bottom.

On this particular occasion I had a kindred spirit as my companion, a Harvard professor who was helping the Rhodesians to set up a computer. His assistant was a Kikuyu from Kenya. The idea of a black mathematician teaching them how to use a computer was too much for the lowbrow Rhodesians and the professor had had a bad time. He had escaped, like me, from Salisbury and like me he was completely overcome by the majesty of the Falls. Together we climbed down the opposite side of the gorge to get a good view and stood on a promontory gazing silently at the white falling flood. Every now and then a cloud of water vapour would rise out of the gorge driven upwards by the trapped air. It would soak us to the skin but so warm was the sun that we felt no cold and would be dry again in a few minutes.

We remembered that this had been going on for millions of years. We knew scientifically that the billion billion water molecules were made of two atoms of hydrogen and one atom of oxygen. We were witnessing the macrocosm of the microcosm and the microcosm of the macrocosm at the same time.

We walked back from the gorge of the Zambezi very silently

182

and were quite glad to meet an ordinary group of human tourists.

'Come and join us on the trip up the Zambezi on a launch,' they cried, 'and see the hippos.'

We took tickets for the trip and were very glad afterwards that we had, for although we didn't meet any hippos we saw something that possibly nobody else has ever seen.

After proceeding a short way upstream from the falls but not so far that we couldn't see the vapour cloud and could still hear a very distant roar, we suddenly came upon a small red speedboat going round and round in wider and wider circles without anybody in it. After a minute it struck the right bank of the river and became caught under some trees. We looked frantically around to find the owner who we thought must have been precipitated over the stern of the speedboat which presumably had started up suddenly when he pulled the starter string violently. We scanned the vast river—no sign—perhaps he had been eaten by a crocodile. Then we saw a man frantically waving on the far bank. Our launch put about and went across the river to him. As we approached he leaped into the water, swam to meet us and scrambled up into our bow. 'Thanks,' was all he said, pointing to his speedboat at the other side of the Zambezi about a mile away. We took him back across. When we were approaching the boat he jumped in again and swam strongly towards it.

'But why don't the crocodiles eat him?' I asked the professor.

'Well,' he said, 'they wouldn't with his hat on.' I looked again and sure enough our man, now doing the trudgen stroke, was wearing a homburg hat. I quickly photographed him and the resulting snap is probably the only picture of a man swimming with his hat on, certainly in the Zambezi above the Victoria Falls.

* * *

Some fifty years after our Rugby days during one of my leaves I met Jamie Hamilton, the publisher, who had been a friend of both Ionides and me in those days. He told me Ionides (see p. 21), now a man of world-wide fame, was in a place called Nualu on the borders of Tanzania and Mozambique, catching snakes as his main occupation. I decided on one of my East African journeys to visit him. So now on my way north from South Africa I stopped in Tanzania. He was waiting for me at the airport. He still looked tall, lean and straight with a face like a Greek god. Within minutes we were in the Land Rover heading towards the setting sun along a dusty, red, laterite road bordered on each side by dry scrubby bush. I glanced behind. The back of the Land Rover seemed packed with things and people:

'I brought the team along,' Ionides said. 'It's ninety miles' drive and we might bag a snake on the way.' 'Oh, yes!' I said. 'They sometimes cross the road, don't they.' I didn't ask how one bagged a crossing snake and Ionides didn't tell me but rather chatted about our school days at Rugby. He reminded me he had played full-back for the house fifteen.

Night fell suddenly as it does near the Equator, no long twilight as in the northern islands. The sun sets; the light is turned off as if by a switch and at the same moment the crickets and the frogs tune in. It seemed now that I had to shout to make myself heard, although it was probably due to the fact that Ionides was deaf in one ear.

We drove on steadily, our weak headlights making queer patterns in the rising dust which gradually covered us so that our faces appeared made up like leading gentlemen in a desert film such as *Lawrence of Arabia*.

After what appeared a very long time, we passed through a straggling village and came to a little house. We got down stiffly, walked round the house and onto a verandah that faced south, and stopped. There in the moonlight the land fell away precipitously for a thousand feet and then for another thousand more gradually towards a faint ribbon of light which Ionides said was the river beyond which was Mozambique. Africa throbbed; a drum beat, a night creature piped; there were rustlings in the dry leaves, and always the high note of crickets filled the air and the deeper croak of the frogs.

We went in and washed. It was cool and exhilarating. I had read all the books about Ionides. Indeed I had only just finished reading Margaret Lane's *Life with Ionides*, and I should not have been surprised when dinner did consist only of dessicated goat and potatoes. I always rather pride myself on being a decently preserved man for my age, but I have to admit to dentures and I had then a rather new set which hadn't quite settled down. The trouble was, I was hungry. With the greatest difficulty I tore off a small piece of goat, the knife having turned in my hand as if I had been pressing it against rubber. As it was clearly impossible to divide the morsel, I put it in my mouth and started to chew. In spite of the pain that this pressure produced I continued for about five minutes by the end of which time I had it gummed between my upper and lower dentures so that when I opened my mouth they flapped. With difficulty I managed to extract the bit of goat and place it back on the plate surreptitiously. It was almost dark as the only light came from a hurricane lamp. I ate the five potatoes. Ionides chatted away, and swallowed his goat without complications, apparently having gastric juices of extraordinary potency.

Next morning I awoke into a fabulous world, for the mysterious view of the night before now lay below us in the early sunlight like a vision.

Ionides gave me an egg and some bread and butter and coffee for breakfast. But hardly had I got started on a second slice when a man entered talking rapidly in Swahili.

'There is a mamba in a tree four miles away,' Ionides said. Within three minutes we were in the Land Rover, team complete, bumping off along a very bush road. We came to a hamlet near which stood a grove of mango trees, their shining leaves closely packed. Under the trees a man was standing pointing upwards.

'There he is,' Ionides said. After some time I was able to make out a slender body with a spearlike head high up amongst the top-most branches.

The equipment was quickly brought out and one of the team started up the tree. When he had got about halfway up he was handed a long pole with an open clamp on the top which was worked by a lever at the lower end, the two being connected by an iron rod which ran up alongside the pole. The pole was gently raised till the clamp was level with the mamba which was holding on to a branch with its rear portion.

A quick movement and the clamp was firmly around the middle part of the snake, which, however, held on firmly with its tail portion while striking at the pole, its enemy, again and again with its death fangs.

'Don't hurt her,' Ionides called. 'Use gentle, firm pressure, don't jerk.' These instructions were carried out by the man up the tree and after a few minutes the mamba let go with its tail and was lowered through the leafy branches of the mango tree. Now both the front and the rear ends of the snake were curling and struggling but the clamp had it firmly by the middle.

When it was about ten feet from the ground Ionides fixed a second clamp to its front end and a second assistant another to its rear end. In this way it was brought down to earth. Then the first clamp was removed, the two others remaining in place. The snake had little more than a foot free at the head end and was greatly cramped in its movements. It looked at us with small implacable beady eyes and its jaws dripped venom.

Ionides came forward holding a pair of tongs in his left hand, a strong canvas bag inside out on his right arm. The mamba's neck was seized in the tongs and Ionides grasped it under the jaw between his right fore-finger and thumb through the bag. The tree-climber now removed the two remaining clamps and pulled the bag down from Ionides' arm, stuffing the body of the snake into the bag, and tied its neck. A third assistant now produced a wooden box and at the correct moment Ionides let go the mamba's jaw and dropped the canvas bag, snake and all into the wooden box. The lid was nailed down. We had 'bagged' our first mamba for the day.

During the morning we got eight more by similar tactics. In one case the snake, which was in a thicket and not up a mango tree, made off through the dense branches of the scrub trees. A fierce chase ensued while the mamba twisted and turned and tried to slip away but in the end Ionides got a clamp on it and after that the procedure was the same as usual.

Ionides also captured a puff adder which was so drowsy that he was able to catch it behind the jaw with his hand only.

'Rather risky,' he admitted. 'Puff adders for all their sleepy appearance can strike like lightning and they are rather bad-tempered. You simply can't trust them.'

During the morning he made me feel a mamba. 'You notice he feels cold,' he said. It certainly did as its green folds wrapped themselves round my bare arm. 'Cold as death,' I agreed, handing over its rear portion to the first assistant as quickly as I could with decency.

'It's perfectly safe,' Ionides said, 'as long as you keep concentrated all the time. If you begin to think about other things it's no good. I taught a friend of mine how to do it but he had a whisky and soda before his first bag and would go on talking.'

'What happened?' I asked.

'He died, of course,' Ionides said.

Later in the day I went up in his estimation, however, when I saw a vine snake before he did. We had gone out for a walk to look at the view from a particular point of vantage and were coming along a sandy path by the edge of the escarpment when I suddenly saw a thin grey snake crossing the path right under his foot.

'Look out, Ionides,' I said, 'and don't step on that snake. You've only got gym shoes on.'

'Oh, thanks,' said Ionides. 'I'll get him.'

And like a flash he did, by the tail. He held up the snake at arm's length. 'Perfectly safe for this kind,' he said. 'They can't turn and bite you, but you can't do that with a mamba. Anyway these vine snakes are pretty harmless, though I knew a man who suddenly died two days after being bitten by one. You can easily tame them. I'll show you this evening.' And sure enough he did later, taking the snake out of its box and running his hands over it gently. It seemed to like it.

All my life I have been pursued by a dream in which I find myself in a marsh full of snakes writhing all round, and am unable to escape, or even move without stepping on one. Thus I began to feel anxious as we sat late talking in the dimly lit sitting-room around whose walls were piled the wooden boxes containing the nine mambas, and also the puff adder and vine snake. The puff adder had woken up after dark and was keeping up a stealthy rustling against the wire.

'Do they ever escape?' I asked.

'A mamba did once, and we had to get it out from under the dresser,' he said.

Finally as a night-cap we drank some strong sugary tea and departed to our separate rooms. Very carefully I closed the door of my bedroom and made sure it was properly fastened so that no loose mamba could slip by in the night. Unfortunately I only slept for some hours and then awoke with a start. It may have been the goat because I had swallowed some out of pure hunger that evening, or it may have been the tea, but in any case I felt impelled to visit the bathroom, though that is a very inaccurate description of that particular hole in the ground.

My hurricane lamp was out. It was pitch black. I groped about and found a box of matches. There were four left. I couldn't get the hurricane lamp to work in the dark, so I crept to the door, my bare feet feeling terribly exposed. I opened it, lit a match and looked around the sitting-room. The boxes were piled up round the edge and looked sinister in the flickering light. The match went out. I lit another and tried to peer into the dark corners of the room to see if they contained any snakes. I thought the light might be reflected from their green eyes. The match burned my fingers. I retreated. 'I can't do it,' I said, and began to retire towards the bed. Nature, however, insisted. 'You can't just lie in bed holding on all night,' I said to myself. So I started off again. I struck match three and ran across the sitting-room and reached the hole, making the return journey in a similar dash. The last match went out as I got to the bedroom. I felt my way to the bed and climbed in palpitating with fear. I quickly tucked the mosquito net in with great care remembering that I had left the bedroom door open while crossing the sitting-room and that in all likelihood a mamba had slipped in while I was away and was no doubt under the bed. However, I was so exhausted emotionally that I fell asleep almost immediately. When

I awoke it was daylight; the sun was shining; the terrors of the night had fled.

'Come on,' Ionides said smiling broadly. 'Good news. They have come from a nearby village with information about a spitting cobra. If we catch him we'll let him loose on the air-strip and you can photograph him.'

'Thanks awfully,' I said. 'I'll be ready in a minute.'

Catching spitting cobras is quite a different kettle of fish from bagging mambas. Spitting cobras spit. They go for the whites of your eyes. Indeed one is advised never to show the whites of one's eyes to a spitting cobra. But when faced by a spitting cobra in person it is extremely difficult, I am told, to keep the whites of your eyes under control. A spitting cobra is a very accurate spitter and can get your eye at five paces.

'Keep clear to five paces and wear spectacles,' Ionides said. But I had left my spectacles behind in the rush and felt very naked when Ionides put on his goggles to approach the disused anthill in which the villagers said the cobra had its lair.

'We'll have to dig him out,' Ionides said.

The team set to work at once with hoes, picks and shovels, working in relays. The laterite had been worked by the ants into a hard cement-like substance and the anthill consisted of passages and chambers four feet above and six feet below the surface of the ground. Hour after hour they worked in the hot sun, the whole male village taking part. The women kept well away but the boys crowded round.

Every now and then the cobra would put out its deadly head from one or other of the passages and give a flying spit. The entire workers and onlookers would then turn and run.

'Somebody will get hurt or killed, if they will crowd around, but what's the good of talking to them?' The fact was, nobody was a bit nervous. Everybody felt perfectly safe as long as Ionides was there in his queer squatting position, watching, waiting, hour after hour.

'He has magic,' they said.

I felt, too, a complete confidence. In the villagers' case the Ionides magic was well known. Once a person had been foolish enough to steal some of his snake equipment. Ionides was very cross. He reprimanded the man with violent gestures and stern voice. On the way home the man was bitten by a mamba. After that there had been no more stealing and very little argument with Ionides.

After four hours' digging the excitement faded and I was able to observe the scene more objectively. The village men were sweating. Some of them were actually in the trench quite near the cobra but seemed unafraid. Then I saw Ionides, saw him really for the first time. He was crouched at the edge of the trench, his grey hair thrown back from his chiselled Greek face. His extraordinary brilliant eyes were taking in every movement of the men. He was ready for any sortie from the snake, but his look was far away, like that of a lion one sometimes sees behind bars in a zoo, looking away into a distance which is unknown to us.

I remembered the stories of his hunting days in Africa. How he had pursued a man-eating lion which had eaten ninety men in three months. It would make a kill, eat a few mouthfuls and clear off for eight miles. Ionides tracked it following its spoor relentlessly, sometimes going without food himself for three whole days and nights at a time. At last they met in a thicket. It fell dead on top of him from his second shot.

I saw him now suddenly as he really was. I understood his two personalities as Jung would explain it: first, his ordinary three-dimensional ego, eccentric maybe, but that was all, interesting, when he was talking about history or snakes but not very profound as both his previous biographers had discovered; second, the creature of the wild akin to the other creations—the trees, the butterflies, the great cats, the elephants, the snakes, the elementals, God's other breaths with Man.

Death meant no more to him than to any of the creatures though he feared the crippling of old age and would, he said, much sooner, 'fulfil his dateless bargain with engrossing death', if needs be, by his friend and enemy the snake. But looking at him then I saw that he knew absolutely where he belonged—the other world in which Man is merely part and a rather irritating part of creation. Maybe it was easier for God to make butterflies, lions and snakes, trees and flowers, all of which obey, than Man who doesn't.

It cannot be said he loved animals for he could hunt and kill with pleasure. There was nothing sentimental in his relationship with them, nothing very human, certainly he never made them into extensions of human beings. Rather he and they belonged together to an elemental timeless world that we know not of. Later thinking on the mystery of Ionides I remembered Robert Louis Stevenson's lines

> The untented cosmos my abode
> I pass a wilful stranger
> My mistress still the open road
> And bright the eyes of danger. . . .

Yet this is too romantic a picture really and Ionides would not have liked it. Certainly his first personality would have disclaimed it altogether and even his number two would have preferred something less emotional.

That evening we talked of many things; of the creatures, of death, of love, of Africa. Africa was his home, had always been his real home, always outside and inside time. This was the mystery of Ionides. Only a small side of him belonged to our world of cities and machines, of built-up areas, dumps, universities of learning, courts of law, cathedrals. Much the bigger side dwelt in an ancient present amidst creatures of forgotten times and those still lingering in a world now overrun by man.

I glimpsed his meaning and a greater meaning of which he was part then standing in the hot midday equatorial sun.

Now what I saw fades and lies in the bottom of my mind like a half-forgotten dream and I cannot answer if you ask me why he went on catching snakes or what he knew about snakes that we do not know.

Maybe he was a little mad about snakes.

Shortly after getting back to Nigeria I received a last letter from him. He died not long after.

'We resumed digging for the cobra on Friday and dug all day only catching a glimpse of the nose in the late afternoon. However, we took two mambas and a puff adder while the digging was going on. This morning we received news of a spitting cobra in an abandoned hut and took him in a matter of minutes, a big adult male. We then continued digging and at about 10.30 a.m. we came up with the cobra at the end of the hole. After one abortive attempt I succeeded in getting a good enough grip on the end of her nose with the tongs to draw her head out for me to grasp her neck, after which we carefully raised her out; a nice adult female.'

*   *   *

During this and other medical journeys I visited several of the great reserve areas where the wild creatures of Africa live free. But it was in Uganda by the Murchison Falls that I got closest to the heart of wild Africa.

On this journey I had two companions, both doctors from the medical centre in Kampala. One was an efficient New Zealander dedicated to the organisation of a large paediatric clinic which he ran every day at the hospital. He took one day off while I was there and drove me in his Land Rover to the Murchison Falls and back. The other was a girl with an Irish-Norman name, who had been in Nigeria at the Wesley Guild Hospital in Ilesha and was now on a research project in Kampala. She was a good companion, gay, at ease. She looked out at the world through grey-greenish eyes of particular brilliance and her presence lit up the day.

The mists were rising from Lake Victoria. It was not yet seven in the morning when we reached the Land Rover. As we set off, still hardly awake, our senses were dulled by the green banana world around. Everywhere were rolling hills and little farms surrounded by banana trees rising out of the red earth. To me it was a new landscape, fresh and pleasant but in no way disturbing or particularly thought-evoking. The New Zealander drove on steadily. It relaxed his mind, strained in seeking the impossible. The girl sat quietly. I talked lazily about Ionides and the places I had left in Tanzania. Gradually the scene changed. We left the tarred road, and the bananas. Hills rose, rocky and beaten like all the little kopjes of Africa, huge boulders worn by the passage of time, countless ages, old, old land. We saw nobody. The red road stretched on and on to the north. After some hours we reached open grass country. Every fifty yards or so a tree or two stood, some gaunt and dead like posts planted in the war to stop enemy aeroplanes landing, others heavily foliaged with dark shade beneath.

Suddenly, looking across a green expanse of tall waving grass I saw two elephants about two hundred yards from our road standing in the shade of a mango tree. One of them flapped his great ears so that their dark forms took shape in the shade—two wild elephants, African elephants! My senses stirred. My mind and memory awoke. I remembered an Indian elephant I had met in a densely crowded Benares street with five laughing children on his back. He was picking his way with great care through the vast throng of pilgrims passing down to the Ganges. As I watched him he came to a place where a ragged fakir sat with his begging bowl. To have gone on would have meant stepping on him. So he stopped, wrapped his trunk round the old man and lifted him, begging bowl and all, to one side and then proceeded slowly up the street, placing his feet carefully so as not to stand on anybody, while the gay children on his back called and laughed. There in India he had seemed to symbolise the whole life of man and creature in that ageless land. Here in Africa elephants were alone, unattached, wild.

Now, as we drove forward we came upon herd after herd of these grey monsters with their fantastic bulk and humorous little eyes set on each side of their incredible heads.

We came to a signboard, 'To Murchison Falls'. I had heard of the Murchison Falls but no descriptions I had read prepared my mind for what was to come. The Victoria Nile here comes roaring down a gorge in a dark torrent. The rocky sides narrow till the main stream carrying about as much water as the Thames at Westminster is pressed into a channel not more than twenty-five feet across. It then suddenly falls a hundred and fifty feet sheer into a boiling cauldron to widen out into a valley half a mile wide, its surface covered with a white lace of foam.

We got down from the Land Rover and climbed up the end of the gorge to the top of the Falls and walked to a point where we could face the falling water. An askari with a loaded rifle had silently attached himself to us. There were great cats about.

We stood on a rock with a precipice on three sides and looked down. The violence of the water, the roar, the foam, the rainbow mist were gathered into our minds almost obliterating thought, though somewhere inside a feeling of awareness stirred and consciousness widened. The New Zealander got lost temporarily fussing with his long-distance camera lens. The askari, the girl and I were alone. The soldier stood motionless, his dark face and rifle silhouetted against the reflected light from the white-foamed valley far below.

As we walked back past the cataract above the Falls we saw a lone bull elephant with immense curved tusks come down the bank and begin to browse in the lush grass by the other side of the rushing water. He was completely indifferent to us. We were small unimportant intruders into his tremendous home.

Next day we decided to take a trip by launch up the Victoria Nile to the bottom of the Murchison Falls, though with some misgiving as the other people at the camp looked horribly like human beings who had strayed out of their own world and whose minds were quite unprepared to comprehend the mystery of the ancient present at Murchison.

The launch was a very plebeian affair with a stuttering internal combustion engine that emitted a foul exhaust. Into it were crowded rather more than such a craft could reasonably accommodate, so that the water-line was very near to the gunwale making us feel uncomfortably close to the inhabitants of the dark water which lapped against the side.

The Victoria Nile runs in such a deep bed that in most places it is possible for the launches to chug along a few feet from the bank. It was not long before on rounding a bend we found ourselves in a hippo world. Here the sand banks were crowded with dozens of hippos whose bodies looked like enormous blown-out balloon pigs surmounted by a flat preposterous head cut in two by a cavity of a mouth containing horrible, huge, yellow teeth. On our approach panic took them and they floundered off through the muddy

verges like hysterical aldermen in an earthquake. Reaching their
second element, however, they were transformed in a moment into
their other incarnation, the river horse, and floated away with the
elegance of ballet dancers.

We travelled on and came to another colony of ancient monsters.
Here mixed up with the hippos were enormous crocodiles and
immense green and grey lizards, remote descendants of the pre-
historic ichthyosauri. It is said that the crocodiles sometimes eat a
baby hippo and that the lizards are particularly fond of crocodiles'
eggs. If so they did not show any such tendencies while we were
there but seemed to be co-existing excellently, hippopotami, lizards
and crocodiles all on the same mud bank.

When you looked beyond the actual river edge you caught
glimpses of still more elephants, huge, immensely powerful buffaloes
and different sorts of deer.

My travelling companions from Kampala were at the other end
of the launch. I looked round my end. There was a faded lady
belonging to the English county classes. She was in some trouble
with an ancient camera.

There was the inevitable American tourist with two or three
cameras. He climbed up and down the launch, leaned over the sides
and continually clicked one or other of his machines in my ear.

'If he falls overboard the crocodiles will eat him automatically,'
I said, 'even if they have never eaten anybody before.'

The faded lady agreed. 'I couldn't care less,' she said.

I half drowsed, then suddenly awoke into a vivid consciousness. I
looked round the boat load, 'piffling' was the only word to describe
us, homo sapiens, my God! I looked out beyond and saw the
implacable eyes of a crocodile looking at me, waiting. I saw the
hippos, the lizards. I felt the presence of the nine thousand elephants
who live at Murchison. I remembered that the crocodiles had been
in this bit of river for thirty million years and that the ancestors of
the lizards had ruled the world for three hundred million years
before that. Time hit me like a blow. I recoiled from the terror of
such knowledge. Suddenly I realised that Time had changed its
pace and that I was looking at something that had been and no
longer was, or, if it was, meant nothing any more. It was like
regarding the light from a star which died a thousand million years
ago. I realised that I was looking at the Creator's other dream, a
breath of God unassociated with man and his consciousness, which
had nothing to do with the God of love and compassion. Here was
the ancient time world of birth and death, life living on the destruction of life. Life unconscious, driven along a predestined path by

instinct activated by some implacable plan. Why had God created crocodiles? Elephants, yes certainly, though difficult to explain in human language, and hippopotami possibly, but crocodiles, *no*. Had something gone wrong in Heaven? What about the Fall?

My mind was still in turmoil when the launch touched the bank below the camp and we disembarked along a slippery plank which literally brought us back to earth.

That evening we drove our Land Rover to a peninsula where the Victoria Nile flows into Lake Albert. There it meets the other great waters flowing north out of the central African rain forests to form the White Nile and flow for thousands of miles to reach the Mediterranean, passing through the Sud, the greatest swamp in the world, passing through the desert to join the Blue Nile from Ethiopia at Khartoum in the Sudan and flowing on through Egypt with man's early written history inscribed on the great stones on its banks. Looking at these early waters of the great river in Uganda in the evening light while hearing the distant thunder of the Murchison Falls coming in snatches with the fitful breeze, my memory stirred and I suddenly realised that I was looking at the true source of the Nile which Burton and Speke and all the others had sought so long, marching on their tired feet day after day for thousands of miles, driven almost to despair by the fever-carrying insects, so that in the end they had lost all reason and quarrelled bitterly.

The track we were following came to an end and we found it difficult to continue as the ground was marshy by the water's edge with its profusion of reeds, green spaces and sandy shores.

Among the reeds the biggest tusker we had ever seen stood up to his knees in the water tearing out the river weeds in great sheaves with his trunk and bundling them into his mouth.

His mate and baby daughter stood on rather firmer ground to one side. When he saw us he flapped his ears, raised his trunk and emitted the elephant's nasal trumpet sound. He advanced towards us slowly, turning his head for a moment towards his family as if to say, 'Stay where you are, I'll settle these people myself.' We retreated rapidly before he had time to reach firmer ground and charge. Seeing us remove ourselves he lowered his trunk and joined his family.

As we came over a rise we came upon six slender antelopes playing a game of 'catch me'. Our presence seemed in no way to disturb them. For a moment they all stood motionless; then one suddenly made a dart at another who bounded away in a long, low, effortless leap to one side and dashed off at what looked like the speed of sound, his feet hardly touching the earth between each stupendous jump. The remaining five now pursued the fugitive who twisted and turned like lightning, returning in a minute to the place he had started from. Then one of the others took his place and bounded away to be pursued by the rest in his turn. We might have been ghosts looking on for all the notice they took of us.

Later three bigger water-buck appeared. They passed close by us. The third who lagged behind was limping badly, and a recent wound showed on one buttock. He looked at us with sad, forlorn eyes, as he struggled past. He reminded me of Ionides and I wondered if his 'dateless bargain with engrossing death' was near also. For a moment a human compassion for the creature filled my doctor's consciousness, but I realised such a thought had no place at the source of the Nile.

Suddenly, remembering that we were a long way from home and that it was getting dark, we turned about. Immediately we saw why the night had come up on us so unexpectedly. The whole of the western sky was covered with dense black clouds which blotted out the last of the evening light. At the same moment an electrical tropical storm burst about us. There was a brilliant flash followed almost instantaneously by an explosion of thunder, and then the rains hit us like water out of a fire hose.

We drove as fast as possible so as to avoid getting bogged. Fortunately we found the track we had come out on. We had not gone very far along it however when there was another illumination followed by a thunder clap, like a cannon shot. There right ahead of us on the road we saw a herd of elephants apparently throwing back defiance at the angry heavens. With trunks raised high and the tusks gleaming in the reflected lightning they were trumpeting wildly. We stopped and turned off our engine. We sat still. Then flash followed flash while the thunder crashed around us. We watched the wild elephants in the flashes of light which grew brighter and brighter. They looked like enormous spectres come to earth from another planet or forms of terror in a nightmare. We sat very still. Fear was all about us. Suddenly I ceased to look ahead and glanced, during a flash, to my right. Perhaps I had seen *it* out of the corner of my eye when I thought I was only seeing elephants. There just off the road at the other side of a small ditch was a bull rhinoceros, nature's ton tank. He was standing with his back to the storm a few yards away. Two enormous horns stuck out of his nose. One was very long and pointed. Of all the creatures in the Wild the rhinoceros has the most preposterous appearance. He looks and usually is invulnerable except perhaps to a heavy gun. He is not naturally vicious but if he comes for you in or out of a car the only thing to do is to get out of his line of vision as quickly as possible, as he has poor eyesight. He is hunted for his horn which when powdered is said to be a potent aphrodisiac.

I remembered all this in that instant but we couldn't advance or retreat or even turn on the engine of the Land Rover. All we could do was sit still. The rain was obviously annoying the rhinoceros as it poured off his armour-plated skin folds for he kept flapping his ears and shaking his head. We remained thus beside him for what seemed like an hour. Then in one of the now less frequent flashes we saw that the path ahead was clear of elephants, though we could see huge dark forms on both sides of our road. Very quietly the New Zealander started the engine and let in the clutch. He silently pushed the gear lever into first. Almost imperceptibly we crept forward leaving the rhino still shaking his ears, passed up the path through the herd of elephants, and left Wild Africa to its night life.

CHAPTER 20

LIFE IN LAGOS

Settled now in Lagos, life moved into a particularly interesting phase for both Han and me. As Professor of Child Health in the new Lagos Medical School and a friend of the Minister of Health, I found myself adviser to the Federal Government on Child Health, indeed on medicine in general. Majekodunmi planned a health service for the Federal Territory which he hoped would spread later to the whole country. Part of this plan was the establishment of the central Institute of Child Health supported by the universities of Ibadan and Lagos and the Rockefeller Foundation. This flourished and produced many invaluable guidelines for the health of the children of the nation, particularly in the field of nutrition, but the fate of the local branches in the Regions was characteristic of the state of affairs at that time. The English Permanent Secretary of Health in the Northern Region took the money and built a quite excellent centre in Kaduna (the capital of the North), but in a forceful letter said the Northern Region would accept no advice, either from the Federal Ministry of Health or the University of Ibadan. Having no paediatric centre at all in the Northern Region and no trained staff the Unit there never functioned beyond being a modern local child-welfare centre and had no influence on the paediatric problems of the North.

In the East an excellent plan was agreed upon at one sitting between the Ibo local health people, the Federal Health Authority and W.H.O., but nothing satisfactory came of it as the young doctor appointed to run it was arrested and then the civil war started.

In the Western Region the money along with other funds was simply stolen by a minister or somebody in Government service who was able to get hold of it. Embezzlement was the order of the day at that time as the subsequent enquiry showed. I tried to get the money out of the Awolowo Government, the Administrator's Government which followed, the Akintola Government and both Military Governors after the coups. They all said the same thing: that that particular moment was not favourable for finding the money. The fact was it had disappeared without a trace. This may sound very outrageous, but it was typical of Nigeria after Independence. Corruption of all kinds was rampant among politicians and their supporters both regionally and federally, only varying with the location and the possibilities for getting rich quick.

*　　*　　*

The general situation was now rapidly moving towards a final struggle for power between the three main tribal groupings in the North, West and East. But for the moment the political situation had very little effect on our personal lives.

The new University Medical School in Lagos which had been set up by Majekodunmi, although affected by the slowing up of direct government support, had been well founded and went steadily ahead. Here I was able gradually to establish perhaps the best paediatric unit in Nigeria, probably in West Africa. In the end it consisted of a complete four-storey block in the main teaching hospital, containing over a hundred beds, teaching facilities such as lecture rooms, a library and professional and lecturer accommodation, medical research laboratories and a milk kitchen. The unit was partly financed by the Wolfson Foundation and partly by the Federal Government. There was also a neonatal unit for newborn babies in the Maternity wing. The Lagos branch of the Institute of Child Health was attached to the local Health Centre. Its function was to study social paediatrics in Lagos. There was also a large children's clinic in the area, apart from the paediatric consultant out-patient department in the hospital itself. All were under the control of the Lagos Professor of Child Health.

More important than the physical equipment, however, was the staffing. This consisted of a professor, four lecturers (consultant paediatricians), registrars (senior and junior) and housemen in the hospital proper. As well as this staff the Institute had a number of medical men attached as full-time research fellows. The nursing staff were also adequate and well trained in paediatrics and able to take considerable responsibility on their own. The doctors were chiefly Nigerian but we always had some expatriates from Great Britain, the U.S.A. or Ghana, some of whom were outstanding. The most remarkable men in the team were two young Nigerian doctors whom I had known four years before at Ibadan. One was Ishaya Audu from Northern Nigeria, a Hausa-Fulani. He was a very clever young man who had come to me one day at Ibadan and told me he wanted to be a children's physician. He had then gone off and obtained the necessary higher qualifications in Great Britain, returned and now had come to join us in Lagos. From the first he was exceptional and later was called to be the first Nigerian Vice-Chancellor of the Ahmadu Bello University in the North. He was one of the few outstanding doctors from Northern Nigeria and as such necessarily involved in the political affairs of the time.

The other Nigerian, Koye Ransome-Kuti, was originally one of our Trinity College, Dublin, graduates who had returned and served as houseman and then as registrar at Ibadan with me. He also had gone later to the United Kingdom and obtained a higher degree qualifying him as a teacher and consultant. He joined me now as Lecturer in Lagos and gradually assumed the position of leading child specialist in Nigeria, indeed by now in the whole of West Africa. He comes of a very unusual family. His mother is a leading Yoruba woman politician and sociologist. One brother is a famous musician, another an excellent doctor. He now holds the Chair of Child Health and Paediatrics in Lagos. Of all the young doctors I have known all over the world he is the best. I can remember no occasion when I have criticised him even in my mind.

Needless to say I was very happy with these young men and the fascinating problems with which paediatrics in Lagos brought me in contact.

*   *   *

Han also was happy. Balewa had given us the house where Awolowo had been 'restricted' in the island suburb of Ikoyi. This and its garden Han made into a very beautiful home where Niall was looked after by a splendid great black nanny. She belonged to a strange African Christian church called the Cherubim and Seraphim, who used to have singing services on the wide sunny Lagos beach with the soft wind blowing in from the breaking Atlantic rollers. She used to carry Niall along with her on her back wrapped in a cloth, African style, his fair hair waving in the sea breeze. Sean, who had now graduated from his Ibadan school with all honours, was at Newtown, the Quaker co-educational school at Waterford in Ireland. During his holidays he used to come riding with me for miles along the silver-golden Lagos beach which stretched away along the coast. I had now several little Arab polo stallions which he rode like a prince with a straight back and happy eyes shining from a tanned face.

Sometimes we would canter for a mile or so along the edge of the sea, the waves coming in and washing round our horses' feet, and then turn inland into the wide open country. Occasionally we came to queer fishing villages where the people would greet us with friendly smiles. Sometimes he would come and support me at some match at the Lagos polo club where were kept over a hundred polo ponies and for whom I now played in many great games against the other Nigerian clubs from Ibadan or the North or against Ghana. To Han he was always her greatest joy. He loved all creatures, birds perhaps most. Boys on the beach used to catch young seabirds and attach a string to one leg and sell them to Europeans. Sean would get his mother to drive him down to the beach where he would spend all his pocket money and hers as well buying the defenceless creatures, often with broken wings. He fitted up a sort of aviary on his balcony in our house where he tended them till they recovered and could be released. Sometimes Han would find him asleep in the morning amongst his birds on the verandah. From the age of five he was always reading, showing unusual likes such as the *Pilgrim's Progress* and the poetry of Blake and Homer. On one occasion, at the age of seven when Han had been particularly defeated by life and was cross, he said, 'Mother, you do always meet Apollyon, don't you?'

He loved Blake's poem of the 'Little Fly' and would sometimes say it.

Little Fly
Thy summer's play
my thoughtless hand
has brushed away
Am not I
A fly like thee
Or art not thou
A man like me

For I dance
And drink and sing
Till some blind hand
Shall break my wing
If thought is life
And strength and breath
and the want
Of thought is death

Then am I
A happy fly
If I live
Or if I die. . . .

In fact he said it so sweetly once in London that Jill Balcon, Cecil Day Lewis' wife, gave him her own inscribed copy of Blake's poems.

His favourite was W. J. Turner's 'Romance', that splendid poem about the great Andes:

> When I was but thirteen or so
> I went into a golden land
> Chimborazo, Cotopaxi
> Took me by the hand.

Most of all he felt an overwhelming compassion for all creatures in pain or distress. Once off the coast of Ireland we were catching mackerel. We had been pulling in the struggling fish for some time. Sean was in the stern of the boat. As a particularly violent fish was knocked on the head to quieten it I saw the pain in his face and remembered how I felt similarly as a child, even for dying fish.

* * *

Han became Assistant Medical Officer of Health in Lagos under Dr Tunji Adeniyi-Jones, a very distinguished African doctor whose family had originally come from Sierra Leone. Her work was very comprehensive: she had to look after the domiciliary midwifery service, the school medical service, and also inspect markets and drains, and deal with hygienic problems generally. This brought her in touch with the people of Lagos in a very personal way. Mamma'Ronke, a huge eighteen-stone Yoruba lady trader, became her staunch friend and supporter after Han had given her successful medical advice for her daughter in the school clinic. She would invite Han to her 'parlour', and show her the family photographs while entertaining her with Fanta or beer. Then they would walk home through the crowded narrow Lagos streets arm in arm. On parting she would kiss Han goodbye much to the astonishment of passing Europeans. Sometimes she would come round to our house, bearing gifts of fruit, drink and bread perilously poised on the head of an attendant 'small-boy'. Mamma'Ronke on these occasions would wear her magnificent local gold earrings, bracelets, and necklaces and an immense Yoruba head-dress of yards of highly coloured cloth.

Much of Han's work was arduous, however: a child dying of sickle-celled disease under her hands in the clinic, the mother having already lost eight from the same condition; or every morning the 'fever clinic' where some thirty children of school age would be stretched out over the floor of a room, suffering from fever with temperatures around 104° F. caused by malaria. They would be sprinkled with water continually while lying under a fan during the period in which the anti-malarial treatment was taking effect. Some would go into convulsions, some had other complaints than malaria. The differential diagnosis was extremely difficult. Han also got to know the street traders who would let it be known that she was a special doctor, to be treated with consideration, so that she was passed from one to another very kindly when on shopping expeditions.

*   *   *

Lagos being the capital of the most prosperous and important West African country had over fifty embassies or missions of foreign countries from both sides of the Iron Curtain. Eamonn Kennedy, the Irish Ambassador, and his red-headed American wife were our friends. We all helped to organise the Ireland–Nigeria society of Irishmen in Nigeria and Nigerians who had been educated in Ireland.

In contrast to people of the Western Embassies were those from the other side of the Iron Curtain. Our contacts with them were equally cordial, if more unusual. The Russians became perhaps the best of all our diplomatic friends. It started when Professor Lapin from Odessa turned up in Nigeria to collect red monkeys. We never discovered if the redness of the monkeys meant anything ideologically or was merely the mark of a special breed. We invited him to dinner. He turned up punctually at eight p.m. accompanied by a second Russian gentleman. They both sat down and conversed very amicably over drinks until after nine p.m. when Han, urged on by her cook who was getting impatient, asked the second gentleman if he would stay to dinner. He accepted immediately. The penny dropped and we realised that he was the acting commissar in charge of the professor. But from that evening on Commissar Alexander became our devoted friend and through him we learned the warmth of the Russian human character, though our differences in outlook and behaviour often led us into amusing situations both in Africa and when we visited Russia. My best moment was shortly after our first meeting when I was invited to the Russian Embassy while Professor Lapin was still there. There were four of us. Three Russians including Alexander, Lapin, one other and myself.

'This is an occasion,' Alexander said, 'we must open a bottle of pink vodka, which means, Professor,' he said turning to me, 'that we must finish it.' After about the third round the Russians who all spoke English fluently forgot to change back into Russian when they began to discuss Stalin, some being anti and others being pro. At last Lapin said, 'We're all peasants' sons, aren't we? If it hadn't been for Stalin, even if he killed a lot of people, none of us would be here—would we?' All agreed. Suddenly they grasped that I had understood their arguments and to cover up their dismay Alexander called on me to propose a toast in the pink vodka. With unusual inspiration, I called out 'Homo sapiens', rising to my feet, somewhat unsteadily. They all rose. We clinked glasses. It was a great moment. 'Homo sapiens.' Tears glistened in the old Muscovite eyes. They clapped me on the back. 'Comrade!' they shouted. When finally I reached home Han looked me up and down. 'What *have* you been doing?' she said.

*   *   *

Lagos in the sixties was a very unhappy place politically. First Awolowo, the leader of the southern Yorubas, was gaoled after his treason trial. Corruption and blatant nepotism were the order of the day both in federal and regional government circles and business was conducted in the worst capitalistic manner; bribes of ten per cent on a deal were common practice. Behind the scenes was great discontent and disillusionment in those hating the corruption in high places. In the purely political arena a struggle for power was in progress. There the Ibos, the most cohesive of the Nigerian tribes, felt left out in the cold particularly when the Northern leader, the Saudauna of Sokoto, seemed to be allying himself to Akintola, the new premier of the Western Region.

Violence broke out towards the end of 1965, but things were at their worst during the first week of January. At the same time the British Commonwealth Conference was being held in Lagos with Mr Wilson and all the other Prime Ministers. At the conference Balewa was hailed as a statesman, his dignity and beautiful voice charming everybody as he took the chair.

During the same week his young son Ali went down with a crisis of sickle-celled anaemia, a deadly blood disease to which Africans in malarial environments are particularly prone. Most severe cases die and all suffer bouts of fever and pain. Ali was a bad case and I was in and out to see him throughout the week. I came in late on one evening after the Commonwealth Conference had wound up and found him responding to treatment and out of pain. As I came out of the women's quarters Balewa was coming down the stairs of the main part of the house. He looked tired but came and greeted me very kindly.

'Come and sit over here,' he said, drawing me to a couch. 'And tell me how you are and how medicine is going. I haven't seen enough of you, my friend, lately.'

'Well, Mr Prime Minister,' I said, 'you are a very busy man. Oh! I must congratulate you on the conference, you were splendid!'

He seemed pleased with my praise which a smaller man might have considered presumptuous to a prime minister of a great country. He smiled and laid his hand on my arm. I told him about Ali and said that though I thought he was going to get through this crisis all right he would have others and would need great care if he was to reach adult life. We talked on. Then fearing to tire him, I rose and took my leave. I was ushered out by his A.D.C., a huge man whom I didn't take to. The guards at the gate were even more unimpressive. They did not appear to be properly armed. The sergeant was very apprehensive about 'the present troubles in the West' and asked me if I thought the thugs were employing juju. I said 'burning' was quite enough. As a sergeant of the Prime Minister's guard I thought him very odd.

I drove home. Next morning before eight a.m. the electricity failed including the telephone which made a queer noise and went dead. Han and I drove into town to report the failure and found soldiers everywhere and rumours of all kinds. The Prime Minister and the Federal Finance Minister had disappeared from their homes and a military junta was in command. Gradually we heard more. During the night a group of army officers had brought about a coup d'état. The Prime Minister of the Federation, Balewa, had been murdered, along with his Finance Minister. Also the Prime Ministers of the West (Akintola) and the North (the Sardauna) had been shot down and a number of others including some twenty army officers. All those killed except one officer who had refused to give up the keys of the arsenal were non-Ibos. There were awful rumours as to how the killings had been carried out. Some said Balewa had been tortured to find out state secrets, others that he had been smothered, one that they had put out his eyes—certainly his guards had put up no resistance. All of them were alive. Akintola and those army officers who refused to join the plotters had been shot down, some in bed with their wives. It was said that the Sardauna and his guards fought it out with the assassins, killing some of them before he was shot through the shoulder (he wore a bullet-proof vest). They then finished him off with a shot through the head and left him lying in his own courtyard.

In Lagos, after taking Balewa away, they went round to the Iloyi Hotel, shot one of the leading army officers there and dragged his bleeding corpse through the lounge much to the consternation of the expatriates present.

Majekodunmi, as a friend of Balewa's, had apparently been on the list to be assassinated but a friend had rung him up and gone round to his house and when the assassins drove up there, they found the two men standing at the door with revolvers in their hands. Seeing them the assassins' car simply circled in and out of the drive and went off without stopping.

In the town that morning nobody seemed to know what exactly was happening. There appeared to be an Ibo take-over. But Major-General Ironsi, the commander-in-chief of the army, though an Ibo, was said to have had nothing to do with the killings which had been carried out by a fanatical young Ibo officer called Nzegwu, a very religious person who went to Communion every morning. We were told that Ironsi had taken over from these mutinous officers and set up a military dictatorship, making himself Supreme Commander and Head of State.

It was difficult to know what to do and thinking that Majeko-dunmi was probably still in danger we made a plan to get him hidden. We drove round to his house which we now found surrounded by Ironsi's soldiers and local police. Han got out and walked through the guards who greeted her cordially as one of the Lagos medical personnel. She saw Majekodunmi but he would not hide. I sat there in the car outside for half an hour, very nervously wondering what might happen to her. I was relieved when she came out walking very straight through the guards around the door. 'He won't come,' she said.

Within a day the Ironsi take-over was complete. The version that a mutiny of some young officers had taken place was now official and Ironsi had to be accepted as new Head of State by foreign diplomats. But it was noticeable that the people now in power were nearly all Ibos and only one Ibo had been killed in the coup. Looking back I think that most probably there were two plots, one a genuine, if mistaken, effort to end the corruption by murdering the leading politicians and anybody who stood in the way, the other a much deeper laid conspiracy for a take-over by the Ibos of the whole state.

To begin with it was obviously necessary to make their coup appear respectable and to hush up the murders which had been taking place. Ironsi played the part of 'honest broker', decent, Sandhurst-trained, British-type, Major-General, excellently. He opened Red Cross fêtes, made little speeches, gave great dinners, appeared to be acting reasonably by appointing local dignitaries as regional Governors, such as Colonel Hassan, son of the Moslem

Emir of Katsina, as Governor of the Northern Region, and not appointing Nzegwu as Governor of the East but Colonel Ojukwu who was said not to have played an active part in the killings. Indeed life in Lagos appeared to return to normal. I found Ironsi pleasant to meet. I looked after his much too fat little daughter and tried to keep her to a slimming diet which was not very easy with the State House cooks.

During the late spring violent disturbances broke out in the North in certain towns, particularly Zaria and Kaduna where organised rioters attacked the Ibo settlements and killed many Ibo residents with machetes, including some actually in hospital. As a result, so it was said, a second Ibo coup was planned to finish off the killings of the first coup and finally destroy the remaining opposition.

To begin with, however, Ironsi's 'pacification plan' was in vogue and life went on normally. In hospital the clinics were crowded and teaching took up most of my spare time.

*   *   *

One day that spring Audu came to me and said that the British Vice-Chancellor of Ahmadu Bello University in the North was about to retire and that his Northern friends wanted him to take on the post as otherwise it would be filled by a very unsuitable Ibo professor. What should he do? I encouraged him to accept. He asked me if I would help him form a new medical school in the North, not founded on a tremendously expensive hospital as at Ibadan, but on a group of government hospitals in different Northern towns. This sounded real sense to me and I agreed.

Through Audu I now met a remarkable young officer called Gowon whose father had been a member of a primitive hill tribe in the Northern plateau. The father had been converted to Christianity at the age of seventeen, and later had moved to Zaria where there was a famous secondary school. There he sent young Yakubu Gowon, who became head boy—no mean feat for an unknown Christian boy from an outside tribe in that traditional, Moslem world. Later he was selected as one of the six young Nigerians to go annually to Sandhurst. There again he had done well, and now here he was back in Nigeria. I spent an evening with him completely fascinated by the brilliance and genuineness of his personality. He said he had had a great escape at the time of the first coup. Nzegwu had asked him to join the young officers' plot. He had refused, saying murder was unchristian and against his army oath. So they had decided to murder him. But at an army party the night of the coup Ironsi had made a remark that made him suspect that they might be after him so that he had not gone home. He had, in fact, seen his house surrounded and entered twice that night by the assassins who however failed to find him.

Now I began to travel up and down to Kaduna, the capital of the North, so as to be able to move north as soon as possible. On one of these occasions I attended a curious party at Government House, Kaduna, given by Hassan for Ironsi who was visiting the North. All the guests were assembled on the lawn behind the Governor's British-built establishment. Colonel Hassan accompanied by General Ironsi appeared in full dress uniform and proceeded down the steps to us. Ironsi knew very few people present and recognising me as his daughter's doctor came up and talked to me. He seemed to be unusually nervous. Then after some perfunctory remarks to other people he re-entered the house and disappeared with Hassan. I was told later that the young Northern officers had plotted 'to get him' that evening but had been prevented by Hassan who, being a Katsina prince, could not allow a guest to be molested in his house.

*   *   *

They did get him the following weekend at Ibadan when he was staying at the old British State House there. That weekend a second coup took place, the Ibo junta being rounded up and shot along with the others who had joined them all over the country, except in their own Eastern Region where Colonel Ojukwu was Governor and had a tight control of all army personnel.

The whole situation was changed. The Ibo junta had been destroyed overnight, except in the Eastern Region. What was to happen now? The next senior officer in the army was a Yoruba, but neither he himself nor anybody else, felt he was a 'Supreme Commander' by any stretch of the imagination. After a considerable search and much heart-burning, Gowon was suddenly made into the Head of State and Supreme Commander of the Army. Before he had time to consolidate his position and get a real grip of things a second wave of communal murder against the Ibos in the other Regions, particularly the North, took place. The local Moslems, now realising fully what had happened, organised themselves and went for the Ibos who had remained in many of the Northern cities. usually living together in enclaves. The killing was done brutally with knives and, where Northern troops were involved, with bayonets. At one point on the airfield at Kano when an international aeroplane landed many of the passengers who were Ibos were bayoneted to death there and then in the customs rooms of the air terminal. A friend of mine saw an Ibo customs officer stuck in the back with a bayonet while he was opening his bag. All over the North the massacres took place. The Ibos fled for home. Whole train loads of them were stopped and slaughtered. The Ibo propaganda put their casualties at thirty-two thousand and repeated it so often that it became the basis of their later 'genocide' slogan. The Northerners said the figure was three thousand five hundred. Both figures are probably incorrect but if only three thousand are knifed to death it is so frightful as really to make little difference. Each man dies alone.

The result of this attack on the Ibos by the other Nigerians was naturally to weld them still closer together. Ojukwu called home all the Ibos who lived outside the Eastern Region and almost to a man they obeyed, leaving their good jobs, their houses and all their belongings behind them.

*　　*　　*

To reconstitute the State after the first coup, the second coup and now the second massacre was an impossible job for the young man, now Head of State. A conference took place in Ghana between Gowon and Ojukwu, but nothing came of it. Both sides accused the other of double-dealing. In fact the position was impossible for the Ibos. Their heart-land was not very fertile and possessed few minerals and could not even support in comfort the large population normally there without money coming in from the outside which had been regularly supplied in the past by their emigrants in the other Regions holding good jobs. And now that tens of thousands of these had come home penniless the position was desperate. There was only one hope—oil. In the delta of the Niger River a great oil-field had been found—a real reserve oil area which the great companies were hungry to get their hands on. Unfortunately, the oil area was not exactly in the Ibo heart-land but rather in the Ijaw tribal area, though this area had been consolidated previously by the British into the Eastern Region and was dominated by the Ibos. Ojukwu now thought that if he seceded with the oil-field from Nigeria he could make it alone successfully even with this extra population. But naturally enough the other Nigerians were unwilling to let their oil-field go which was already bringing some two hundred million pounds a year into the Federal Exchequer.

Gowon was in a difficult position. He was very conscience stricken as a compassionate man and a Christian over the massacres. But he knew that it was the Ibos who had struck the first blow. Nor could he contemplate secession, with all it meant, not only in the loss of oil revenues, to the state of Nigeria. So, supported wholeheartedly by the Northern tribes and half-heartedly by the Yorubas, he refused to recognise 'Biafra' as Ojukwu christened his new state, and civil war broke out.

At first it took the form of mere pressure from the North by the Federal troops which was held up pretty successfully by the Ibo army. Ojukwu turned out to be a first-class leader, of the ruthless variety, abiding no opposition. Those who opposed him he had shot. He managed to obtain considerable financial and other aid from outside sources with promises of oil grants if he won. He realised early on the great power of propaganda in the modern world and obtained the services of a well-known advertising firm with head-quarters in Switzerland at an initial fee of what was said to have been more than two million pounds. These advertising people were real professionals and before long they succeeded in making the Biafran cause into a world tragedy. The cry went up all over the world that genocide of the Biafrans must be prevented.

However Ojukwu was in no position to sustain a long campaign. He had lots of able officers but very few trained private soldiers. So now he and his friends concocted a most daring plan to hold off the Northerners while organising a flying column and making a dash to capture Lagos and cut off the North from the sea.

They collected about two thousand men in a flying column, got them across the mile-wide Niger by the new bridge at Onitsha, raced to Benin, capital of the Mid-West State, and pressed on into the forest area in the Western Region. But it was a forlorn attempt. To reach Lagos they would have to pass along a road through a thick forest intersected by creeks for several hundred miles, leaving their right flank open all the time to attack from the North, which was likely to happen if they were held up by a road block, such as a blown bridge. This was exactly what happened in the end. When they got stuck at Ori in the forest, Colonel Mohammed, leading a Northern brigade of hard fighting men, came in on their right flank and rolled it up. All Ojukwu could do was retreat as fast as he could for hundreds of miles, through the Mid-West and back across the Niger where Ibos were fortunate enough to check the Federal Army who rashly tried to cross the barrier of the great river without enough preparation.

Driven back into their heart-land the Ibos could now only try and endure a prolonged siege. This they did gallantly for more than a year while the Federal forces gradually closed in from all sides. The whole thing could have ended quite quickly if it had not been for the foreign aid founded on oil hopes and false propaganda. Food and ammunition were poured in nightly by foreign mercenaries.

In the end, however, their best air-strip came under artillery fire and the Mid-Western commander of the Ibo forces saw the red light and insisted that Ojukwu and one or two other Ibo leaders take themselves off in an aeroplane he placed at their disposal.

Gowon now really came into his own. He called for no reprisals, no trials of war criminals, no revenge.

During these years whenever I visited Lagos I used to go in and see Gowon who seemed to find in me a person he could talk to. He often told me things about the war which were not generally known. For instance once I asked him why the civil war was dragging on so long. He said that if he ordered an all-out offensive by the Nigerian forces through the thick forest in which the fighting was taking place the Ibos would shoot from the rear from behind trees. They would probably not be in uniform and the Nigerian soldiers might get wild and kill all before them. He wanted to avoid unnecessary savagery so that the wounds of the civil war could be healed when it was over.

CHAPTER 21

INTERLUDE IN ISRAEL

Amongst our other diplomatic friends was Dr Chelouche, the Israeli Ambassador. He arranged that on one of our journeys we should visit Israel and contacted his government so that our old Belsen companions who had managed to reach the country should be informed of our proposed visit.

As we walked towards the usual airport reception room at Lod we saw people waving. Suddenly we were surrounded. First came Chava and Mariana, then a representative of the Belsen committee. There stood Hermina, enormous in billowing pink silk, and twenty-five other ex-Belsenites. An old rabbi took our hands in his. They kissed us, the tears running down their faces. We cried too. It was like coming home after a long, long journey. We were suddenly transported from the ordinary world of cares and worries into a realm of loving kindness.

We spent the evening with Mariana and her mother. Mariana was now happily married and was a beautiful young woman with golden hair and big eyes shining with happy affection.

Later we visited Hermina and her husband whom we had met last in Košiče in Slovakia. His appearance was changed so that it was hard to recognise him. In the old days his entire dentures were crowned with gold. It is a mystery how he had escaped the gold-hungry Nazis who had extracted that precious metal from every Jewish mouth they spotted. Now the gold was gone, replaced by clean white dentures.

They lived in a poor but spotless house and presented us to a splendid young son and a daughter of fifteen. Hermina looked fifteen stone. She now was dressed in green silk and wore a hat. Her face was a full moon, all smiles, if a little plethoric. On leaving they bade us God's speed very sweetly, the handsome young son bending and kissing my hand as a touching gesture of thanks for helping in their deliverance.

Next day we set out for Jerusalem along the road which gradually rises two thousand feet, through the smiling land of Israel. Everywhere were crops, vines or planted forests. It was said that to settle a family in Israel then cost about twenty thousand pounds. The organisation was stupendous, perhaps the most interesting method being the Kibbutz community cooperatives, and village settlements.

Back home to their historic land had come the Jews from all over the world, from the remnants of Hitler's Europe, from Japan, U.S.A., Russia. Perhaps the Yemenites were the easiest to settle being the only Jews who had maintained their agricultural tradition and not become urbanised.

The people had arrived in every imaginable way, at first evading the British blockade and slipping in often quite destitute. In most of the countries from which they had come they had been disliked. In many they had been persecuted, chiefly because they insisted upon remaining themselves with their own traditions and religious belief, and hence were unassimilable into the various cultures in which they lived. In many countries they were not allowed to own land and therefore had to become traders. And as they were more quick-witted than the average they tended to become rich and then money-lenders. To 'Jew' in England had come to mean to take in somebody for your personal gain. They were regarded in most countries as undesirable citizens so that apart from the mad Hitlerites most people looked at them askance. Only when one got over this prejudice and actually entered their homes, as we had done now, did one realise that they are in fact among the most intelligent, warm-hearted and truly upright people in the world.

Here in Israel we now found a new people, no longer Jews as we had known them, but people with a real soil of their own, no longer semi-nationals, or outcasts in other people's lands. At the King's Hotel in Jerusalem this was very obvious, particularly with visiting American Jews who seemed unsure and over-compensated, not very polite, rather arrogant and rich beside the fine, straight, upstanding young Israeli waiters.

Old Jerusalem at that time was mostly held by the Arabs except for the David's Tomb area. Beyond the valley of Gehennah was a kind of no man's land, containing a dogs' hospital, and then the British Consulate and a Scottish church containing The Bruce's heart. Outside the Old City the Israelis had built a splendid modern city including the great Hadassah Hospital in the centre of which is a perfect place of worship, a little synagogue with twelve stained-glass windows designed by Chagall to represent the twelve tribes of Israel. These windows are so arresting and the emotion in the mind which they engender so intense that they defy objective description. For us everything else in Jerusalem was overshadowed by the reception we were given by Yad Vashem (Association of Survivors of Concentration Camps) in their Memorial Hall. They first showed us the huge photographs of the concentration camps—suddenly we were back in the horrors again. Here was a life-size photograph of Jewish school-children in a crocodile trooping into a gas-chamber. Among them a little boy with one sock up and one down his legs, another in a sailor-suit. Or that of a German SS guard pointing a sub-machine-gun at a little Jewish boy. We saw these and others before they took us into the Hall of the Flame. It is made of rough granite stone. The roof is low. On the flat floor of white marble are inlaid black slabs bearing the names of those who were murdered in Belsen, Auschwitz and all the other camps and nothing else except the Eternal Flame itself.

Now into the gallery around poured the concentration-camp survivors, a thousand of them. My name was called and I walked out and stood beside the flame. Next to be called was Han. Then our beloved children: Mariana, Chava, Hella, and the others and, of course, Hermina. We stood in silence. An old rabbi who himself had been in Belsen prayed and the Kantor sang a prayer which rose and filled the air around us. As the old Hebrew words rose up we felt the presence of the six million murdered Jews who had died in the camps. It was terrible, beautiful, heart-breaking. Eternity stood before and behind us.

Then they took us to another hall where the president of Yad Vashem spoke. He had read both our books on Belsen and quoted the passage where we had said that the children's hospital in the centre of Belsen by June 1945 had become a place of shining happiness. He presented us with a beautiful modern Menorah (candlestick) inscribed in Hebrew. Then the representative of the Belsen men gave me a beautifully wrought little gold medal and thanked us gently for helping to save the remnant of the children of Israel. They called on me to speak. I was almost too moved.

While in Israel we travelled throughout the country. In Jerusalem the most impressive human representation of the Eternal God is not the Church of the Holy Sepulchre or any Jewish synagogues but the great Mosque of Omar. In the seventh century Omar, having defeated the Crusaders, came galloping down to Jerusalem. The Patriarch of the Orthodox Church came out and knelt down before him expecting to be decapitated. 'Rise,' said Omar, 'you are more holy than I. And please show me round the sacred city.' The Patriarch showed him round. When they came to the Church of the Holy Sepulchre Omar said, 'I will not enter here lest my followers make this church into a mosque. Where else can I build a mosque?'

'What about the site of the old Jewish Temple?' said the Patriarch. 'We have never liked to use it since Jesus said "I'll destroy this temple in three days!"'

'Very good,' said Omar and he sent for his best architects from India who came and first made a little model which stands there to this day and then commenced to build the great Mosque which took one hundred and fifty years to complete with its great dome, three hundred and fifty feet high covered with shining gold leaf. Inside the Mosque there is nothing except a great carpet and the Rock of the Covenant. The building represents in stone the desert peoples' feeling for the Eternal God without 'graven images' or other human interpretations to lessen its majesty.

The most moving place, perhaps, in all Jerusalem is the Garden of Gethsemane. There the old olive-trees still stand, said to have been there when Jesus spent his last long agonising night under them before he went out to die in the greatest pain a human body can endure so that mercy and forgiveness might come into the world. Nothing I have ever seen anywhere has felt so tragic as those olive-trees.

Later we stood in the field where Jesus had preached the Sermon on the Mount overlooking the Sea of Galilee above Capernaum. The sun shone from a cloudless sky. The lake was bright blue. The pink distant mountains formed a frame. We stood alone surrounded by perfect beauty and realised that it was right that the Eternal God had sent his Messenger, his most beloved Son, to proclaim there by the lake that 'love is the key which alone unlocks all doors and to command us therefore to love one another'.

Later that day we drove to Tel Aviv once more. After supper we were sitting in a hotel lounge. Suddenly I felt someone behind me and turned round. There stood a woman with a man and two children. I recognised her, the girl I had left fifteen years before at a Pilsen hospital, I thought to die.

'Ludmilla,' I cried.

'Doctor,' she answered, running across the room and throwing her arms round me and bursting into tears.

When we had to leave a complication arose due to our air tickets as we had to get into an Arab country. The Iron Curtain is nothing to the barrier between Israel and the Arab States. However, I found a young Alexander in Jerusalem as the British Consul-General.

Like all the Alexanders, including, of course, the Field Marshal whom I knew of old as Colonel of the Irish Guards in World War I, he could do anything. He was accustomed, in those days, to drive from one side of Jerusalem to the other each day. On these journeys his pockets were full of notes to people on the other side—young men's girls, and so on.

'Oh, I'll arrange it,' he said, 'if you don't mind joining the Church of England for the day! I hope your wife doesn't belong to one of those queer, determined Dutch sects and will not object.'

'Oh, not at all,' I said.

So we got across into the Jordan side of Jerusalem where we immediately contacted Dr Majaj, one of the world's greatest paediatricians. He was also Minister of Health and knew everybody. He took us to the children's hospital in the Arab city of Jerusalem which had been built by the Kaiser who, if you remember, had had part of the old city wall knocked down so that he could ride in. In remembrance of this great German event he had built them a children's hospital in which he had included a chapel and a memorial of himself and the Kaiserin, life-size bronze statues, dressed as Crusaders in armour. However, the saving grace of German *Kultur* is always their inimitable music and true to tradition they had placed in the chapel a beautiful organ at which Dr Majaj now sat down and began to play. As the waves of Bach filled the air around us I was transported almost out of my body standing there listening to a Christian Arab physician playing here in the Moslem part of Jewish Jerusalem.

CHAPTER 22

THE NORTH

My promise to help Audu to form a Northern medical school and our subsequent move to Kaduna, the capital of the Northern Region, came at as difficult a moment as it is possible to imagine. We were on leave in Europe when the second Ibo massacre took place. When we returned, though civil war had not actually broken out, we found ourselves in a very troubled world. Uncertainty was in the air and it was difficult to get people to concentrate their thoughts on ordinary matters, such as health.

In Kaduna, the capital of the North, the Sardauna's ministers had been Moslems. As orthodox upper-class Moslems they were expected socially and religiously to have four wives at a time and therefore the ministers' houses were built with special wives' quarters. These were separated by almost fifty yards from the main house but connected to it by a long covered passage. The main house consisted of two storeys, chiefly large rooms and balconies. On arrival in Kaduna we were allocated one of these ministerial houses.

Audu asked me to start off at the new government hospital in Kaduna which had been built on pavilion lines, each department having its own block. He himself at Zaria had about the most difficult job that a comparatively young man could take on. As Vice-Chancellor he followed a professional professor of the English don class. The staff of the University were mostly expatriates from different outside countries who didn't easily get on with each other, and to find a teaching staff for the new medical school was a herculean task.

However, while at Kaduna, I had a most interesting medical experience. The staff of the hospital were completely international. The senior physician was a very good Egyptian doctor who understood people, the leading surgeon a brilliant Indian. The obstetrical department were a very interesting trio. There was an eccentric

216

English gynaecologist who had been some ten years or more at Ibadan and knew her African young women. She was an outstanding person in her speciality if perhaps a little eccentric about her creature pets. When she came to stay with us for a weekend she arrived with half a dozen black Abyssinian hissing geese in the back of her car. two cats, several parrots and Charlie the dog with one ear up and one ear down. She had left her baby lion behind.

In the same department there was a charming Irish sister-doctor and a good Yoruba male gynaecologist. Perhaps most notable of all the departments was that of 'Eyes'. The Unit had been presented by Guinness and was the best in West Africa. It was run by a splendid bearded and turbaned, young, Sikh ophthalmologist. There was a Facio-Maxillary Unit, including an excellent dental section, run by a remarkable Iraqi doctor, which developed into a first-class department for treating facial wounds during the civil war. Psychiatry was situated in the dilapidated old Government hospital and managed by a Yoruba doctor of wisdom. Among his other duties he had the unpleasant job of sorting the real murderers from the homicidal maniacs. The difference between manslaughter and murder is often very hard to decide among peasantries anywhere in the world, but almost impossible in Nigeria. Hence every psychiatric unit and prison was full of men who had killed somebody but to whom the epithet murderer would have been a misnomer. On one horrible Saturday morning a Pakistani doctor who was in charge of the prison came into my room in a state of jitters. He had just attended six hangings. When I complained later to the prison governor that this seemed excessive he said it was not his fault. He had been keeping all those men alive for years by helping them to appeal but at last he had been ordered by some civil servant in the Department of Justice 'to get on with it'. 'But,' he said, 'I don't know what you doctors are complaining about, it all went off very well.'

They made me Chairman of the Medical Board of the hospital and I was able to get a group of newly qualified young Nigerian doctors to come up from Ibadan and Lagos and man most of the departments as housemen. Every week we had a clinical meeting to which the whole medical staff came. These meetings were amongst the most interesting clinical demonstrations I have ever presided at. Usually such affairs are confined to one's own speciality but here we had a complete mixture from every discipline, and with the unique clinical picture of disease in this sub-Saharan world one learned something new at every meeting.

My paediatric department consisted of a separate block in the hospital and an enormous daily out-patient clinic of some hundred sick children a day. The wards were supervised by a beautiful Fulani sister who had the bearing of a princess. It was the custom to admit all the mothers to the wards with their children. In consequence things sometimes got very untidy and the mothers not uncommonly got into bed and put the baby on the floor beside them. But one word from our sister and things would instantly improve. They would obey her command immediately for this was a world where everybody knew their place. There was none of your modern 'I'm better than you' attitude in this old Moslem sub-Saharan ancient world which, if largely medieval, had an old-world charm provided you yourself had the necessary manners.

One day I found three children with two mothers, wives of the same Moslem husband, admitted to the unit with cerebro-spinal meningitis, a condition which in northern Nigeria sometimes assumes epidemic proportions. The history was that two other children in the family had already died from the same condition the previous week. When the three children had recovered after modern treatment and the father had turned up, I suggested to my Nigerian houseman that we should try and find out how the infection had started. So on the children's discharge they all got into my car. We proceeded by road for an hour in a north-westerly direction and then for another hour on foot into the bush. Finally we began to smell cattle and came to the father's camp with its herd of a hundred hump-backed cattle. He also had a flock of sheep, some donkeys and a horse which he showed us with some pride. He was particularly delighted to exhibit his gun.

I failed to gain any clear epidemiological data and so after a number of very polite visits including one to his sleeping quarters where he explained he put his wives in the tents at night but slept outside himself with his cloak about him and the gun at his side, I said I would like to see the children again soon. Well, he said, not very soon as he was due to start for home when the moon came out in a day or so. 'Where's home?' I asked. 'Sokoto,' he said, pointing to the north.

When the moon came out he was planning to walk home to Sokoto, some two hundred miles away. He was going to bring with him over a hundred head of cattle, a flock of sheep, some goats, three donkeys and a horse, not to speak of his wives and children. He would not drive the flock, rather he would walk in front, letting out a cry every few hundred yards. He knew the way. He knew where grass was to be found, he knew the water-holes. They would all follow—the horse, the cattle, the sheep, the goats, the donkeys and the wives and children. He was a patriarch straight out of the Old

Testament. He walked back with us to the road, there he made an obeisance, touching his head on the ground, and presented me with five pounds of Fulani butter. A year later, almost to the day, he turned up again with his youngest son who still had a limp. He had walked home to Sokoto and back.

*   *   *

Life in Northern Nigeria below the Sahara Desert, as we saw it coming from the forest lands along the West Coast of Africa, was like entering a completely different culture, an old civilisation of great manners and traditions, of princes and peasants in the old-fashioned sense, where the upper class were aristocrats and the poor near serfs only just removed from actual slavery. It was a man's world.

Being a horseman was the best introduction I could have had into this world where the most appreciated gift of the British Raj to the Fulani princes had been that of polo. Up here were half a dozen famous polo clubs patronised not merely by expatriates as in the south, but by the Northerners themselves, particularly the Fulani.

Unfortunately I had brought up with me from Kaduna one of my Lagos polo horses, named Owen Glendower by his recent Welsh owner. While I was on leave he had acquired an infected eye which had been treated wrongly so that he was blind to all intents and purposes in that eye when I got back. Horses' eyes, being set on the outside of their pointed heads, each keep control of a visual field and if one eye is lost the horse is blind on that side. I knew that ponies blind in one eye were not allowed to play in polo matches but I did not think it would matter in ordinary games. However when I was being 'ridden off' by a fierce young Northerner, Glendower went down with a crash. I landed on my polo helmet but was completely stunned, knocked unconscious. They took me to the hospital where Han found me rambling some hours later. The only effect the accident had on me was a complete loss of memory of the incident or the following two or three weeks afterwards, of which, although I recovered enough to fly to Boston and read a paper, I can now remember nothing.

Those years we spent at Kaduna were amongst the most interesting from the world-citizen point of view. All my life I have heard Englishmen deprecating Irishmen and Irishmen Englishmen, and not uncommonly unkind remarks about Jews, Egyptians or Portuguese, whom the brisker Nordics tend to despise. Here we were now in the middle of Africa with a complete mixture of nationalities sharing the vocation of doctoring. We found we could work together, like each other, even be close friends. Outside the medical group the polo-horse world with its hard-riding Northern gentlemen was also one in which I was able to feel happily at home.

*　　　*　　　*

After a year I had to move from Kaduna to Zaria to help get the University medical school going at the Centre. The medical work in Zaria, after Kaduna, from my point of view, was not very satisfactory. I was made Clinical Dean of the Medical School but at this stage it meant little as clinical teaching had not yet commenced. However, Han now found herself a Lecturer in the University Department of Social Medicine, with the fascinating if very strange job of also being medical adviser to the Old City of Zaria.

The walled city of Zaria is built of laterite, baked reddish mud, with narrow streets between the houses. In the centre the Emir's palace stands facing a rectangular open space. It is also constructed of laterite but with great skill and artistry, its halls having beautifully arched tall ceilings which give dignity to the cool spaces below. The whole town is completely enclosed by a laterite rambling rampart about thirty feet high through which had been constructed a number of splendid gateways.

It is run on feudal lines by the Emir and his staff like a medieval city state. From the modern health point of view the conditions are utterly unhygienic. There is no proper drainage or sewage system. There are a number of water hydrants but no piped water to the houses so that every form of enteric infection is rife. Worst of all are the numerous pits from which the laterite has been dug out. These are filled up in the rainy seasons with water, and are used by the boys as bathing pools. They are all infested by the snails which carry the bilharzia parasites so that this infection is almost universal among the young males most of whom appear to harbour the parasites in their bladders. By puberty the boys are said to have 'periods' like females (blood in their urine).

In the centre of the city was a dispensary and health centre run by a Health Assistant, a sort of male field-nurse. He was a Moslem, had four wives at a time, and had already produced fifty-two live children among whom were six pairs of twins. He was usually too worn out in the daytime to be much use and was often to be found asleep on the dispensary floor. To keep his family going he became involved in a number of doubtful transactions. When eventually sacked by the town secretary and sent to an outlying village it took two buses to transport him and his offspring.

Han had to sort out the sick here every morning, after which she would take the bad cases to me in the hospital clinic. One morning on arriving at the clinic she found the usual large crowd of patients waiting around under the mango-trees. In their midst she saw a tall, oldish man dressed in a flowing white regal garment pouring water from a cup into the mouth of a baby with a sunken face. A woman was sitting beside him holding another emaciated child. Han came forward to remonstrate lest the man choke the baby. As she approached he turned towards her and she saw a fine, triangular, bearded face in which the eyes were opaque. He was blind, as was his wife. As soon as possible Han set out for the hospital with them and their small guide Saibu, aged five, carrying a long thin stick, a kettle and an umbrella. Arrived at the hospital they got out of the car with difficulty, striking their heads against the top of the back door and upsetting their kettle of water. Now they lined up in the strangest of processions. First Han came holding Saibu by the hand whose other hand was holding the end of the blind man's long stick which was grasped first by the tall father who was also holding his son high up in his left arm. Behind them came the woman, with the other child on her back, also grasping the stick. The hospital compound was large and it was a very long way to the children's department which meant traversing sunken drains, tree roots and up and down steps over the broken ground. The blind couple followed their small guide with difficulty tripping, half falling over the obstacles and getting their long garments caught, their blank blind eyes turned upwards unseeing. The whole scene was like Breughel's sixteenth-century painting of 'The blind leading the blind'.

Zaria was our last home in Africa. We had a charming house built in Moorish style round a courtyard in which was a fountain surrounded by flowering shrubs and overhung with a 'golden shower' creeper. I was due to retire but until the civil war ended this was impossible. But there in this almost forgotten world we felt at home with Emir and servant alike.

CHAPTER 23

SEAN

Sean was now fourteen, a very promising boy at his Quaker school in Waterford. Han and I spent our summer vacations at Bo-Island with him or in Holland. When he was with us life seemed brighter. His smile would lighten up the day for us.

With Han he played Scrabble, patience, and Mah Jong, would read or chat with her. With me he was a perfect boyish companion, particularly on horseback in Nigeria, Ireland or in the wooded country round Arnhem in Holland.

He came out to us in Zaria for Christmas 1968. He was particularly gracious in his Sean-ish way that Christmas. He turned our court-yard into a Christmas garden, placing a crèche under the papyrus, candles on the shrubs, coloured glass containers with more candles on the rocks. When all were lit up before dawn on Christmas day and again at seven as the tropical night started, the little garden, with its fountain giving out myriad shooting stars, looked like a dream out of the Arabian Nights.

I remember that Christmas he was given an encyclopaedia and a dictionary to help with his O-levels next term, and he and I together gave Han a silver Hausa brooch.

By now he had become a horseman in the tradition of the family. We used to ride across country from the University outside Zaria to the great rock of Rufena which Queen Amina in the old days had made into a fortress. To this day on an overhanging ledge some hundreds of feet up you can see the oval holes cut in the granite rock where the guards used to sit and play the game of Eyo while keeping watch over the plateau for miles around. A rampart still runs round the foot of the rock so that it was easy to imagine the fortress in the old days when it would turn back the savage raiders as they came up on their little stallions. To reach the rock we had to cross a river whose bed was of treacherous sand, proceed across rough savannah with here and there cultivated fields of cotton, ground-nuts or tall millet, then slither down the side of a gulley, cross a shallow pool and pass up the opposite side. Our little horses were strong and used to such terrain and would clamber up the steep slopes like goats. Occasionally we would pass through a hamlet where the people would come out smiling and bow to us in welcome and we would smile and bow back.

The polo club at Zaria got up a gymkhana, British fashion. Sean won three rosettes. Glendower, my last little stallion, had never jumped till then but picked up the idea three days before the event. But above all of the memories of Sean on horseback is that of the Sallah at Katsina when the Emir invited him to ride with his young princes in the famous procession when more than two hundred horsemen take part in that great Moslem ceremony.

For one month each year the orthodox Moslems neither eat nor drink from dawn to sundown. The very orthodox endeavour not even to swallow their own saliva. The period is a lunar and the next month cannot start until the new moon is seen by one of the faithful. The month is different every year and the seeing of the moon somewhat variable. The end of the period of fasting is celebrated by a tremendous festival, both religious and secular, the 'Sallah'.

In Nigeria it varies considerably from place to place. The first part of the ceremony, however, is everywhere an open-air gathering where all the men prostrate themselves before Allah.

Katsina is the most northerly town of importance in Nigeria being but a few miles from the border of French-speaking Niger which itself gradually relapses into the desert which divides it from the Mediterranean by twelve hundred miles of sand.

The province of Katsina, or better the Emirate, is an area of about seven thousand square miles and holds about one and a half million people.

The Emir of Katsina is a prince. In some way he manages to be both a modern leader of his people and prince in the old-world sense. He represents something in the subconsciousness of the people which combines a respect for the past and a feeling for the future, called progress, so that when he proceeds through the town everybody bows and makes the spear salute and smiles up at him in gladness.

On the first day of the Sallah, the Emir, on a white stallion, followed by his guards, local chiefs, village heads, and thousands of males rides out to the Prayer grounds in the early morning, where he prostrates himself and all bow down before the Infinite God. He then rides back through one of the old gates in the ramparts of Katsina to the square in front of his palace in the middle of the old town (one hundred by three hundred yards). He now takes up his position surrounded by his personal guards dressed in chain armour on black stallions. On one side is a troop of turbaned lancers in red tunics, on the other the young Katsina princes on white stallions, and behind stands a band of kettle drummers on camels. A durbar now takes place, each chief or village head, gorgeously attired in flowing robes of white, green, scarlet or blue, with his mounted guards, galloping across the square and drawing up his horse on its haunches in front of the Emir while giving the clenched-fist spear salute, with a yell. The Emir, himself dressed in white and black robes embroidered with gold, sits motionless on his milk-white stallion while a crimson embroidered umbrella of immense size is held over his head by one attendant, and two others fan him with colourful plumed fans. Occasionally he raises his sword in a special greeting to a chief he wants to honour or a member of the family who has pulled up before him.

On the second day of the Sallah, all the horsemen, the Emir himself, the bodyguard, the lancers, the chiefs and village heads and the princes together with the footmen (the bowmen, the gunners, the dancers) ride in procession in the opposite direction out of the town to the Residency to show respect for the Government. In the old days it was the British Resident, now it is the Nigerian Provincial Secretary. The route is lined by all the townspeople—men, women and children. There are few visitors and no tourists. The Sallah at Katsina is still the real thing carried out by the people and led by their Prince as an integral part of their lives.

At this time Han and I held a very personal position with the Katsina family. Both being doctors, we had looked after many of their children of all ages. Han's diagnosis of a complaint which had ruined the health of one of the Emir's wives for ten years and her subsequent successful treatment and cure had given us a very particular position at Katsina so that we often visited there. This usually meant for me playing polo as well as both of us doctoring the family. My last game of polo in Nigeria was played with the Emir's grandsons against his sons. It was natural, therefore, that when the Sallah fell during the Christmas holidays in 1968 we should bring Sean, now fourteen, along with us and that I should present him to the Emir. On presentation, the Emir put his hand on Sean's head and said he must ride with the princes in the Sallah procession.

At seven on the morning of the ride out of town to the Residency, I brought Sean to the palace. Here preparations and bustle were in full swing. In one courtyard the archers were donning their red smocks, in another the gunners were gathering, in a third the Emir's nine personal stallions were being dressed in every sort of horse accoutrement including inlaid silver trappings.

A young prince came forward and took Sean off and dressed him in a scarlet tunic with golden epaulets, wide, white belt, long, light-blue tight trousers, and a 'Clive's style' white Indian turban over a gold cloth cap. The princes' horses were all white stallions with manes plaited with red ribbons and tails bound in red. Their saddle cloths were black and gold.

I slipped out of the palace and went and picked up Han. Together we stood at a point where we could view the procession as it proceeded towards the Residency outside the town. It was a splendid spectacle: the lancers, the Emir, his guards, the nine milk-white stallions, each held by a colourfully attired groom, the bands (fife, drum, pipers in yellow coats and red kilts playing Celtic airs, the camel kettle drummers, the long trumpeters), the gorgeous chiefs and their followers.

One moment held us spellbound. In front of the Emir rode the nine princes, all boys, in their scarlet tunics and white turbans. And there in their midst, the middle of the front row of five, rode Sean, his pale Friesian complexion slightly touched by the sun, shining in splendid contrast to the handsome dark faces around. He was riding his white stallion well. His back was very straight. He held the reins with his left hand and carried a switch in his right, perfectly controlling his horse which now and then swung an arched neck to try and nip those on each side of him. He was riding like a prince among princes of the Sub-Saharan savannah world. He neither looked to the right nor to the left. His chin was not arrogantly high or uncertainly low but straight and steady. His bearing was neither superior nor inferior. His fair pale complexion in some way heightened the beauty of the scene around so that the spectators gasped in wonder at the spectacle before them, enquiring who he might be.

It seemed right that the only white person in the whole of that vast procession that day should be an Irish boy who was quite unaware that he was performing a part of any great significance in the second half of the twentieth century, though his bearing suggested that subconsciously he knew he was carrying on his shoulders some of the tensions and troubles of the world.

On January 8th, 1969, the Christmas holidays were over and Sean had to fly back to school. We drove him to Kano across the then quite dry and crackling northern savannah. His presence lightened the journey for us as it always did. He had only to be in the room with us for any feeling of ennui which might be besetting us to evaporate. As we approached the airport, however, the parting came closely into our conscious minds more forcibly than ever before and when he walked out on the tarmac to the plane and then turned on the aeroplane steps and waved back to us I found my eyes were full of tears. Han hid her face in her hands and would not look up till the plane had taken off and then could only glance at its disappearing form, as the haze swallowed it up.

We drove back to Zaria and continued our work of building up the new Northern Nigeria Medical School during my last year before retiring.

*   *   *

Suddenly, on April 9th, I found Eldred Parry, our charming and brilliant Welsh Professor of Medicine, standing at the door of our house. He had a look on his face I could not understand. He said: 'Colonel Robertson wants to speak with you. He has a message.'

Colonel Robertson had been House Governor to the new great hospital at Ibadan and was now in Zaria as general secretary for the new medical school. He was one of those Englishmen whom I once described in *The Silver Fleece* as 'the gentlemen of England, the envy of the world'. He died shortly afterwards.

Now I saw him walking up and down in obvious distress outside the house.

He came up to me.

'What is it?' I asked.

'Your son, Sean, has had an accident.'

'Is he dead?'

'Yes,' he said.

I found myself in the house beside Han, who was resting. She saw my face.

'Is it Sean?' she asked.

'Yes,' I said, 'he is gone.' 'Gone' was the word then and afterwards—not dead.

We flew back to Ireland. How we did so is still quite obscure. All plane tickets both to London and from London to Dublin were booked out but at the last moment we were on both occasions put on the plane.

We arrived in Dublin much spent after our three thousand mile rush. At Dublin Airport all had been arranged by Oliver Hone, my sister's son, who was traffic manager at the airport. And on the tarmac stood Zoltan. He had managed everything. He had taken Sean's body from Waterford himself, had arranged that he should be buried up on Calary in our little, beautiful churchyard surrounded by our smiling, purple mountains. Now Zoltan stood waiting for us with love in his eyes. He took Han's arm with gentle affection like the elder son should on such an occasion, and she was comforted. We were brought through the customs area and taken out to Professor Thompson's house outside Dublin. He had been in Lagos with us.

Next morning still numb, we got up and looked out at a grey sea under grey clouds. We set out for Calary in the Wicklow mountains. We had to meet the coffin at Bray below.

They led me into the room where he was in his little oaken coffin. There he lay with the most beautiful smile upon his lips, simply as if asleep. As I gazed upon the beauty of his beloved face something happened to me which I cannot even now put well into words. I had a moment of revelation which time has not dimmed. From the first moment when he lay unbreathing in my arms till now when he had gone equally mysteriously back from whence he had come I had never said a hard word to him or even indeed been angry with him in my heart, and he had been the very meaning of Han's life.

For a moment I stood and gazed at him while my whole life swayed around me. Then I ran and fetched Han from the car. She came and stood silently looking at his smiling face, holding my hand.

'When I was but thirteen or so / I went into a golden land.'

As we walked again to the car the grey sky lifted and the sun came out.

As we passed out of the Rocky Valley to go up the long hill to Calary a complete rainbow shone out touching both sides of the valley. It moved with us up the hill and across the plateau so that it stood over the church while the beautiful burial service was read, and remained until we had lowered Sean into his grave when it, too, seemed to sink slowly into the earth around us.

My brother Jack knew Sean from his first days and now wrote: 'He seemed to me a star. The light shone and went away. The time it was here is immaterial. The life was complete.'

All fear of death has now left us and our hope is simply that some-how, somewhere, inside or outside Time and Space we may meet Sean again and unravel the mystery of love. So above his mountain grave I've made a little garden of daffodils and primroses and placed a rough granite stone with his name on it and the words which he had quoted to Han: 'The greatest of these is love.'

CHAPTER 24

THE RETURN

We flew back to Nigeria and during the next eighteen months we wound up our work there and handed over our departments in the university and medical worlds.

The strain was almost too much for Han but in some strange transcendental way Sean's smile and his rainbow have remained with us ever since so that when we say the Lord's Prayer together every night as we used to do with him we see them again and sometimes it seems as if he is still conscious of our love.

The civil war was over when at last we had to leave Nigeria where we both had laboured and had loved the people so well. I met Zik again for a brief moment and though somewhat discredited in most Nigerian eyes he still retained his charm and I bid him farewell sadly. With Awolowo I spent a last hour. He talked with candour about his people, the Yorubas, and his hopes for the future. General Gowon received Han and me at his headquarters in Ikoiyi in Lagos. He had been recently married and he introduced us to his young wife. He said he wished he could go back to being just a soldier and hoped that it would be possible to introduce a reasonable form of democracy again soon. I do not know what I said in reply as it is exceedingly difficult to think of any form of government being a success in a country where the majority of the people, the voters, cannot read. It is certainly easier to run a country authoritatively if the Head of State is a person like Gowon, without personal animus, but even benign men such as the self-effacing professor-dictator Salazar of Portugal in the end grow too old and the State begins to run aground under his steersmanship.

As I write Gowon has just been received in London by Queen Elizabeth, the Royal Family and the Prime Minister with the full pageantry of England. In the photograph of him sitting beside the

228

Queen driving to Buckingham Palace he looks the most charming of national leaders today. It is a joy to remember that not so long ago he was a clever boy going to school at Zaria, from a small hill tribe away up in the Nigerian mountains. He bid us farewell with open friendliness and thanked us simply for having helped his people.

Before I left I was given a final lunch by Majekodunmi in his house in Lagos. He had invited many of my Nigerian friends and he said goodbye with warmth and charm. The Nigerians have since remembered that I served them as a physician and have given me an Honorary Doctorate of Science at Ahmadu Bello University.

*   *   *

Back in Ireland Han and I have remodelled the house at Bo-Island. She has now made it into a place of great beauty. Opening windows through the old farm walls has lightened up the interior and at the same time given us incomparable views of the Wicklow mountains seen through the trees standing up on the *rath* behind the house.

On returning to Ireland, to my surprise, I have been welcomed home in the most unexpected ways. On one occasion when I was crossing the road by O'Connell's Street Bridge, I had avoided one bus and was just about to sidestep another when the bus driver pulled up with a screech of brakes. I looked up apprehensively expecting the usual busman's forceful comments. But instead he leaned out of his seat, and stretched out his hand. 'Dr Collis,' he said, 'welcome home, you remember me. I was little Charlie in the Children's Hospital, you remember, with rheumatic fever.' I clasped his hand. His features stirred a memory in my subconscious, of a boy with curly black hair and monkey eyes whom we had cured in the Harcourt Street Children's Hospital twenty years before.

I have been asked to act as examiner in the medical finals in both Dublin University (Trinity College) and the National University (University College, Dublin) and have been made consultant to the National Association of Cerebral Palsy and asked to reorganise their service and make a national plan for the physically handicapped all over the Republic from Cork to Donegal, as well as in the big Dublin area with its eight hundred thousand population. It is now realised after World War II that the only logical answer to the Nazis' doctrine of the survival of the fittest, implying the elimination (murder) of the handicapped, is for society to support them in such a way as to give each handicapped child or adult the greatest fulfilment possible during his sojourn in our world.

Niall being a handicapped child himself has made it possible for both Han and me to understand very well the family problems produced by the appearance of a mentally or physically handicapped (or both) child in a family. It is hardest of all for the parents of the autistics to cope with their children who cut themselves off from all communication with those about them and live entirely inside themselves. How to help such parents by providing homes or at least day centres where they can be managed for most of the time is one of our most urgent problems. It is not too difficult in big centres of population but it may be extremely difficult to help families in the remote areas of the southern and western seaboard of Ireland.

In the case of Niall we have been particularly fortunate. I was asked to visit the Glencraig (Camphill) Settlement for the handicapped at Holywood near Belfast. I found their approach the best I had seen in Ireland, Great Britain or on the Continent. To begin with the staff all appear to have a vocation of service and an extraordinary aura of loving kindness. Secondly their method of having a mixed group of children of different ages, sexes and handicaps in houses looked after by a house-mother and father, maybe married with normal children of their own, is by far the best arrangement. They took on Niall at once and he has been so happy there that he sometimes cries when he leaves his Glencraig house-mother to come back to us for holidays, though it must be said he also cries at the end of the holidays when he has to leave Han and go back to his school.

*   *   *

These journeys up and down to Northern Ireland to bring Niall backwards and forwards, have brought the present turmoil in the country very much into the forefront of our lives. Four or five times a year we have made these journeys throughout recent years when the violence has steadily mounted. I always carry a stethoscope beside me when crossing the border into Northern Ireland, as I used to do in the civil war days in Nigeria. If I am stopped by a patrol of any kind I pick up my stethoscope and say something about being a doctor and always after a minute or two my interrogators say, 'O.K., Doc' and I drive on. We have driven through boarded-up town areas recently bombed and met many patrols of soldiers. The last time we were driving back with Niall we found ourselves stuck behind an 'Orange' procession in a border town. A long file of youths with orange sashes were marching through a Catholic area. Behind were following a number of jeeps in which were seated groups of young British soldiers with sub-machine-guns in their hands. Otherwise they were quite exposed to snipers. I called to one jeep saying I was a doctor in a hurry. The young Englishman in it smiled back at me with the most candid unaffected friendliness. I remembered the kind British soldiers at Belsen in 1945 helping the despised displaced persons there. Now these were no 'Black and Tans', no imperial troops of the old British Empire, but rather ordinary English boys who had been ordered here to stop us Irishmen from killing each other. I felt ashamed.

Recently I overheard a discussion in Dublin between two intelligent Southerners, one Protestant and the other Catholic. A particularly nasty bomb outrage had occurred the previous day, a number of women and children being killed without warning. It had seemed quite senseless and utterly brutal.

'Southern Protestant': What do you think should be done to stop this senseless killing in Northern Ireland?

'Southern Catholic': It looks as if the British Army can't do it alone. Even if it defeats the I.R.A. temporarily, what about the future? One cannot contemplate a return to the status quo when the Northern so-called loyalists gerrymandered the elections and kept all the best jobs for themselves.

'Southern Protestant': Yes, but you must admit the fault was not only on their side.

'Southern Catholic': Agreed.

'Southern Protestant': What can be done now? Mr Whitelaw's reasonableness did not seem to get anywhere in this beautiful island of ours!

'Southern Catholic': I agree—I think a completely new approach is required. What is necessary is to go back to 1921 and rethink the treaty between England and Ireland. At that time, after World War I and the 'troubles' in Ireland, men's minds were too confined by events to be sufficiently free to understand the underlying causes of the differences between the two islands and the subsequent settlement was bound to lead to future unhappiness as has proved to be the case.

'Southern Protestant': I think we'd all agree to that but even suppose we manage to get a group of people on both sides to make a new start how are we to stop the extremists from continuing to kill each other, not to speak of innocent people who may be in the line of fire.

'Southern Catholic': A settlement is only possible in a peaceful atmosphere.

'Southern Protestant': But how do you produce a peaceful atmosphere?

'Southern Catholic': I see only one way. The English and the

Irish Governments must agree to settle it together. After all now that both are Europeans in the Common Market and England is no longer an Imperial Power what are the differences? Economically there is nothing dividing them and culturally and politically not much. Now surely it doesn't really matter in Ireland what flag men wave or what song they sing? They can have double nationality, British and Irish, or be British or Irish as they like. There is no border any more. What's it all about then? Surely it would be possible to compromise now?

'Southern Protestant': But what about the two to three hundred million pounds the British subsidise the six counties with yearly? The Northerners won't want to give that up—will they?

'Southern Catholic': Perhaps that is the most sticky problem as money usually is. But when all is said the British are spending a lot more at the moment, and not only not succeeding but having their boys slaughtered. Wouldn't it be much simpler for Britain to make a generous gesture even now to Ireland? After all remember the past, if only the famine. A little restitution on their part might not seem out of turn!

'Southern Protestant': All right! But all the same how do we get the boys to stop shooting? They're being paid to keep it up.

'Southern Catholic': If the extremists won't stop the only course would be complete martial law imposed not by the British Army alone but by the Irish Army as well, and perhaps a foreign Brigade, say Canadian or Swedish. Ultimately the only solution will be a compromise. The key to the whole situation is to realise that compromise on both sides is inevitable. The question is how long will it take the extremists to realise this: we desperately need to reach a compromise *now*.

This probably puts the situation as straight as it is possible to express. There are a lot of hurdles still to get over. For instance one continually hears demands for the ending of internment. It is obvious that internment without trial is a temporary measure open to many criticisms. But it has one advantage which most people don't realise. Without internment you have no alternative way of dealing with young men captured and known to be implicated in the guerrilla organisations, such as the I.R.A. and the U.D.A., or those actually involved in armed robbery, especially when somebody has been hurt or killed. These young men imagine themselves as adventurous patriots of one sort or another. If they are tried they will be sentenced as criminals to long terms of imprisonment. You destroy their lives, whereas if they are interned they can be released and many rehabilitated when the 'troubles' are over. Of course internment is very unsatisfactory, even as a temporary measure. Their guards, also young men, whose job it is to prevent them escaping and to gain as much information from them as possible, will tend to become violent, and however controlled officially, will on occasion over-step the bounds of decent behaviour.

The most dangerous development of the situation here would be if the British got fed up and just walked out. If they did, a bitter internecine conflict would break out in the North of Ireland in which a lot of people would get killed. And it would be difficult for us in the South to stand by idly and watch the U.D.A. murdering the Catholics without intervening. In which case a real Irish civil war would result with every sort of horrible bitterness, violence and killing. Having experienced just that in Nigeria, I, as a doctor dedicated to healing, hope still that all the cousin peoples in these islands can yet forget their ancient antagonisms, compose their religious and tribal differences, and become at last homo sapiens.

* * *

During the time when I was in Africa I always spent part of my annual leave in Dublin; and always one of my first joys was to visit Christy Brown whose mind seemed to grow in stature every year. Some people thought that his first book was just a flash in the pan, that his story was so good that the book had sold for that reason only. But I gradually discovered that Christy was not just a magnificent cripple breaking his bonds but an artist and a writer in his own right. I read some of the beginnings of his next book *Down All the Days*, which has now placed him among the great Irish writers of this period along with Joyce and Beckett. It has been translated into fourteen languages, the French edition alone selling some fifty thousand copies.

I have met young American writers engaged in completing Ph.D. theses on *Finnegan's Wake* but I still do not know what Joyce was trying to tell us. I am still 'Waiting for Godot' having sat out the whole Beckett play, although John Stewart, my excessively literary twin, gave up before the end. Perhaps I am too much a clarity-man and a doctor trained to make clear diagnoses to be able really to appreciate obscure writing, however good. Christy's writing is not obscure but it's *avant-garde* all right. The fact that he did not go to a good Catholic school like Joyce and therefore have to spend most of his literary life de-brainwashing himself is perhaps his great advantage. Not being conditioned into any ordinary life-form Christy is free of restraints that beset most of us whether we know it or not. His work has an extraordinary lyrical quality and the scenes and the people he describes stand out with almost terrifying clarity and truth. Never has the life of a people been more vividly portrayed than in his work except perhaps by some of the great Russian novelists. That this tremendous artistic achievement has reached the wide world is due in no small way to David Farrer, one of the most perceptive of editor-publishers, for he has contended with Christy's manuscripts and his thousands of left-footed adjectives so well that the final printed text has received the world-acclaim due to the genius of the author.

Christy has also published several books of poetry and has published a new novel, *A Shadow on Summer*, based on his visits to America, on the first of which I accompanied him on the air journey which in those days took some fourteen hours' flying time. It was not a very simple business especially in matters of hygiene during the long hours of the flight. However in some ways it was for me a little like accompanying royalty, for the staff of the Aer Lingus plane were unbelievably helpful and even the immigration officials at New York Airport who are usually notoriously brusque, were kindness itself, being all Irish Americans.

I left Christy in a house by the sea in Connecticut which looked out on Long Island Sound with some friendly admirers of his who took him in and showed him several sides of American life which he has subsequently turned to advantage in his writing. Apart from his steady literary work he has continued his painting and there have been several exhibitions of his pictures. I still like some of his earlier paintings best, however, particularly his head of Christ which seems to me to contain all the tragedy of the world.

While I was in Africa both Christy's parents died. His father was buried with full military honours as an Irish patriot in their resting place at Glasnevin, firing-party and all. Mrs Brown had no firing party. She died as she had lived with proper dignity. One day when I was in Dublin they rang me up to say she was very ill and had collapsed. I found she had acute abdominal trouble and was in considerable pain. We got her into the old Meath Hospital right away and she was operated upon for acute abdominal obstruction the same evening. But she was a very poor subject for such major surgery what with her incredible obstetrical history and her blood pressure. The operation was difficult enough and took a long time as I stood there in the big, old operating theatre built by my grandfather in the early days of modern aseptic surgery. She was hurried back to the ward as soon as possible after the operation. She rallied and seemed a little better next day and smiled her old smile again but the improvement didn't last and she began to sink slowly and a few days later she just 'took her leave'. Her body had taken enough for one lifetime, though her spirit never flagged till it left us. As we stood bare-headed by her grave, also in Glasnevin, I remembered John Bunyan's description of Christian as he came out of the River of Death: 'And all the trumpets sounded for him on the other side.'

After his mother's death Christy was looked after by his younger sister Ann who had always seemed to me almost a second version of her mother whose twenty-first pregnancy she was. She has a house on the outskirts of Dublin where to begin with she looked after Christy and her own family—charming young husband Willie and three sons. With his new money Christy built himself a house in the garden of Ann's house and joined the two by a covered passageway which he has planned to make into a picture gallery.

Suddenly, recently, he got married to Mary. Marrying a cripple is never easy and where the cripple is a genius to boot it must be more difficult still. There could be stormy times ahead, for Christy has a mind and a temper of his own, but certainly Mary seems to be able to satisfy his longings for love and to be loved. Christy has said to me often, 'I am happy, Bob!'

Our strange friendship goes on unchanged down the years so that I feel deep in my consciousness that in some way our Karmas have been intertwined. I imagine that if in eternity one has other existences then Christy and I will tend to find each other again wherever we are.

Recently I got a letter from Christy in which he said he had suddenly remembered Sean and felt constrained to sit down at two in the morning and write a poem about him. Here it is.

For Sean Collis

You who went so innocently before us
Do not forget us in that green-gold world of yours.
You, the gay laugh upon the Wicklow wind
Smiling boy upon a rainbow
Galloping over the morning of your life
Blessedly unmet with crippling remembrances
Shaming us with your enthusiasms,
Spare us now a thought of quiet love
In all your fourteen-year-old wisdom,
You whom death has so dismally failed to possess.

I did not know you well, knowing only your eyes
And knowing your eyes, knew you
In some other better time, boy on rainbow,
Beyond the brittle dimensions of now
Sup with me again at the same table
And crumble between us the bread of brothers.
Sean of light gentleness and boyish wayward ways
The cloud that darkens your last green hour
Hangs over us all.

For Han and Bob
Christy

INDEX

INDEX

Abbey Theatre, Dublin, 93, 94
Abrahamson, Professor, 91
Achill Island, 50
Accra, 160–1
Adeniyi-Jones, Dr Tunji, 201
Adrian, Dr, 29
Ahmadu Bello University, 146, 199, 206, 229
Aiken, Frank, 67
Akintola, 203, 204
Aladar (Belsen child), 107, 108
Alexander, Commissar, 202–3
Allergy, thesis on, 54–5
American Army in Europe, 110
American football, 32–3
Apartheid, 166, 171, 172, 173, 174–5, 176
Arnhem, 101, 105, 113, 114
Asthma, 54–5
Audu, Dr Ishaya, 198, 206, 216
Awolowo (Yoruba leader), 145, 197, 203
Azikiwi, Dr (Zik), 145

Bafut, the Fon at, 149–51
Baganwanath Hospital, 166–7
Balcon, Jill, 141, 201
Balewa, Abubakar Tafewa, 142, 145, 146, 149, 199, 203–4
Balewa, Ali, 203
Bantu, the, 165–6, 167, 171
Barton, Robert, 90, 91
Barton, Stoirin, 92
Baumöhl, Mariana, 109, 113, 128, 211, 213
Baxter, W. D., 173

Behan, Brendan, 89
Belderig, 79–82
Belsen, 101–23
Benett, Louise, 92
Benson, Robert, *The Light Invisible*, 9
Berger, Dr, 112–13
Berlin, Franz, 120
Bernadotte, Count, 113
Betjeman, John, 78
Biafra, creation of, 209
Biafrans, *see* Ibos
Bingham, Arthur, 35–6
Blake, William, 'Little Fly', 200
Bloomsbury, 82–3
Bo-Island, 13, 129, 130, 229
Bonsel, Annie, 105, 106, 113
Boxwell, Dr, 69, 74
Bray Hunt, the, 85–6
Brennan, Mrs, 93
Brevée, Dr, 113–14
British Army: author's time in, 22–3, 35; garrison at Belsen, 102–3, 110
Brock, Professor, 172
Bromley, 98
Brompton Hospital, 137
Brown, Christy, 132–6, 233–6; *My Left Foot*, 136
Brown, Horsey, 89
Brown, Mrs (Christy's mother), 133–4, 135, 136, 234–5
Bull, Dr, 32, 33
Bunyan, John, 235
Burroughs, Mrs, 106–7
Byrne, Alfie, 92

Calary, 226, 227

Cambridge University Officer Training
Corps, 27–8
Cameroons, the, 149–51
Canavan, Father, 91–3
Cape Times, 173
Cape Town, 171–3
Cardiac disease, 55–6
Carshalton Children's Hospital, 132
Caulfield, Padraig, 79
Cerebral palsy, 132–6
Cerebro-spinal meningitis, 218
Cheatle, Sir George Lentel, 42
Chelouche, Dr, 211
Cheshire, Group Captain, 147
Childers, Erskine the elder, 43, 90, 92
Childers, Erskine the younger, 90
Childers, Robert, 92
Citizens' Housing Council, Dublin,
91–3
Clinch, Jammie, 15
Cockneys, world of the, 41
Colles, Abraham, 3, 57
Collins, Michael, 35, 43, 66, 71, 90
Collis, Mrs (author's mother), 1–3,
131–2
Collis, Dermot (author's son), 83, 84–5,
129, 130, 141, 142
Collis, Eirene (author's sister-in-law),
132, 135, 141
Collis, Han (author's second wife), 105,
106, 107, 109, 112, 116, 120, 121,
124, 125, 127, 139–41, 143, 149, 152,
153–4, 199–202, 205, 213, 220–1,
222, 227, 228, 230
Collis, John Stewart (Jack, author's
twin brother), 2, 4–5, 6, 14, 15, 19,
20, 22, 23–4, 25–6, 96, 98, 132, 141,
227, 233; *Bound upon a Course*, 5;
Farewell to Argument, 89
Collis, Joyce (author's sister), 1, 5–6;
A sparrow findeth her nest, 6
Collis, Mary (author's sister), 1, 5, 50,
51
Collis, Maurice (author's brother), 1,
4, 5, 9, 19, 96, 130; *Way Up*, 5;
Siamese White, 89; *Trials in Burma*,
96, 146
Collis, Niall (author's son), 152, 153,
154, 199, 230
Collis, Phyllis (author's first wife),
82–4, 86, 129, 142, 143

Collis, Robert (author's son), 83, 84–5,
129, 130, 141, 142, 158
Collis, Sean (author's son), 141, 143,
152, 153–4, 199–201, 222–7, 228,
235
Colombia, nutrition conference, 148
Commonwealth Conference 1965, 203
Connolly, James, 16
Conway, Geoff, 26, 27
Coué (French auto-suggestionist), 45
Coventry, 98
Crawford, Ernie, 15
Crighton, Dr, 70
Curtis, Edmund, 90
Czechoslovakia, 100, 125–8; internees
return to, 109–10

Daggett, Bill, 30
Daragh (author's Irish wolfhound),
48–52
David, Dr, 19, 20, 21, 46
Davison, Harry, 31, 32, 33
Davison, H. P., 36–7, 38
Davison, Kate, 37, 121
Davison Scholarships, 31, 34, 37, 38
Davison, Trubee, 37
Dawson of Penn, Lord, 98
De Valera, Eamonn, 66–7, 97
Dillon, Professor Theo, 91
Displaced persons, 124–8
Doctor's Nigeria, A (African Encounter),
145
Doherty (flyer), 99
Donald, C. S., 40
Doogort, 50
Dublin College of Surgeons, 2, 69
Dublin Medical School, 3
Du Maurier, Daphne, 82
Durban, 170–1
Durrell, Gerald, 150–1
Duval, Professor, 163–4, 168, 169

East Africa, 177–96
Edit (Belsen child), 108, 109, 120, 130
Edwards, Hilton, 94
Ellis, William Webb, 20
Elmina Castle, 161–2
Emmett, Robert, 18
Erythema nodosum, 30, 36, 64–5
Ewell, 141

Fairy Hill Hospital, Dublin, 121–2, 129
Fanucane (ace flyer), 99
Farrer, David, 234
First World War, 22–3
Fleming, Sir Alexander, 121
Fletcher, Sir Walter, 63
Flying bombs, 99–100
Fons, the, 149–51
Foxhunting, 85–6

Galway, 49
Garden of Gethsemane, 214
Gas chambers, 117–19
Ghana, 159–62
Glencraig (Camphill) Settlement, 230
Glendower (author's polo horse), 219, 223
Glenlossera, 79
Goebbels, Josef, 112, 117
Gogarty, 58, 69–70, 72, 76
Gowon, General Yakubu, 67, 146, 206, 208–9, 210, 228–9
Great Ormond Street Hospital for Sick Children, 42, 45–6, 62–5
Greese, Irma, 118, 119
Gregg, Dr, 91

Hadassah Hospital, 212–13
Haemolytic streptococcus, 63–5, 75
Halloran (British Navy boxing champion), 43
Hamilton, Jamie, 183
Hansen, John and Joy, 172–3, 175
Harlequins, the, 43
Harris brothers, 8
Hassan, Colonel, 205–6, 207
Hastings, 'Tiger', 19
Head, Lord, 146–7
Himmler, Heinrich, 117, 118, 119
Hitler, Adolf, 97, 108, 117
Hogerzeil, Han, see Collis, Han
Hogerzeil, Lykle (Han's brother), 152, 153
Holt, Professor Emmett, 52, 148
Holy Ghost Fathers, 145
Home Rule Bill, 1912, 68
Hone family, 5
Hone, Oliver, 226
Horder, Lord, 98
Horne, Lord, 28, 29
Horse-riding, 85–6, 199–200, 222–5

Hudson, Noel, 26, 28
Hutchison, Sir Robert, 64
Hypnosis, 45

Ibadan, 142, 151–4, 207, 164–5
Ibadan Teaching Hospital, 158
Ibadan University, 146, 147, 153, 197
Ibos (Biafrans), the, 145, 146, 151, 203, 205, 207–10, 216
Institute of Child Health: Ibadan, 148, 153; Lagos, 197, 198–9
Ionides, 21, 183–90
Irish affairs, 28, 35, 43–4, 66–9, 78–9, 230–3
Irish Free State, creation of, 35
Irish Land Act, 43, 68
Irish rebellion of 1916, 16–17, 19, 35, 134
Ironsi, Major-General, 145–6, 205–7
Israel, 211–15
Ives, Burl, 137, 138
Iyangur, Omio, 30

Jerusalem, 212–14, 215
Jewish Hospital, London, 152
Johannesburg, 165–8
Johns Hopkins Hospital, Baltimore, 47, 52–6, 63, 148
Johnston, Colonel, 102, 103, 104

Kaduna, 207, 216–20
Kano, 207–8
Katsina, Sallah ceremony at, 223–5
Kennedy, Eamonn, 202
Kezmarok, 128
Killiney, 1–12, 38, 50, 75–6, 132
Kilmore, 6–8, 51, 132
King's College Hospital, 40–2, 45–7, 63, 152
Kinnear, Nigel, 105
Kinnear Wilson, Dr, 45
Kosiče, 127, 211
Kramer, 106, 118–19
Krantz, Hermina, 106, 111, 112, 113, 116, 127, 211, 213
Kwashiorkor, 147–8

Lagos, 154, 197–210, 228, 229; University, 146
Lake Victoria, 191
Lane, Margaret, Life with Ionides, 184

Lapin, Professor, 202–3
Lawson, Professor John, 142, 156
Lee Wilson, Dr, 71
Leeuwarden, 113
Leigh, Boughton, 19, 22
Leixlip, 50–1
Lenner, Dr, 72
Leprosy, 152–3
Lewis, Cecil Day, 90, 136, 141, 201
Liammóir, Micheál Mac, 94
Lightwood, Reggie, 46
Limerick, 139–40
Limerick, Lady, 101
Lloyd George, David, 23, 35
Lockhart family, 48
London Chest Hospital, 137
Longford, Lord (Frank Pakenham), 90, 136
Lough Bray, 13
Lough Dan, 13, 24, 83–4
Lüneberg, war crimes trials, 116–19
Lyons, Professor, 8

MacClancy, Patrick, 101, 105
McCormack, John, 8
McCurd Hospital, Durban, 170–1
MacDonald, Malcolm, 147
McHale, Anthony, 79, 80, 81
McIntosh, Maevis, 135
McIntosh, Rustin, 52, 55
Maclay, Joey, 60
Magee brothers, 86
Majaj, Dr, 215
Majekodunmi, Ade, 141–2, 145, 147, 154, 197, 198, 205, 229
Malahide, Lady Talbot de, 50
Malan, Mr, 173
Mandela, 172
Marrow Bone Lane, 94–5; fund associated with, 129, 132
Masaryk, Jan, 100, 125–7
Meath Hospital, 3, 16–17, 69, 71–6, 234
Meningitis, tuberculous, 122
Mennonites, the, 124–5
Mike (author's Clydesdale), 130
M.B. examination, 38, 39
Mohammed, Colonel, 209
Moncrieff, Alan, 46, 91
Montagu, E. A., 19, 89, 93
Moore, Henry, 57

Moore, Sir John, 69, 71, 72
Moore, Tom, 95
Moran, Sister, 77
Morgan, J. P., 31
Mosse, Bartholomew, 70
Mountbatten, Lord, 147
M.R.C.P. examination (English), 46–7; (Irish), 74–6, 91
Mulu (author's horse), 155–6, 157, 158
Murchison Falls, 190–4
Murphy, Dr, 72

Natal, 170, 171
National Association for Cerebral Palsy, 129, 229
National Children's Hospital, Dublin, 70, 71, 76, 95
New Hampshire, 35–6
Newton, John, 162
Nigeria, 141–2, 144–58, 197–210, 228–229; violence in, 203–10
Nigeria in Conflict, 145
Nkrumah, 159–60
Northern Nigeria Medical School, 216, 226
Nutrition Conferences, 148
Nzegwu, 205, 206

O'Brien, Conor Cruise, 159
O'Brien, George, 90
O'Casey, Sean, 58, 92
O'Connor, Frank (Michael O'Donovan), 90, 93, 94; The Big Fellow, 71
O'Connor, Rory, 43
O'Faoláin, Sean, 90, 94
O'Flaherty, Liam, Famine, 67–8
Ojukwu, 146, 206, 207, 208, 209, 210
Olivier, Laurence, 94
Oosterbeek, 105, 113, 114
O'Shaughnessy, Miss, 87
O'Sullivan, Maureen, 8
Owen, David, 120

Park, Ned, 52–3, 55
Parry, Eldred, 226
Paterson, Dr Donald, 64
Pearse, Padraig, 16, 18, 134
Phelps, Billy, 34, 132
Plumer, General Lord, 29
Polo, 155, 200, 219, 223, 224
Potts (author's dog), 156–8

Powerscourt, Lord, 71
Poynton, Dr John, 62
Prague, 126–7
Pretoria, 168–9
Price Thomas, Mr, 136–8

Rags (author's Cairn terrier), 11
Ransome-Kuti, Dr Koye, 199
Red Cross, the, 101, 102, 104, 107, 116, 121
Rheumatic fever in children, research into, 62–5
Rhodesia, 175–6
Richards, Shelagh, 94
Richardson, Ralph, 94
Roberts, Frank, 100
Roberston, Colonel, 226
Robinson, David, 90
Robinson, Lennox, 94
Rockefeller Foundation, 56, 57–8, 127, 148, 197
Rockefeller Research Fellowships, 47, 60
Ronke, Mamma', 201
Rosenzweig, Ludmilla, 109, 113, 214
Rotunda Hospital, Dublin, 43, 44, 70, 76–8, 129
Royal College of Physicians, 98
Rugby football, 14–15, 19, 26, 28, 36, 43, 89, 163
Rugby School, 4–5, 15–16, 18–21, 98
Russell, George (AE), 56, 57–60; 'The Wings of Angus', 59
Rusty (author's red setter), 87–8, 132, 142, 156
Ryan, Rachel, 93

Salisbury, Rhodesia, 175–6
Sallah ceremony at Katsina, 223–5
Saudauna of Sokoto, the, 203, 204
Schlesinger, Dr, 63
Schwarz, Evelyn, 120
Second World War, 96–100
Sheldon, Wilfred, 46, 63–4, 65, 91
Sickle-celled anaemia, 201, 203
Silver Fleece, The, 16, 89, 226
Skite (author's horse), 86, 130
Sobukwe, Robert, 172
Solomons, Dr Bethel, 43, 70, 76–7, 78

Spaight, Robert, 94
Steen, Dr, 71
Stellenbosch University, 173–5
Stevenson, Robert Louis, 189
Still, Sir Frederick, 42, 45, 46, 62
Stokes, Henry, 69, 72
Straight On, 120
Streptomycin, 121, 122
Strong, L. A. G., 89, 90
Susie (Belsen child), 107, 108, 109, 113, 120

Tanzania, 183–90
Tatters (author's Cairn terrier), 11–12
Taussig, Helen, 52, 55
Thompson, J. J., 29, 38, 227
Tibor (Belsen child), 107, 108, 109, 113, 116, 120
Tim (author's hunter), 131, 142, 143
Trinity College, Cambridge, 23, 25–31, 34–5, 38–9
Trinity College, Dublin, 18, 23, 57, 69
Triszynska, Luba, 106, 112, 113, 116
Tuberculosis, 5–6, 30, 36, 38, 64–5, 72–3, 107, 109, 120–3, 136–8
Turner, W. J., 'Romance', 201

Uganda, 190–6
United Nations Organisation, 120, 124
University College, Dublin, 57, 69
University Medical School, Lagos, 198

Verwoerd, Dr, 174
Victoria Falls, 182
Victoria Nile, 191–4

Wakely, Sir Cecil, 42
Wallace, Professor, 170
Wayburne, Dr, 165–8
Wesley Guild Hospital, Ilesha, 190
Wicklow mountains, 7, 9, 13, 24, 50, 83, 130, 132, 227, 229
Williams, Cecily, 147, 148
Wilson, Sir Henry, 28
Wolfson Foundation, 147, 198
Woodham-Smith, Cecil, The Great Hunger, 67–8

Wough (author's Airedale), 86–7

World Health Organisation, 158, 197

Yad Vashem (Association of Survivors of Concentration Camps), 213

Yale University, 32–9

Zambezi, 182–3

Zanzibar, 177–80

Zaria, 216, 220–1

Zoltan (Belsen child), 107, 108–9, 113, 116, 120–1, 121–3, 125, 128, 130, 136–8, 226–7